The Philosophy of Comics

The Philosophy of Comics

What They Are, How They Work, and Why They Matter

Henry John Pratt

Illustrated by

Kurt F. Shaffert

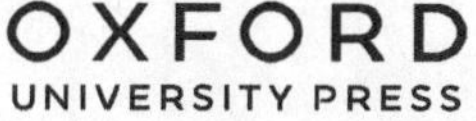

OXFORD
UNIVERSITY PRESS

Oxford University Press is a department of the University of Oxford. It furthers the University's objective of excellence in research, scholarship, and education by publishing worldwide. Oxford is a registered trade mark of Oxford University Press in the UK and certain other countries.

Published in the United States of America by Oxford University Press
198 Madison Avenue, New York, NY 10016, United States of America.

Library of Congress Cataloging-in-Publication Data
Names: Pratt, Henry John, author. | Shaffert, Kurt F., illustrator.
Title: The philosophy of comics : what they are, how they work, and why they matter / Henry John Pratt ; illustrated by Kurt F. Shaffert.
Description: New York, NY : Oxford University Press, [2023] |
Includes bibliographical references and index.
Identifiers: LCCN 2023004887 (print) | LCCN 2023004888 (ebook) |
ISBN 9780190845438 (paperback) | ISBN 9780190845445 (hardback) |
ISBN 9780190845469 (epub)
Subjects: LCSH: Comic books, strips, etc.—Philosophy. | Comic books, strips, etc.—History and criticism. | LCGFT: Comics criticism.
Classification: LCC PN6710.P73 2023 (print) | LCC PN6710 (ebook) |
DDC 741.5/9—dc23/eng/20230201
LC record available at https://lccn.loc.gov/2023004887
LC ebook record available at https://lccn.loc.gov/2023004888

DOI: 10.1093/oso/9780190845445.001.0001

Paperback printed by Marquis Book Printing, Canada
Hardback printed by Bridgeport National Bindery, Inc., United States of America

In Memory of Lee B. Brown

Contents

LIFE IN COMICS

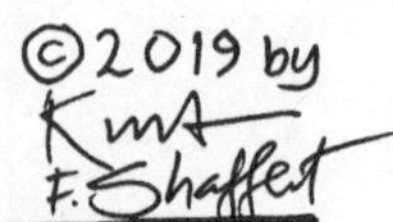

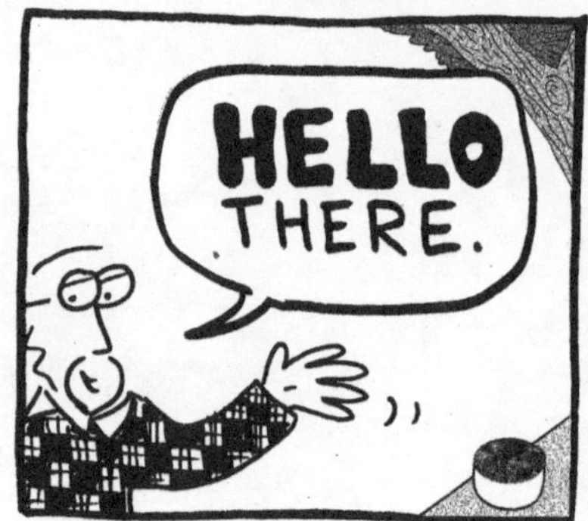

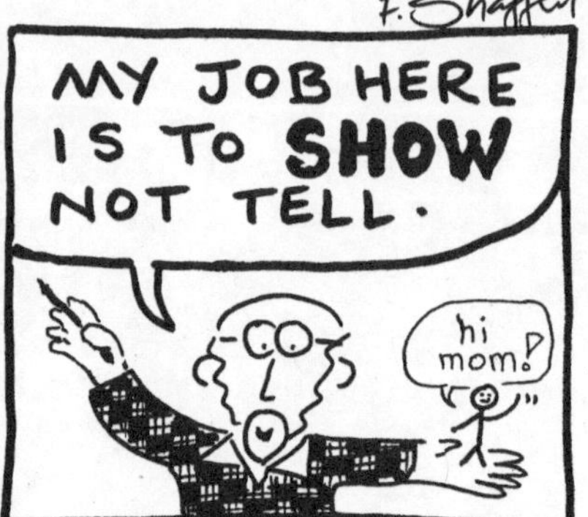

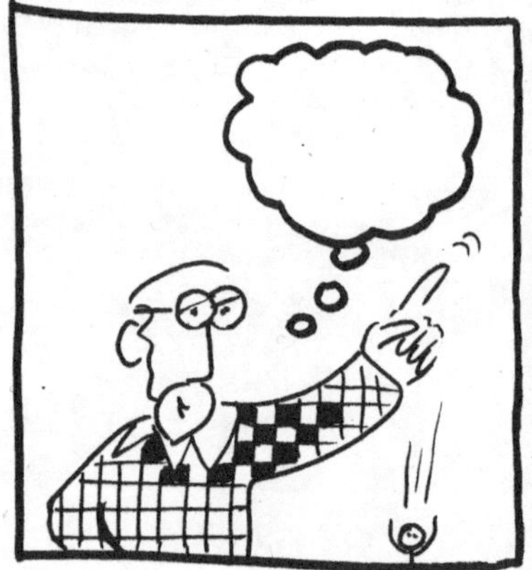

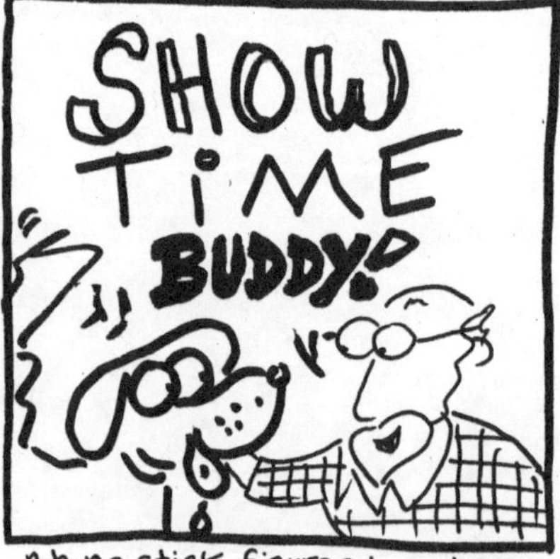

fig x.1.

n.b. no stick figures have been harmed in the production of this comic.

Preface

P.1. Why the Philosophy of Comics?

Comics are fun. I expect you agree with that. If you don't, I can't promise that this book will change your mind, but I can always hope. For me, reading comics produces a lot of effects. Generally, enjoyment and relaxation. Sometimes, challenge, disappointment, or enlightenment. And frequently, a sense of guilty pleasure.

That sense of guilt is interesting. It used to be practically obligatory for anybody who wrote about comics and took them seriously as an art form to preface their work with a specific type of disclaimer. It would start by pointing out that comics are disreputable, lowbrow, and written for audiences of misfit geeks, children, perverts, artsy European types, or various overlapping subsets thereof. Then it would go on to mention ways in which comics have achieved some form of significance or influence—typically in the world of high art (museums exhibit comics!) or within academia (there are college courses about comics!)—in an attempt to justify studying comics further.

I've had occasion to write disclaimers of this ilk myself. Happily, we've advanced to a stage, I think, at which I merely feel compelled to mention that they *used* to be commonplace, but aren't any more. While it wasn't that long ago that the situation was quite different, it's now pretty well accepted that comics and, in fact, all aspects of popular culture are worthy of investigation, critique, and analysis. I'm not well qualified to offer any definitive account of this shift in opinion. But I'd guess that it has something to do with three factors, listed in order of most to least cynical: (a) the persistent need within academia to find new subjects about which one might publish, (b) the increasing penetration of geek culture (e.g., superhero movies) into the mainstream, and (c) the very real, if belated recognition that comics and other works of popular culture present a host of distinctive theoretical puzzles and challenges for the intellectually curious.

It's to that audience of the intellectually curious that this book is addressed. If you like comics but have ever wondered what makes something a comic in the first place, or how comics function to tell stories, or why movies based on comics never get it exactly right, or what makes some comics better than others, or whether you're a terrible person just for liking comics, then this book, ideally, will help you think through those problems. If you like comics but have never really thought about any of the above, then this book, ideally, will convince you that it's worth your time to do so. And even if you don't like comics at all, perhaps this book will provide an entry point into comics readership: maybe you'll even realize that comics are, to reiterate, fun.

In what follows, I'm not going to presume that readers are rabid comics fans with an exhaustive knowledge of their subject. Some of you, undoubtedly, fall into that category, and that'll provide you with richer resources and test cases for confirming or contravening the arguments I offer. But even casual readers shouldn't feel left behind. Although I refer to comics that you might not have encountered before, I've made every effort to describe those comics and to explain why they're relevant to the arguments I construct. Then too, the illustrations by Kurt Shaffert provided in each chapter were designed and commissioned specifically to convey information that isn't easily articulated through words. They'll help you understand what I'm getting at even if what's depicted in them is new to you.

I'm not going to presume that you're highly trained in philosophy either. Familiarity with at least some philosophical concepts and methodology will certainly be helpful at points. It's hard to find an entry point into any philosophical text with no background whatsoever, simply because any philosophical problem, no matter how introductory it might seem, is always the tip of a very large and craggy iceberg. That's why in some ways Philosophy 101 courses in college—which typically introduce philosophy to students for the first time (at least for those who have been educated in the United States)—are among the hardest for philosophy professors to teach and for their students to take. Accordingly, I'm going to be careful to explain any technical terminology and to provide, to whatever extent is feasible, as much background context as is required for working through the topics we'll cover.

A professor of mine in my undergraduate days at University of Vermont, Don Loeb, always encouraged his students to consider what he termed the "Smart Roommate Test" before submitting the final draft of a paper. The idea is relatively self-explanatory: if (hypothetically speaking—for some of us, this was more hypothetical than for others) you have a smart roommate, that person should be able to understand what you've written, regardless of their particular field of study. This book is intended to pass the Smart Roommate Test.

That said, a caveat is in order. It's more or less unavoidable for me to write in the style of a professional philosopher, because I am one. If it means anything to you, I'm an analytic philosopher by training, and the influence of that tradition has played out in my work in part through the tone, vocabulary, and methods I adopt. I think that the virtues of this style include clarity, rigor, and optimally an appropriate level of modesty in my aims and commitments. It's always possible that some potential readers will find this book inaccessible for stylistic reasons, but I hope not.

Even though one of my goals is that this book can pass the Smart Roommate Test, that shouldn't be taken to indicate that there's nothing in here for trained philosophers. There should be plenty of interest for experts who work in aesthetics and the philosophy of art, not to mention the more specialized few whose research touches comics. Comics have received a good deal of theoretical attention from the academic areas of cultural studies, literature, and linguistics, as well as from comics practitioners themselves. But the philosophy of comics is really in its infancy, as shown by the relative paucity of publications about it, especially in the English language (continental Europeans have been thinking rigorously about comics for longer than those of us in the United States and United Kingdom). While we'll encounter content from many fine thinkers as we go along, comics is severely underexplored, which leaves lots of open territory and room for development.

I've published earlier versions of some of the material in this book elsewhere, but this is the first time I've tied it all together systematically. In addition, I offer what I believe to be novel arguments for novel positions about comics. It's my hope that experts in the field will find much to think about, to build on, and, naturally, to dispute. Philosophy done well invites debate, which, with some optimism, I expect that this book will provoke.

Before offering a brief chapter-by-chapter summary, let me quickly address a terminological issue. "Comics" is both a singular term for a general category of objects and a plural term for multiple individual works or printings thereof. In this book, I'll do my best to disambiguate these usages, where necessary, by referring to the former in terms of "the category of comics" or similar, and the latter in terms of "particular comics" or "individual comics."

P.2. The Structure of the Book

Overall, this book is divided into seven chapters, each of which concentrates attention on a different area of philosophical interest in comics. The first several chapters are about what sorts of things we typically think of as comics and what it is to be a comic. The discussion flows naturally into topics about how comics work, as well as crucial similarities and differences between comics and other art forms like film, nongraphic literature, and theater. The book closes with a host of issues about value—both the value of particular comics in contrast to each other and the ethical and social values of the category of comics as a whole.

While each chapter could be read on its own, they do accumulate. Reading through them in order will be the most productive way to read the book since ideas and terms are developed progressively. I have deliberately planned it so that a college course on comics could be constructed using this book as the primary text. In a standard semester with fourteen weeks of classes and a week of final exams, one could spend two weeks on the topic of each of the seven chapters, complementing and contrasting the arguments advanced in this book with additional reading material.

In Chapter 1, "The Category of Comics," I begin with a list of what I take to be uncontroversial exemplars of the comics category, prompting questions about *why* we take them to be comics. The answers have to do, in part, with their fit into what I call the "standard history" of comics, an account of the development of the category from protocomics into newspaper comics, comic books, graphic novels, underground and alternative comics, and webcomics. While somewhat different in length, style, and delivery system, I hold that each of these is a proper subcategory of comics and that it's worth seeking a unified theoretical understanding of all of them. Being part of the standard history is insufficient for making something a comic, as we can see by attending to the relation between comics and cartoons. I argue that while they have common roots, comics is a distinct *category* from one-panel cartoons (not to mention animated cartoons). At the same time, I acknowledge that it's legitimate to refer to a range of common *styles* that are used for drawing comics as cartooning, and offer reasons for why this is so. I close the chapter by investigating the intersections and overlaps between comics and art, which depend on what sense of art one has in mind. In the evaluative and premodern senses of art, most (possibly all) comics turn out to be artworks. But in the sense central to the Western modern tradition, fewer comics are artworks. I show that although some comics occupy the right kind of context for art—the artworld—the fit of the comics world into that context is uneasy.

Chapter 1 establishes an understanding of the sort of works any definition of the category of comics ought to cover, and so in Chapter 2, I turn to whether a definition can be formulated that encompasses all of and only those works. After explaining what essentialist definitions are, I draw from Morris Weitz and Aaron Meskin to outline the case for why the category of comics cannot be defined using an essentialist strategy. I argue that Meskin might well be right, but that attempting the project of definition is important and worthwhile nonetheless. I then list a number of extant proposals, and from these extract various candidates for necessary conditions that comics have.

I assess each condition in turn, moving from the less plausible to the more plausible. Ultimately, I demonstrate that the best strategy for an essentialist framework is to advert to the comics' pictorial representationality, the sequence of spatially juxtaposed images, narrativity, and (to a lesser extent) historical considerations.

In Chapter 3, I turn attention to the media of comics. Conspicuously, the best definitions proposed in Chapter 2 home in on comics' formal features, without making any commitment to their material (or, indeed, immaterial) constitution. This is as it should be: comics can be made on paper of any type, drawn on a blackboard, hewn into marble, painted, exist only in electronic form, and so on. Comics, like film, have no characteristic set of physical media (unlike, perhaps, an art form such as painting). However, I propose that it will be useful to construe "media" more broadly in this case, to encompass not only the tools and substances with which creators work, but also the basic constituent elements from which they compose their works. For comics, media typically include pictures, a panel sequence, and words. These produce medium-specific tendencies, an idea that I explain by making the case against the more standard strong medium specificity and for a more moderate alternative, on which the media out of which a work is created affect its capacities for representation and expression (as well as being evaluatively significant). While I take up these tendencies in more detail in later chapters on narrativity, adaptation, and evaluation, here I argue that the combination of pictures, the panel sequence, and (optionally) words explains the effectiveness of comics when used for education and instruction, as well as in graphic medicine.

Paying close attention to how the sequence of panels functions as an organizing device for pictures (and, frequently, words) is vitally important for understanding how comics work. In Chapter 4, I address the ways in which the arrangement of media characteristic of comics exerts strong pressures toward narrativity: storytelling is perhaps the most natural organizing principle for a comic. I break down two of the main media that comics use for storytelling into a verbal dimension and a pictorial dimension. I describe in detail how each of these dimensions guides the reader's perception and understanding of narratives. Comics employ a range of complex techniques in order to portray temporal and spatial relations within the diegetic world. Explaining these techniques, I show how the narrative is constructed within individual panels, in the gutter between panels, and through the layout of panels on the page. I also consider the impacts of serial publication on narrative structure in comics that employ it.

The media of literature are words; the media of film are (moving) pictures and (generally, audible) words. The prevalence of the verbal and pictorial dimensions of comics has contributed to a number of adaptations—the focus of Chapter 5—where comics, paired with works of literature or film, are either the *source* (the adaptation proceeds from comic to x) or *adaptation* (the adaptation proceeds from x to comic). While other art forms can use techniques similar to those in comics to tell stories, they also have some notable differences, which spring from differences in their respective media. Because of the characteristic narrative devices produced by comics media, a number of theorists have suggested that adaptation into or out of comics is impossible. After giving prominent examples of such arguments, I conclude that perfect viability of adaptation into or out of comics is unachievable, but that adaptation is not thereby futile or impossible in any strong sense of the term. Moreover, though there are notable differences, there are also notable similarities among the media of comics and film. I trace out these similarities in defense of the thesis that comics are especially apt, in comparison to works of literature and theatre, for adaptation into film.

A view I endorse in Chapter 5, that it's possible to preserve the value of the source in the process of adaptation, brings another consideration to the fore: what makes a comic good or bad? That is, for works in the category of comics, are there any general principles that can be adopted that, when applied, yield good judgments of comparative value? I begin Chapter 6 by investigating whether the value of comics is completely relative to its context. I develop an argument influenced by David Hume to the conclusion that while some degree of relativism is inevitable, not every evaluation of comics is of equal quality. The standard of taste for comics, I hold, is fixed by true judges—expert critics of comics (which may or may not be hypothetical ideals). Subsequently, I extract from the writings of actual comics theorists four types of properties relevant to the value of comics: narrative, pictorial, historical, and referential properties. I argue that what these have in common is their capacity to afford valuable experiences, and defend a subjectivist account of the value of particular comics. In addition, I attempt to explain how the comics world came to select these properties as evaluatively relevant rather than others, tying the answer to medium specificity.

Among the referential properties relevant to the value of comics are those contributing to their social and moral value, the topic for the seventh, final chapter. Here, I begin with Plato, who notoriously objected to mass-media narrative arts like poetry on grounds having to do with pernicious effects on the upbringing of just citizens. While Plato was writing some twenty-four hundred years ago and was unfamiliar with comics (at least in their contemporary format), his overall strategy has persisted, culminating in Fredric Wertham's *Seduction of the Innocent* (1954), which was instrumental in motivating the notorious Comics Code Authority. I inquire into whether these sorts of charges have any grounding in medium-specific or other considerations. First, I consider the idea that the authors and audiences of comics are prone to immorality, due to marginalization of the comics category and the ways in which comics are created and marketed. Second, I look at the ways in which the formatting of comics has driven the reading process, making it private, antisocial, and prone to violent resolutions of narratives. For both of these worries, I acknowledge that individual comics can be morally problematic, e.g., in the attitudes they invite about race, sex, gender, and violence. But I argue that it is much more difficult to make a case against the category itself. The media of comics are content neutral, with one complication, which brings us to the third potential source of trouble: the cartoon style of depiction involves the use of caricature. I take up Christy Mag Uidhir's argument that media using caricature are epistemically defective, and conclude that while vigilance is warranted, such considerations provide no ultimate reason to condemn comics as a category.

And that's the book. Share and enjoy!

Acknowledgments

The genesis of this book occurred in an independent study I did in graduate school in 2000 at The Ohio State University, along with Greg Hayman, supervised by Lee B. Brown. It was Greg's idea, and it resulted in a paper I coauthored with him (Hayman and Pratt 2005) that has, much to my surprise, become a canonical part of the philosophy of comics literature. Many of the ideas I develop in the first two chapters were originally discussed with Greg and Lee. The former left philosophy (if you read this, Greg, I'd love to find out what you think), and the latter has since passed away. I've dedicated this book to his memory, and hope that he'd find it worthy of his legacy as a teacher and mentor.

In general, the philosophy of comics would not be in its present form if not for the welcoming environment provided by the American Society for Aesthetics. Previous versions of material in Chapters 1, 2, 4, 5, and 7 were presented at the ASA's Annual and Eastern Division meetings. I wish to extend my gratitude to the organizers of those conferences and to the participants of the sessions at which I presented my work. In particular, ASA members Roy T. Cook, Christy Mag Uidhir, and Aaron Meskin have greatly informed my thought over the years, and their continued attention to comics is inspiring. I expect they'll find plenty in this book to criticize.

I also presented early versions of Chapter 5 at the International Conference on Narrative in 2011 and at the United States Military Academy in 2014. My thanks go to those organizations for the invitations and feedback.

Much of Chapter 7 was developed as a part of a National Endowment for the Humanities Summer Seminar, "Narrative Theory: Rhetoric and Ethics in Fiction and Nonfiction," which took place at The Ohio State University in 2008 under the direction of James Phelan. I would like to acknowledge the generous support of the NEH, and the abundant help I received from James Phelan and the other seminar participants, including David Herman.

Portions of this book contain extensively rewritten versions of the following articles, used by permission of the respective copyright holders:

Chapter 1 contains material originally published as "Relating Comics, Cartoons, and Animation" in *Aesthetics: A Reader in Philosophy of the Arts*, 3rd ed., ed. David Goldblatt and Lee B. Brown (Upper Saddle River, NJ: Pearson Prentice Hall, 2011), 369–73.

Chapter 4 contains material originally published as "Narrative in Comics," *Journal of Aesthetics and Art Criticism* 67 (2009): 107–17. Copyright 2009, The American Society for Aesthetics (Wiley-Blackwell, Publisher); and "Why Serials Are Killer," *Journal of Aesthetics and Art Criticism* 71 (2013): 266–70. Copyright 2013, The American Society for Aesthetics (Wiley-Blackwell, Publisher).

Chapter 5 contains material originally published as "Making Comics into Film" in *The Art of Comics and Graphic Novels: A Philosophical Approach*, ed. Roy T. Cook and Aaron Meskin (Malden, MA: Wiley-Blackwell, 2012), 147–64.

Chapter 7 contains material originally published as "Medium Specificity and the Ethics of Narrative in Comics," *Storyworlds* 1 (2009): 97–113. Copyright 2009, University of Nebraska Press.

All illustrations except Figure 6.4 (which is my own work) are copyright by and used by permission of Kurt F. Shaffert.

I crafted the framework for this book during my sabbatical in the spring of 2016, made possible by Marist College. Thanks go to the Dean of the School of Liberal Arts, Martin Shaffer, and the Vice President for Academic Affairs, Thomas Wermuth, for approving and encouraging my project. Other colleagues at Marist provided invaluable feedback on earlier drafts of various chapters, including but not limited to Andrei Buckareff, Joseph Campisi, Kevin Gray, Gregory Machacek, and Thomas W. Zurhellen.

Of course, I was not the only person who worked directly on this book. Without the endlessly patient Peter Ohlin and his team at Oxford University Press, the book would have been rather different, and not as good (though any lapses in quality are my responsibility alone). And it goes without saying that this book would have been impoverished dramatically without the cover and interior illustrations by Kurt Shaffert, with whom I have been collaborating off and on since he was five and I was four. (That's not when we started working on this book, for the record.) His thoughts and expertise were crucial to the shape this book eventually took, not only for the illustrations but also for the content of Chapter 3 in particular.

Preparing the illustrations did not occur in a vacuum or any other appliance. Kurt and I extend our gratitude to Al B. Wesolowsky and to other associates of the Center for Cartoon Studies, including Michelle Ollie, James Sturm, Steve Bissette, Jason Lutes, Glynnis Fawkes, Hilary Mullins, Alec Longstreth, Luke Kruger-Howard, Jon Chad, Sarah Yahm, Marek Bennett, Jarad Greene, Dave Lloyd, M. K. Czerwiec, Elise Dietrich, and Rainer Kannenstine. We also offer a tip of the nib to Matt Groening, whose *Life in Hell* was a significant influence on the style and format of the illustrations.

A number of friends, relations, and acquaintances produced and sustained my enthusiasm for comics. Among these, special thanks go to my parents, John and Mary Pratt, for reading so much *Pogo* to me at an early age that they thought I'd end up talking funny on a permanent basis. And I'm grateful to have had the opportunity to interact with the denizens of various comic book shops over the years. Gratitude is extended to The Professor, Stomp Winchester III, and above all, Ian R. Hummel for, among other things, allowing me the opportunity to play shows with them in the back room of the Laughing Ogre in Columbus, Ohio.

There are most certainly others whose contributions I've neglected to mention. To them, I apologize. I'd be remiss, however, if I didn't close by mentioning my colleague and wife, Cathy Muller. Without her love, encouragement, tolerance, thoughtful commentary, and willingness to indulge my eccentricities, completion of this book would have been impossible.

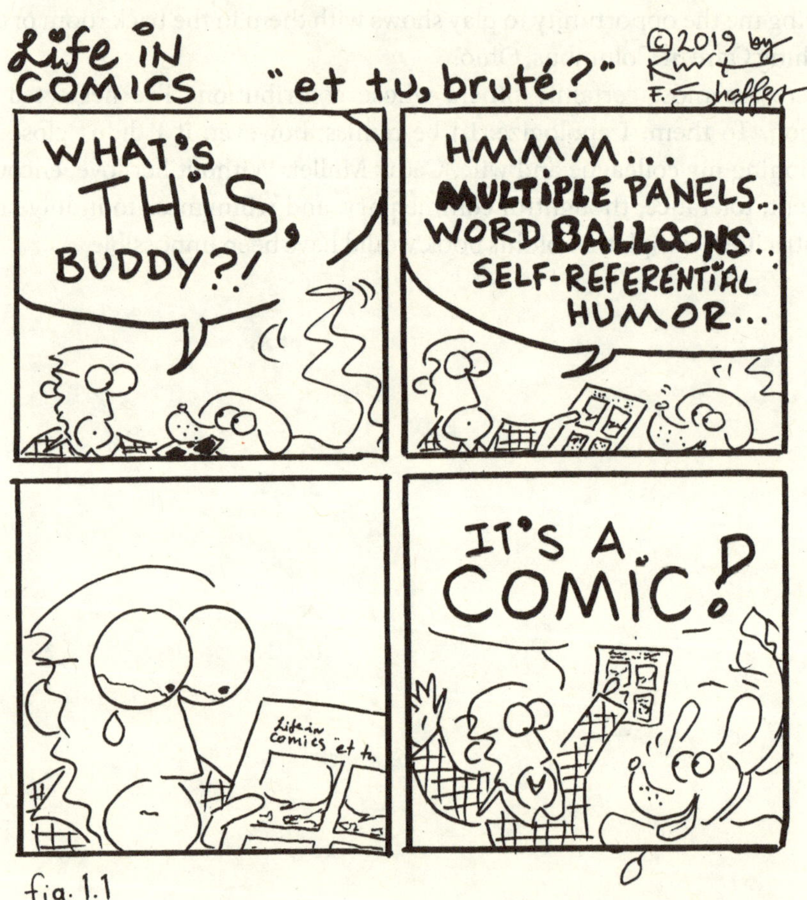
Life in COMICS
"et tu, bruté?"
©2019 by Kurt F. Shaffert
WHAT'S THIS, BUDDY?!
HMMM... MULTIPLE PANELS.. WORD BALLOONS.. SELF-REFERENTIAL HUMOR...
IT'S A COMIC!

fig. 1.1

1
The Category of Comics

1.1. Exemplars

Philosophers are notorious for rejecting positions that pretty much all normal people believe are correct. Do you think you have free will? A whole host of philosophers think you don't. What about your confidence in the reality of the material world? Plato held that it was a pale imitation of abstract forms, which are more real; Berkeley rejected the existence of the material world as we know it altogether. Do you believe in change, or causation? Parmenides and David Hume, respectively, didn't. J. M. E. McTaggart even argued that there's no such thing as time.

All of this is a roundabout way of emphasizing that one person's common sense, or even one person's indisputable fact, is another's theoretical anathema. I'm about to give a short list of works that I'll call "exemplars"—works that strike me as situated uncontroversially within the category of comics. Even if they strike you that way as well, it's worth remembering that some people might disagree, perhaps even for very interesting reasons.

- *The Adventures of Little Nemo in Slumberland*
- *Krazy Kat*
- *Dick Tracy*
- *Peanuts*
- *Garfield*
- *Action Comics* #1
- *Bone*
- *The Dark Knight Returns*
- *Watchmen*
- *Ghost World*
- *Frank*
- *Tintin*
- *Astro Boy*
- *Maus*
- *Fun Home*

The Philosophy of Comics. Henry John Pratt, Oxford University Press. © Oxford University Press 2023.
DOI: 10.1093/oso/9780190845445.003.0001

- *Palestine*
- *Persepolis*
- *Tom the Dancing Bug*
- *XKCD*

There are notable differences among these works. They're rendered in a variety of styles. They're printed in a variety of formats, or sometimes not printed at all. Some are serialized, and some are not. Some have multiple authors, while some are singly authored.[1] Intended audiences range from the very young to the very weird. They are written in different languages, and one doesn't even use a written language.

These differences explain why these exemplars can be correctly placed in different subcategories of comics: newspaper comics, comic books, superhero comics, alternative comics, graphic novels, webcomics, manga, autobiographical comics, and so on. The subcategories are nondiscrete, in that a given work might fall under the scope of more than one. But they're all comics, and my hope is that agreement on this point is widespread, if not universal.

It'll take a goodly portion of this chapter and the next to offer my take on the complex reasons why these works are exemplars of the comics category. Fundamentally, I think that they're comics because they fit into a particular historical tradition as well as satisfying (particularly well, it should be noted) certain evaluative criteria. By making this claim, I'm gesturing toward a definition of the category of comics. Typically, one of the first actions philosophers take when they turn their attention to a new concept or category of object is to see whether they can define it—whether they can specify what properties are held by it and only it—or, on the flip side, to show why it can't be defined at all in that way. Chapter 2 takes up the project of definition in earnest, and this chapter sets the stage for it. I want to think about why we might have come to agree (if I'm right that we do agree) that the list above is of good examples of comics, and to explore how these examples stand in contrast to related categories and with respect to the broader category of art itself.

1.2. The Standard History

The term "comic" is in many ways unfortunate in origin and persistence. The most glaring problem is that, in other contexts, "comic" is associated with humor, as well as with jokes and the people who tell them. Not all comics (in our sense) are comic (in that sense): referring back to the list of exemplars, less than half are primarily geared toward humor.

Early on, then, we should recognize that we're unlikely to capture what it is to be a comic by referring to an affective response that they either do trigger or are intended to trigger. That is, comics—like works in other categories such as film, music, and dance—do and are intended to produce a broad range of emotions and feelings. There's no single response or narrowly circumscribed group of such responses typical of comics as a whole.

Nor do our exemplars have a common subject-matter. What they're about covers such subjects as the adventures of talking animals, crime, politics, dreams, history, sexual identity, science, and so on. Comics as a category appears to be neutral among subjects, so that's a nonstarter if we're looking for an explanation of our willingness to apply "comics" to all of those exemplars.

A better starting place is to consider their ancestry—their placement in the same tradition and their evolution from similar roots. Let me be clear: I'm not arguing that this ancestry, without augmentation, captures why they *are* comics, but that it helps us understand why most people *believe* they are comics.

Historians of comics tend to offer similar accounts about the origins of comics. What I'll call *the standard history*—the story that's typically told about the origins of comics and the general contour of their development—is, roughly, the following.[2]

Comics had several precursors, "protocomics," if you will, that appeared in the early and middle nineteenth century. These included works of social satire by the likes of Francisco Goya, Honoré Daumier, William Hogarth, Thomas Rowlandson, James Gillray, and Rodolphe Töpffer. Typically, they consisted of single or multiple images with captions or descriptive titles that either commented on political issues of the time or were designed to produce laughter. In 1894, the first true comic appeared in the pages of the *New York World* newspaper Sunday supplement: Richard Outcault's *Hogan's Alley*, whose breakout character was the Yellow Kid. It was wildly popular, and soon a whole host of imitators and competitors sprang forward. (Subsequent newspaper wars for circulation, driven partially by the Yellow Kid, resulted in the origins of the term "yellow journalism," which is still with us.) Other important examples of early newspaper comics include Rudolph Dirks' *The Katzenjammer Kids*, Frederick Opper's *Happy Hooligan* (incidentally, the first comic to be adapted for film—in 1903), Bud Fisher's *Mutt and Jeff*, Winsor McCay's *Little Nemo in Slumberland*, and George Harriman's *Krazy Kat*.[3]

The well-established category of newspaper comics rapidly evolved into a number of overlapping subcategories that can be identified in terms of content: gag-a-day (Ernie Bushmiller's *Nancy*), adventure (Milton Caniff's *Terry and the Pirates*), fantasy/sci-fi (Alex Raymond's *Flash Gordon*), crime

(Chester Gould's *Dick Tracy*), soap opera (Allen Saunders and Dale Conners' *Mary Worth*), and so on. As newspapers changed format (reducing size initially because of newsprint shortages in World War II) and television became the dominant narrative form, the comics changed as well. Continuity comics—those with plots stretching over multiple days—waned, and pictorial styles simplified dramatically to maintain legibility at a smaller printing size.

Meanwhile, a parallel strand of comics had evolved outside the newspaper. In 1933, under the auspices of Maxwell C. Gaines, Eastern Color printed the first comic book (in a format we'd recognize—color printing, at 7.5 by 10.5 inches), which was a collection of reprints of newspaper comics. Originally free advertising giveaways, comic books soon were sold on their own. Eventually, given the success of this format, there was a demand for original content. National Publications released an anthology comic book, *Action Comics*, which contained the first appearance of Jerry Siegel and Joe Shuster's Superman.[4] This was the first real superhero story. Comics featuring Superman attracted unprecedented attention and sales numbers, and soon a whole host of imitators and competitors sprang forward. Early "Golden Age" superheroes in the comics, still with us today, include Batman, Captain Marvel, Submariner, Green Lantern, Plastic Man, and Captain America.

The category of comic books, now well established, rapidly evolved into overlapping subcategories that can be identified in terms of content: crime (EC's *Crime SuspenStories*), war (Quality/DC's *Blackhawk*), horror (EC's *Tales from the Crypt*), Western (DC's *Tomahawk*), funny animal (*Walt Disney's Comics and Stories*), romance (Crestwood/DC's *Young Romance*), and so on. Before television took over, the sales and readership numbers for comic books were staggeringly large, particularly among children. This led to some concern about their corrupting influence, producing serious threats to the comic book industry. By 1954, publishers began to self-censor, establishing the Comics Code Authority (CCA), which forbid certain content deemed controversial.

In reaction to the standards of the CCA, superhero comics transitioned into the "Silver Age" with arrival of the new Barry Allen Flash in DC's 1956 *Showcase* #4, rendered in a novel style and with new thematic focus. DC's Golden Age superheroes were largely reworked. By the early 1960s, Marvel Comics (formerly Timely) began publishing popular titles that challenged DC's supremacy. Under Stan Lee, Marvel concentrated on human drama and relationships, grounding superheroes in more psychologically realistic and relatable circumstances, and DC soon attempted to follow suit. Later, as the influence of the CCA waned, and spurred by the impact of comics like Alan Moore and Dave Gibbons's *Watchmen* and Frank Miller's *The Dark Knight*

Returns, superhero comic books in the 1980s entered a "grim and gritty" era in which we are still largely embedded.

The focus of the above is mainstream comics designed and marketed for mass consumption. The rise of the counterculture movement in the late 1960s was accompanied by the rise of underground comics that defied prevailing cultural norms and values. *Mad Magazine* popularized comics created in rebellion to the strictures imposed by the CCA: since it wasn't a comic book, it avoided the CCA entirely and was able to publish content on the more controversial end of the spectrum. Subsequently, often influenced by *Mad*, authors like Robert Crumb, Art Spiegelman, Trina Robbins, Gilbert Shelton, Lynda Barry, and Gary Panter created comics in a range of depictive styles (sometimes crudely drawn) that dealt directly with sex, drug use, violence, radical politics, and other adult themes the CCA forbade. Largely ignored by mainstream publishing houses, many of these works were self-published. The raw style and content of underground comics transmuted into alternative comics—produced for limited, serious, adult audiences. Alternative comics branched into nonfiction (e.g., comics journalism from Joe Sacco) and biography (e.g., memoirs by Marjane Satrapi and Allison Bechdel) and began to attract significant attention as works of literature. The apex of literary comics is the graphic novel (the term coined by Will Eisner in 1978 as a marketing euphemism to try to avoid comics' disrepute), a long-form narrative comic with typically mature themes.

Finally, the rise of the internet, particularly at the end of the 1990s, enabled authors to publish webcomics electronically and deliver them directly via computer. Since their costs of material production are low, webcomics allow comics authors to create and disseminate their own work: currently, there are at least twenty-five thousand webcomics available to readers. Traditional newspaper comics are now accessible online as well, and comic book publishing houses have developed a range of mobile apps so that their comics can be read on smartphones.

Most or all of that standard history is going to be familiar to a lot of comics readers. And astute and well-informed comics readers will no doubt have misgivings about some of it—rightly so. A work of history is an account of the past drawn from evidence of documents of the past. Any explanation of the significance and meaning of past events is going to be selective and, in the interests of simplification, create what are in effect errors.

Careful historians of comics have written books that try to minimize these errors and correct some of the common misconceptions that I've parroted above. Harvey (1998, 17) notes that Outcault didn't really invent the newspaper comic: citing Coulton Waugh, he applies what he calls the "Columbus

Principle": Outcault, like Columbus, wasn't the first, but because of his influence, he gets all the credit.[5] The Columbus Principle can be invoked in other cases as well. Depending on how you understand what it is to be a superhero, Superman might not have been the first. Peter Coogan (2006) raises the possibility that little-known characters such as Hugo Hercules, the Phantom Magician, Dr. Occult, and Olga Mesmer (all of whom preceded Superman) might be superheroes. Paul Levitz (2015, 138–41) relates that Eisner didn't invent the graphic novel or even the term for it, but merely popularized it.

Plus, the standard history probably leaves out many of your favorites. Where's *Calvin and Hobbes*? Or *The Avengers*? Or *Jimmy Corrigan: The Smartest Kid on Earth*? Or, for that matter, *Captain Carrot and His Amazing Zoo Crew*? No history is going to serve every audience.

More importantly, the standard history, as I have related it, completely ignores comics outside the American tradition, several of which (*Tintin* and *Astro Boy*) are mentioned in the exemplars with which I started the chapter. Comics are sometimes asserted to be one of the distinctively American art forms. We didn't invent or perfect painting or sculpture or ballet, Americans might claim, but we did come up with jazz and comics, and this we can be proud of. The truth is rather more complicated.[6] Comics traditions are rich and complex in Europe, and arguably the comics category has been advanced further there: in Europe, there is a long-standing, prevailing cultural assumption that comics are primarily for adults and are capable of conveying sophisticated content. And the standard history omits mention of non-Western comics, most conspicuously leaving out manga. Modern manga shows a Western influence, due to the occupation of Japan after World War II, but the history of manga goes back at least as far as Western comics, and probably farther. Manga titles currently have much larger audiences than American comic books, and subcategories of manga arguably cater to a greater range of readers.[7]

If the standard history is simplified to the point of inaccuracy (albeit in ways that will strike familiar chords with many comics fans), what's the point? One easy answer is that it catches up any readers who don't have a "thumbnail sketch" of the history of comics in their head. If you're new to comics, this might help.

We can also see now that apparently disparate subcategories of comics—newspaper comics, comic books, underground and alternative comics, and webcomics—fit into a single, standard, familiar story. There are significant differences among these subcategories: length, content, format, and style. But an overall theoretical understanding of the whole lot is not out of the question. While books could (and have been) published that concentrate exclusively on only one of these subcategories, an approach that considers what comics have in common in terms of media, storytelling devices, value, and social roles is warranted. And that's exactly what the rest of the book you're reading is an attempt to do.

Finally, remember that surveying the ancestry of comics is intended to afford a rough idea of the tradition in which our exemplars are embedded. Let's grant that the standard history gives us at least an approximation of the development of comics, and that more comprehensive and more careful histories are capable of addressing its omissions and errors. We can now explain why it's uncontroversial to believe that the exemplars are comics: they're either among the central pieces of the standard history, heavily influenced by the innovations of those central pieces, or otherwise embedded in that history. This, I think, is why we're comfortable believing that they're comics and uncomfortable with anybody whose beliefs run to the contrary. But even if that's right, we need to be careful about the connections we draw between being a comic and occupying any specific historical context, as the rest of this chapter shows.

1.3. Cartoons as Style and Category

Merely being part of the standard history is not enough to make something a comic. Some of the reasons why are obvious: Stan Lee is part of the standard history, but he's a person, not a comic, even though fictionalized versions of him appear in actual comics like *Stan Lee Meets Superheroes* (2007). Now, everybody knows that people are not comics,[8] but there are more problematic cases—works that people have created, meant to be read or seen, that fall within or are at least on the edges of the standard history but that are not comics. To see what I mean, it's going to be important to consider not only the history of the application of the term "comics," but also the application of the term "cartoons." While—for good reason—there tends to be overlap between our applications of the former and the latter, it will be desirable going forward to disambiguate the two.

Harvey offers a succinct chronicle of how "cartoon" entered our culture (2009; see especially 26–29). As he relates, originally, "cartoon" derived from the Italian word *cartone*, which translates into English as "card." Cartoons were the sketches that painters made, often on cardboard, in preparation for a final artwork. In 1843, the magazine *Punch* extended the term to humorous, single-image drawings. By the late 1800s, "Punch's cartoons," later simplified to "cartoons," won out over rival terms such as "pencillings" and "illustrated

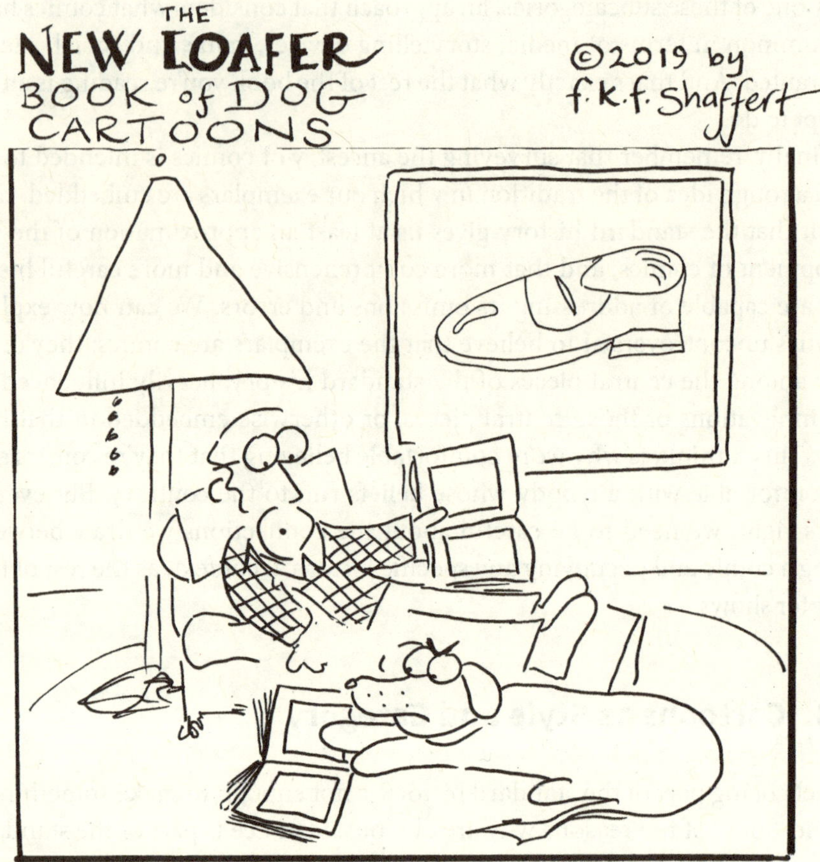

fig. 1.2 "Don't worry, buddy; I don't get it either."

anecdotes." These drawings, usually accompanied by a caption and rarely featuring word balloons, are what we are typically talking about when we use "cartoon" to refer to a category of work. In contemporary context, the cartoons published in the *New Yorker* might be the most familiar example (compare Figure 1.2), but cartoons also still appear in newspapers in the form of editorial or political cartoons.

Daily installments of humor features like *The Family Circus* and *Dennis the Menace*, both cartoons, also show up in the comics section of the newspaper (though, as I'll argue, they aren't comics any more than the *Jumble*).

The modern sense of the term "comics," Harvey continues, arrived at about the same time as "cartoon," but its origins are quite different (2009, 36). Multiple-picture comedic works with captions and word balloons initially attained popularity in humor magazines such as *Life*, *Judge*, and *Puck*, which were commonly known as "comic weeklies" or just "comics." When newspapers started to publish similar works in imitation, the name "comics" came with them, even though the works were not all intended to be humorous. The term "comic books" is a natural extension of this process, since these began as collected reprints of newspaper comics, only later featuring original work.

So what, if anything, differentiates comics from cartoons? The challenge is complex, in part, because comics are occasionally *called* cartoons, and their artists are often referred to as cartoonists. Harvey has even advocated for a wholesale terminological revision in which "cartoonist" and "cartoon" are used as umbrella terms into which subcategories of what we now call "comics" fall (1998, 164–65).

One ready difference is in the number of panels: cartoons have one and comics have more than one. But this is a controversial claim and stands in need of a good deal of defense. I'll undertake that project in the next chapter, in which I reveal the difficulties inherent in lumping single-panel works into the comics category. In this chapter, however, I'll explain why I think Harvey wants to combine the categories of comics and cartoons, and why this move commits an error that has nothing to do with number of panels.

The key is that "cartoon" is used not merely to refer to a *category* but also to a grouping of *styles*. McCloud (1993, chap. 2) analyzes this grouping in detail, contrasting it with others used in comics and, indeed, across visual art forms. In brief, McCloud proposes that cartooning is at root a matter of simplification and abstraction. There is a spectrum of representational styles that lie between the simplest and the most realistic. Consider the human face: the most basic cartoon you could make of it would be a circle with two dots and a line in roughly the appropriate places for eyes and a mouth. Maybe you could even leave out the mouth. (I think you'll find that it's much harder to leave out the eyes—they're *very* important for faces, as you can see in Figure 1.3.)

Cartoons do not all have to be quite so simple. As we move away from abstraction, we can introduce more detail and realism. But nobody is going to confuse a cartoon with its antithesis in representation: a standard, well-focused photograph. Figure 1.4 demonstrates this contrast with a basic cartoon bone (on the left), a somewhat more realistic cartoon bone (in the middle), and an x-ray photograph of a bone (on the right). You might be able to imagine a continuum of bones between those pictured.[9]

With this backdrop, we can explain why comics and cartoons are connected, and why Harvey wants to think of the former as a subset of the

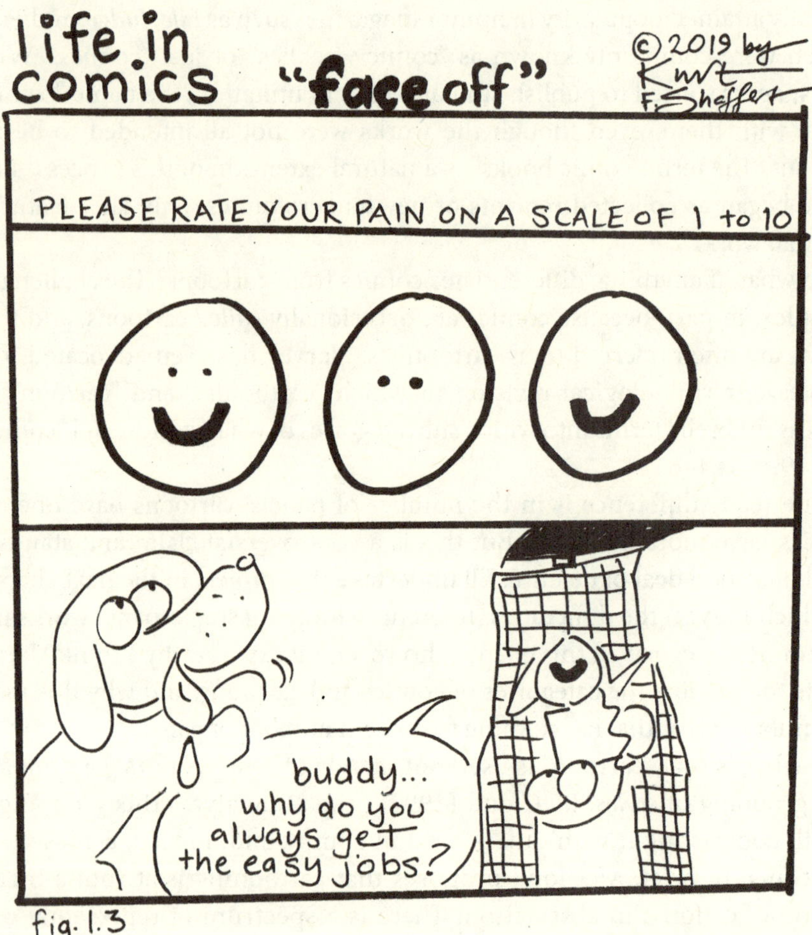

fig. 1.3

latter: a significant proportion of comics are drawn in cartooning styles, including nearly all contemporary newspaper comics.[10] We can also see why it's a mistake to conflate or nest the categories of comics and cartoons. Not all comics are rendered in cartoon styles. There are hyperrealistic comics and even comics constructed out of photographs (a tradition more common in Europe than it is in the United States). If you're familiar with American superhero comics, you'll probably be acquainted with the art of Alex Ross—nobody is going to confuse his painterly images for cartoons.[11]

Obviously, not everything rendered in a cartoon style is a comic, either. Aside from one-panel cartoons (where "cartoons" refers here to the category, not a style), which are generally also cartoons in style, there are *animated*

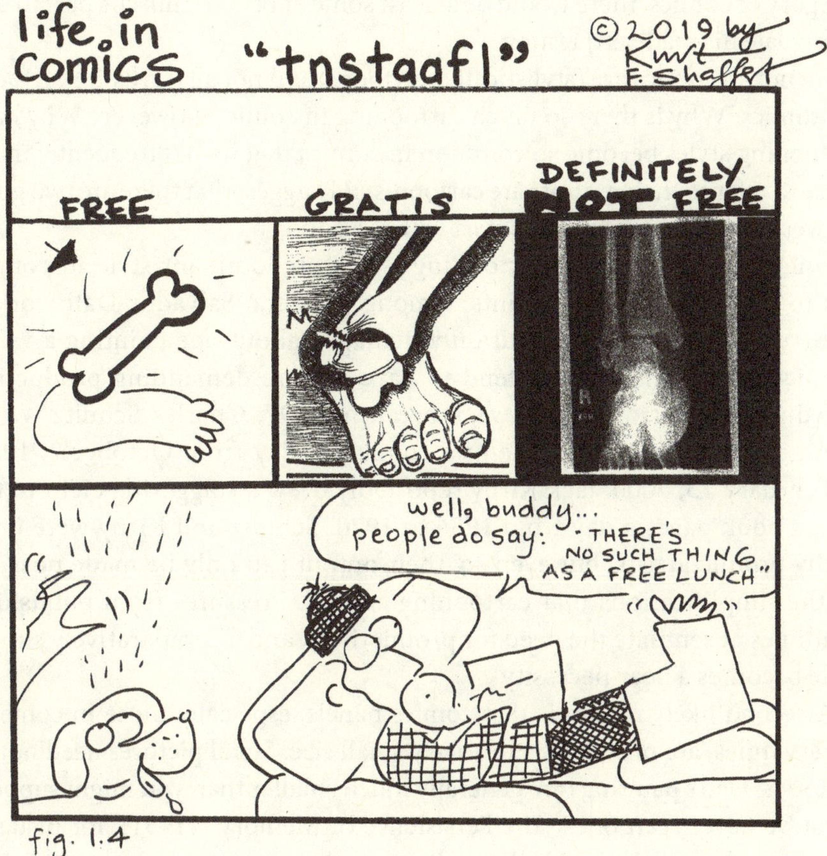

cartoons. *A Charlie Brown Christmas* (1965) is rendered in the same cartoon style as *Peanuts*, on which it is based. But it's not a comic—it's an animated television special. In fact, I'm confident that in contemporary parlance, when most people use the term "cartoon," they're talking about animation. Case in point: a feature that used to appear on my local comics page (but which, I assert, isn't itself a comic) is *UCan with Beakman and Jax*, in which Jok Church answers science questions from children. If you're old enough to remember back far enough, you might recall *Beakman's World*, a children's television show based on it. In one installment (Church 2016), the question is "What was the first cartoon? How did they figure it out?" The answer makes immediate reference to the history of film, and traces the birth of animation to Emile Cohl and James Stuart Blackton. But there's no mention of comics whatsoever. You'd think that if the term "cartoon" was used primarily to refer to the category of comics, there would be at least some effort on Church's part to disambiguate his reader's question.

So: not all comics are (stylistically) cartoons, and not all (stylistic) cartoons are comics. Why is there so much cartooning in comics, however? Why have cartooning styles become so common in comics that it *does* frequently make sense to refer to their authors are cartoonists? I suggest that there are two good answers and one bad one. Let's start with the good.

One likely reason why cartooning is the predominant style in comics has to do with time constraints. Among painters, Salvador Dali worked at a truly remarkable pace but only managed about one painting a week. Comics artists, in contrast, tend to have a more demanding production schedule. Aside from a five-week break in 1997, Charles Schultz wrote, drew, and lettered an average of a comic per day from October 2, 1950, to February 13, 2000. Jack Kirby reportedly drew a staggering eight to ten comic book pages a day from 1956 to 1970. Schultz and Kirby were unusually prolific artists, but even so, their output can only be made possible by the simplifications that cartooning affords. Pressures from publishing deadlines accentuate the need for productivity, and a comparatively simple style becomes a near necessity.

A second likely reason is that comics panels, especially those in contemporary times, are printed at a relatively small size. Small pictures need not be cartoons. Dali's paintings are generally much smaller than you might suppose if you've never seen one. "The Persistence of Memory" (1931), for instance (that's the famous one with the melting clocks), measures in at only 9.5 by 13 inches—not much bigger than a page in a comic book. But Dali is working in oil and his work is intended for close and lengthy scrutiny, rather than instant legibility before the page is turned.

Cartooning as a style is perhaps the easiest way to make images legible to readers. This point is amply borne out in the history of newspaper comics. As comics pages got smaller and smaller, the art got simpler and simpler, the cartooning more abstract and less detailed. Compare Scott Adams' *Dilbert* to Windsor McCay's *Little Nemo in Slumberland*. The former is printed according to current conventions. In my local newspaper, the entire Sunday strip is 6.75 inches wide and 3.25 inches tall. The latter, published from 1905 to 1916, was printed at 16 inches wide and 21 inches tall. *Little Nemo*, in effect, was over *fifteen* times as large as *Dilbert*. While Adams presumably has a number of reasons for his stylistic choices, he could never draw as elaborately as McCay even if he was capable of it: intricate comics like *Little Nemo* would simply be illegible at *Dilbert*'s printed size. I'm guessing that legibility of drawing is likely to continue driving comics styles as they move increasingly into digital formats, but I could be wrong: anticipating technological developments and the uses to which they are put is risky business.[12]

I mentioned previously that there is a bad explanation for why most comics are cartoons in style. It's worth discussing this reason, not because of its quality, but because of its prominence and the amount of controversy it has attracted. Start with something that does seem to be the case: most comics with which typical readers are familiar are produced for mass reproduction. That is, the goal is to churn out as many copies as possible—products that will make a profit rather than products that aspire to the pinnacle of artistic expression. The epitome of the comics industry is neatly captured by Golden Age comics editor Sheldon Mayer's dictum, "Don't give me Rembrandt, give me production" (quoted in Wright 2001, 22). The reason why these are the comics with which we're most familiar, of course, is that there are an awful lot of them.

To move copies, comics are often produced with an eye to broad marketability, and this is where cartooning comes in. McCloud proposes that in contrast to photorealistic styles, cartooning has an immediate appeal for an extensive range of readers (1993, 30–37). Cartoons have found a fundamental place in comics, he argues, because their simplicity allows for the possibility of almost universal identification with the characters therein. The more realistic that a picture of a person is, the more difficult it is to relate to that person as you relate to yourself.

Refer back to the previous illustration in this chapter. The less you are like a bearded fellow or a dog, the less you'll be able to think of yourself as being in the shoes of those characters. But they're still easier to identify with than people (or creatures) depicted via photograph. Correspondingly, as long as you have eyes and a mouth (the vast majority of us), you'll be able to identify with the most cartoonish way of representing people—the face with dots for eyes and a mouth line (see Figure 1.3). McCloud, in effect, claims that comics facilitate reader identification through cartooning. Combining this idea with the profit motive, we have a simple and prima facie compelling argument:

1. More people identify more closely with characters that are depicted via cartooning than characters that are not.
2. People buy comics that contain characters with whom they identify with most closely.
3. So more people buy comics that depict through cartoons than buy comics that do not.
4. A primary (if not exclusive) goal of comics authors and publishers is to sell a lot of comics.

5. Given premise 3, cartooning is an effective way to satisfy the goals mentioned in premise 4.
6. Therefore, cartooning dominates the comics category.

Let me be careful to emphasize that this isn't McCloud's argument. Strictly speaking, only the first premise is. I'm not *sure* he'd accept the rest of it, but the other parts appear to be independently plausible, and my hunch is that this explanation for the prevalence of cartooning in comics is one that he's find amicable to his views.

Let's evaluate the argument. While McCloud's ideas about identification are trading in speculative psychology, with no scientific basis for his claims, this itself is not inevitably damaging—other philosophers employ similar methods with a certain frequency. But there are other difficulties. He might have the wrong way of framing the issue: is identification is the best way to cash out our relationships with characters? After all, as Noël Carroll points out in his discussion of fiction films (2008, 161–70), identification seems to involve sharing the same types of emotional states with the characters with whom we identify, something we rarely do. More typically, the emotional states are asymmetric (e.g., while the protagonist of a horror film is blissfully ignorant, viewers are scared because they know the monster is around the corner).

Even if identification is the proper way of understanding our involvement with comics, there are worse problems with how McCloud's approach is expressed by premise 1. If two characters are depicted at the same level of abstraction, we should identify with them equally well, for McCloud—but we don't. Similarly, we should invariably identify with animated cartoon characters more than we identify with characters in photographically based film and television programs—but we don't. It's not even clear that in comics, we identify with characters the more cartooned they are. It's more plausible to think that we identify with characters (again, if identification is even the right relation to discuss here) based not on depictive styles, but on the similarities each character bears to us in personality, circumstances, or values. My guess is that you don't identify with the persons depicted in *any* of the three pictures in the preceding illustration, because they're decontextualized. You don't know anything about them other than (roughly) what they look like.

Not only that, but pending empirical research, it's unclear that premises 2 and 4 are true. Is identification a significant driver of sales? Perhaps, but perhaps it's no more significant than other factors having nothing to do with identification, such as escapism. Are sales a significant driver of comics creation? Probably: everybody likes to get paid. But it might also be the case that creating comics just to move issues can be secondary to more noble aims having to do with artistic expression and fulfillment—wanting to make something that's not just popular, but good.

For these reasons, we should conclude that McCloud's theory is unlikely to ground a plausible explanation for why so many comics employ a cartoon style. We've seen, however, that there are other good ways of making sense of the tight connection between cartooning and comics.

When comics use a cartooning style, they fall, after a fashion, under the same umbrella as the one-panel works we see in the *New Yorker*. Each employs a style of art in a similar range of simplification and abstraction. But this does not by itself imply that comics should be thought of as being in the same category as cartoons across the board, or that they should be referred to as equivalent, as per Harvey's suggestion.

1.4. Are Comics Art?

Comics is its own category of object, distinct from cartoons and animation. I mentioned at the beginning of this chapter that when philosophers bend their attention toward a new kind of thing, one of the first projects they tend to attempt is a definition, or, alternatively, the development of arguments about why that thing can't be defined. Before we get to an extensive treatment of that topic in Chapter 2, I want to take up another that's a natural question for those philosophers who work in aesthetics: as put in the title of a 2004 exhibition of Robert Crumb's work at the Museum Ludwig in Germany, *Yeah, but Is It Art?*

Fundamentally, this is a question about the overlap between comics and art, and whether there is any. As Bart Beaty details in his comprehensive book on the subject, *Comics versus Art* (2012), it's an apt and provocative question in our postmodern era where boundaries between high and low have become increasingly blurred. On the one hand, the category of comics has, by reputation, been emblematic of disposable, trashy, mass culture. Comics are read by children, delinquents, and outsiders, not art-literate sophisticates (or so the stereotype goes). As even some comics authors assert, comics seems like the antithesis of The Arts, construed as the stuff you encounter in museums, galleries, concert halls, college classes on great novels or poetry, and so forth. On the other hand, because of its basic ingredients—drawing and storytelling—comics bears a *lot* of similarities to esteemed and well-established art forms like painting and literature. And when this topic comes up, a lot of people seem pretty comfortable listing as artworks comics by the likes of George Herriman, Will Eisner, Art Spiegelman, Robert Crumb, Gary Panter, and Chris Ware.[13]

We can focus our attention on the overlap between comics and art by attending to a more specific question that we'll refine increasingly as we go on: Are there any particular comics that are appropriate to classify as artworks? My short answer is, "It depends on what you think it is to be an artwork," but that's a bit of a cop-out, so let's dig deeper.

Perhaps the art status of particular comics has to do with the skill with which each is made: as long as it made by a qualified craftsperson with some degree of aesthetic competence, a comic is an artwork. On this view, lots and lots of comics (maybe even the majority of them) would be artworks. Imagine that you were to see the image shown in Figure 1.5 on the back of a cereal box.

Is this cereal comic (not to be confused with a serial comic!) an artwork?

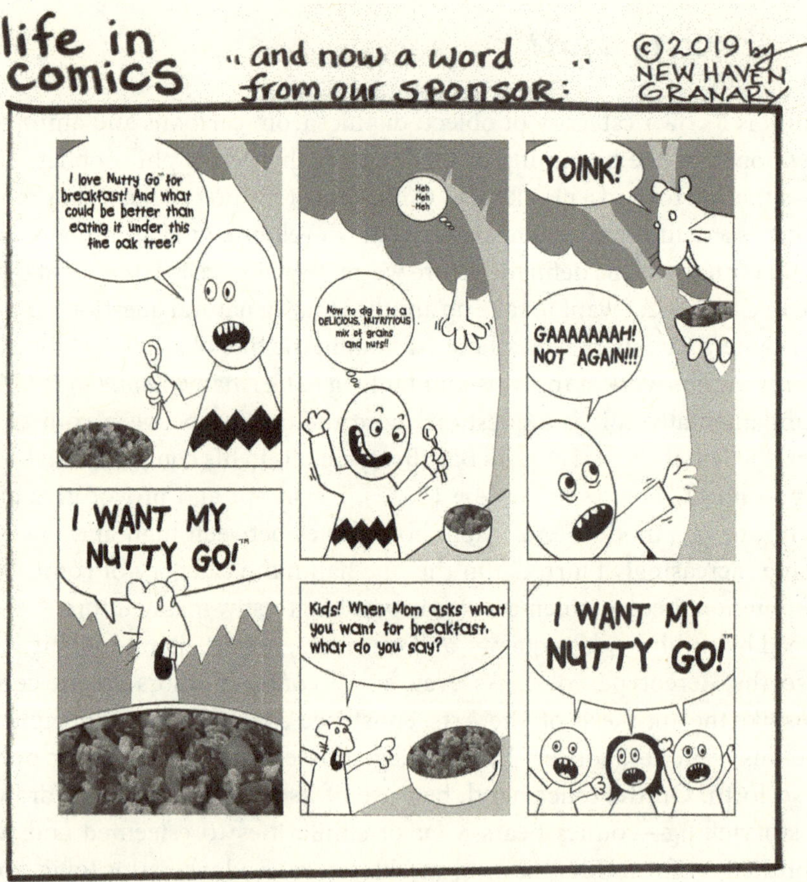

fig. 1.5

Some of you might answer in the affirmative, on the basis that it was intentionally drawn and designed, with a reasonable amount of skill and craft, using typical art-making tools and technologies, and has some degree of aesthetic merit. It's art, just like a hand-built guitar, a quilt, a custom hot-rod, figures and masks carved by the Baule people, haute couture, well-made cabinetry, gourmet food, and so on.

Denis Dutton (2008) offers one possible way to support that position. Dutton argues that the concept of art is stable across cultures—that "their" concept is the same as "ours," and that members of all cultures create artifacts and performances that deserve application of the concept of art. While he is not advancing a definition of art, Dutton gives a list of characteristic features that artworks share around the world. In summary, artworks are created by their makers, using special skills, to give pleasure by representing or imitating the world, thereby engaging the imagination. And while artworks are not primarily for practical or utilitarian purposes, they do occupy a privileged place in culture, and are surrounded by a special language and practice of critical discourse and evaluation (2008, 459–60).

While Dutton does not mention comics specifically, it's relatively clear that on his view, most of them—including all of our exemplars, as well as the cereal comic—are going to turn out to be artworks. Even the most quotidian comics are made using special (if not always virtuosic) skills of drawing, composition, and writing. Comics are representational, at least the ones that are the most familiar to mainstream audiences. The imagination is engaged: as we'll see in Chapter 4, the imagination is *necessarily* engaged by the panel format. Pleasure is important, even though some (including the cereal comic) are ultimately for purposes of information or commerce. Comics are set apart from everyday life in much the same way as works of literature and film. And they've occasioned a robust critical discourse, as any fan will tell you.

Following Dutton produces a serviceable answer to our question about the art status of comics. But we might crave more. Dutton's application of the concept isn't the only option, and if we get more precise about our applications of "artwork," we might get a rather different sort of answer about comics.

To add more nuance, we might introduce the distinction, not recognized in Dutton's list, between the *evaluative* and the *classificatory* senses of art.[14] Sometimes, if works are made well enough or actions are performed with enough skill, we extend the term "art" to them as an honorific. This is the evaluative sense, and it applies, I expect, to the cereal comic in some degree. But it's not the same as the classificatory sense.

An analogy might be helpful. The term "chair" also has an evaluative and a classificatory sense. If I asked you to give me a list of chairs in a given classroom, you could complete this task without much difficulty. In a medium-size classroom typical of most colleges, you'd count about thirty, and you would have properly classified those chairs as chairs. But unless the classrooms you've seen are very different from those I teach in, you wouldn't think much of these chairs—they're hard, uncomfortable, not much to look, encrusted with gum, and so on. Suppose, however, that you encountered a chair that was upholstered with fine leather, heated, reclining, with a built-in massage option and a refrigerating unit in one arm. "Now that's a *chair*," you might say, quite rightly. With this claim, you wouldn't be classifying it: chair classification is pretty easy, and nobody would have been in doubt about what type of furniture it was or whether it was actually a coffee table instead of a chair. You'd be using "chair" evaluatively, to mark out its quality in contrast to other chairs like those in a classroom. If it was good enough (imagine that the leather had been hand-tooled with elaborate, nightmarish designs by H. R. Giger), you might even call it "art."

With the distinction between classification and evaluation in mind, then, if you are inclined to claim that the cereal comic is an artwork, you might be stressing its evaluative aspects. Depending on how good it is, you might make your claim more or less emphatically. But you wouldn't necessarily be intending to *classify* it as an artwork. If I turned you loose in an art gallery and instructed you to make a list of everything in it that's an artwork, I bet you'd make the same list that I would, even if we had very different ideas about which works in there were good and which were bad.

With the distinction between the classificatory and evaluative senses in mind, our question of this section now becomes more precise: as we cast our minds around the world together, which particular comics (if any) should we *classify* as artworks, irrespective of their merits? (We'll consider the issue of which comics are good and what makes them good when we get to Chapter 6.)

But the refinements of our question about the overlap between comics and art don't end here. We might be interested not only in classification, but also, contrary to Dutton, in culturally specific classification. The debate over the existence of a concept of art that crosses cultures is far from settled, and we might want to side with those like Larry Shiner, who take the position opposed to Dutton's. Shiner argues (2008) that Dutton's list applies to the "premodern" concept of art, which has persisted since at least the time of the ancient Greeks. The premodern concept contrasts art with nature; the modern concept of art, which arose in the West in the eighteenth century, contrasts art with craft. As Shiner puts it, "'Art,' once a general term for all human making and performing, had now become a high-status word for only certain kinds of making and performing" (2008, 467). If Shiner is right, and the modern concept of art is distinct and worthy of attention, then we have a final precisification of our question about comics: which particular comics (if any) should we classify as artworks in the modern sense, irrespective of their merits?

Now we do have to be a little careful here. There's a very real risk of accusations of ethnocentrism or even straight-up racism, on which Western standards are used as a yardstick for assessment of the works and practices of premodern, small-scale, Indigenous, nonwhite, or non-Western cultures.[15] Using such a yardstick creates the possibility of evaluative comparisons that unfairly diminish the achievements of those who, for various reasons, fail to conform to the criteria set forth in the Western, modern tradition. More close to home, if the comics classified as artworks are just those that are found in the Western tradition, then that has the potential to wipe out attention given to and esteem earned by comics authors from other cultures.

We should bear in mind, however, that we're just dealing with the classificatory sense, not the evaluative sense. Consider an analogy. What it is to be a sumo wrestling match is determined by a very particular set of culturally specific rules and practices. Being a sumo wrestling match doesn't mean that it's a good wrestling match. And wrestling matches that fit into other traditions—like Greco-Roman—can still be good even if they violate all requirements of sumo wrestling. Similarly, just because something is an artwork in the (modern) classificatory sense doesn't mean that it's a good artwork, and just because something isn't an artwork in the (modern) classificatory sense doesn't mean that it's without value.[16] So: yes, the Western, modern sense of art is ethnocentric. But with appropriate caution, we can acknowledge that it's just one way among many of classifying objects, and shouldn't be taken to occupy any particular space of privilege.

Do comics fit into that classification? This is more specific question, but it's still hard, since philosophers have come up with a wide range of candidates for understanding the modern concept of art. One way to proceed would be to summarize each of the most popular and plausible definitions of art, then apply them to comics. If a given comic satisfies most or all of these definitions, then there is some plausibility to the claim that it is appropriate to classify it as an artwork. That project, however, ends up being a bit tedious, and (as philosophers sometimes say in such situations) is best left as an exercise for the reader.

What I'd like to do instead is narrow down the range of acceptable definitions of the modern concept of art, and then see how comics fit in. Briefly put, until the middle of the twentieth century, the three dominant strategies for defining art were:

1. *Mimetic* theories, according to which artworks are imitations of reality: a mirror held up to nature, as it were.
2. *Expressivist* theories, according to which artworks are expressions of a characteristic emotion (the aesthetic emotion, as some put it) or according to which artworks expresses ordinary emotions in a very characteristic way (specified within each expressivist theory).
3. *Formalist* theories, according to which artworks have characteristic, aesthetically significant formal features such as unity, complexity, and intensity.

Each of these types of theories has it that artworks could be identified—whether by the artist or the audience—through sensory or introspective experience. Internal and external senses, in conjunction with the affective responses sensory information provides, can tell you whether a work is imitative, or expressive, or has the right kind of formal features.

Gradually, philosophers began to realize, due to some dramatic evolution in the arts, that the mere presence of any given feature accessible through perception or introspection was no longer a reliable guide to art status. This led some (see, most famously, Weitz 1956) to argue that art was just the wrong sort of concept to be defined anyway, and that the definitional project was pointless and futile. (We'll look at Weitz's arguments in our next chapter.) But it led others to posit that we'd just been looking in the wrong place.

The right place to look, according to this new theoretical trend, has to do with what I'll call the *context hypothesis*:

> Whether any given *x* (where *x* can be anything—an object, performance, idea, and so on) is an artwork at a particular time *t* is deeply connected to *x*'s context at *t*.

Let me say a little more about why I think this is a plausible way to narrow the definitions of art that we apply to comics.

The context hypothesis is an innovation from the mid-twentieth century, most influentially in the work of Arthur Danto. Danto draws our attention to *counterparts*: qualitatively identical objects that cannot be differentiated from each other merely by using our senses.[17] Of a pair of counterparts, it is possible, Danto thinks, that one is an artwork and another is not. One of Danto's examples (1964, 580–81) is Andy Warhol's *Brillo Boxes*. While these are in fact screen-printed on wood, they could have been made on cardboard, in which case they would be exact counterparts of boxes actually used by the Brillo

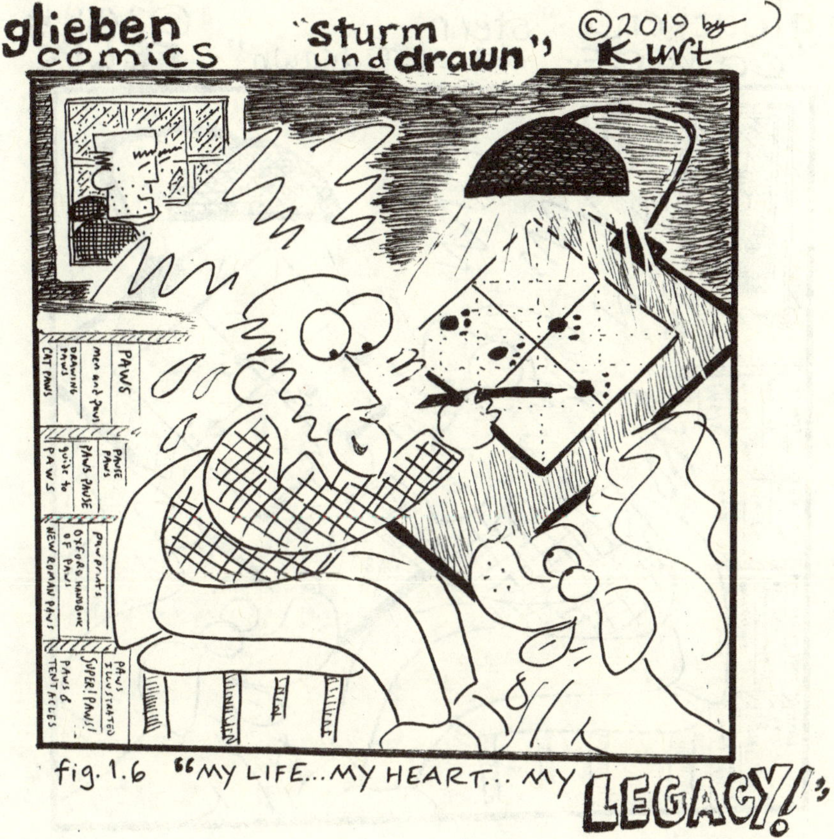

fig. 1.6 "MY LIFE... MY HEART... MY LEGACY!"

company for shipping their soap pads. *Brillo Boxes* (or at least a cardboard version of them) are artworks, but Brillo boxes are not. If sensory experience is insufficient for differentiating the two, then the only alternative is context—something about who generates art objects, what social roles the objects (and/or their creators) occupy, and the like.

I propose that whether a particular comic counts as an artwork needs to be determined with the context hypothesis in mind. Let's just assume for a moment that the fellow depicted in Figure 1.6 has successfully completed an artwork (the comic that you can see on his drawing table).

Now look at Figure 1.7.

Here, in an incredible coincidence, a cat, walking through some ink and then across the artist's drawing table, has produced an image that's perceptually identical to the artwork depicted in Figure 1.6. That is, nobody can tell

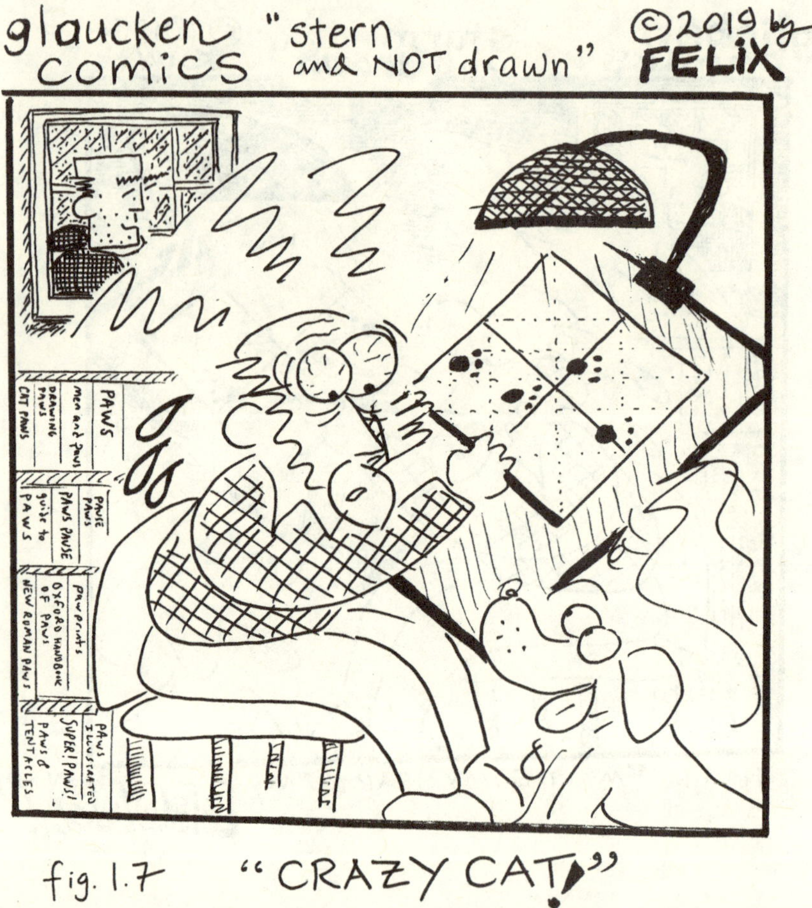

just by looking what the difference is between the two. Yet the first, the result of the artist's creative skills, is an artwork. Or, if you don't buy that, it's at least a comic. The second image isn't an artwork and it's probably not a comic either—it's just a random series of cat tracks that happen to be arranged in a pattern that looks like a comic.

Context explains why: the latter image wasn't created under the right conditions. At a minimum, artworks (and comics) are artifacts—works whose immediate causes are human activity—and the accidental image is no artifact. But artifactuality isn't going to be enough to ground a theory of art, since there are plenty of artifacts (e.g., this book) that aren't art.

Here's what Danto has to say about the context in which artifacts need to be found in order to be artworks:

> To see something as art at all demands nothing less than this, an atmosphere of artistic theory, a knowledge of the history of art. . . . So it is essential to our study that we understand the nature of an art theory, which is so powerful a thing as to detach objects from the real world and make them a part of a different world, and *art* world, a world of *interpreted things*. (1981, 135)

This passage highlights the importance of three keywords: theory, history, and artworld (I'll follow George Dickie in spelling this last term with one word rather than two, as Danto does). How these are understood, combined, rejected, and otherwise used to specify the proper context for artworks is a matter of great debate,[18] but there now seems to be something approaching a consensus that has developed around the context hypothesis (see Matravers 2000). Accordingly, if we pay close attention to the context that comics occupy, we should be able to arrive at a reasonable position about their status as artworks—at least, artworks in the modern sense of the concept.

Beaty offers for our consideration the useful notion of the *comics world*: "the collection of individuals necessary for the production of works that the world defines as comics, [including] writers, pencillers, inkers, colourists, letterers, editors, assistant editors, publishers, marketing and circulation personnel, printers, distributors, retailers, and retail employees" (2012, 37). To this list of those who comprise the comics world, I'd add comics readers (much as the artworld includes a public comprised of people who receive art). Beaty thinks of the comics world as *an* artworld. Does it overlap with *the* artworld that interests Danto?

Sometimes, but the fit is uncomfortable. Comics authors, especially working in alternative comics, have a tendency to position their work as antiart, in direct opposition to the artworld. Examples cited by Beaty include Robert Crumb, Art Spiegelman, Peter Bagge, and Daniel Clowes. As Crumb puts it, "I'm not interested in a bunch of cake eaters that go sniff around museums. . . . That world is phony, repugnant, and sick" (quoted in Beaty 2012, 207). By intentionally rejecting the artworld, these artists appear as nonconformists, maintaining their independent credibility. The rejection goes both ways—critics of the visual arts have historically held up comics as everything that fine art is not, which is why Roy Lichtenstein's paintings of panels from romance and war comics were so provocative; literary critics, until recently, were of a similar disposition (see, for example, Schwartz 2004).

It isn't just that comics authors and art critics agree that their worlds are separate. The contexts in which comics are encountered and disseminated are quite different as well. The stereotypical readership for comics—kids, delinquents, and geeks—does not appear to be the same demographic as art connoisseurs. And the distribution models for comics, which are largely accessed in the United States through newspapers, the direct market, and the internet, lies apart from what we generally think of as the typical venues for acquiring or experiencing art.

Nonetheless, comics have increasingly penetrated the modern Western artworld context. While comics have had a presence in this context since at least 1922, they are now increasingly the subjects of major exhibitions at art museums and galleries, as Beaty relates in detail (2012, chap. 8). The treatment of comics in these exhibitions can be belittling. Sometimes, they are presented merely as influential source material for genuine art, and not the genuine article themselves. Perhaps more commonly, comics are presented in a (relatively obvious) attempt at a cash grab, akin to an exhibit of *Star Wars* paraphernalia. They get a large audience in the door that wouldn't otherwise come. But at least sometimes, comics are treated with genuine respect in museum and gallery context, especially when they're made by the canonical authors cited at the beginning of this section. Crumb alone had seventeen major shows devoted to his comics in the 2000s (Beaty 2012, 200): his rejection of the artworld, quoted earlier, is suspiciously two-faced.

Furthermore, comics are now frequently the subject of study from a perspective that concentrates heavily on widely acknowledged works of art: literature departments in academia.[19] Comics, as Aaron Meskin writes, are

> typically full of text, commonly found in bookshops where they are often sold in book form under the "Graphic Novel" heading, appreciated (at least in part) by means of reading, taught in literature classes, occasionally discussed in academic journals devoted to literature, and often reviewed in the book review sections of newspapers and magazines. (2009, 1)

Meskin is skeptical about straightforwardly classifying comics as literature. Raising considerations both pro and con, he argues that the best way to understand comics is as a hybrid between literature, printmaking, and pictorial narrative. Nonetheless, he seems to agree that the use of words (in many comics) is salient enough to give them what I will call later (in Chapter 4) a verbal dimension, such that "we appropriately appreciate the literary [i.e., verbal] aspects of a comic book (where they are present) in light of the norms and styles and concerns that attach to literature" (2009, 21). If at least some comics are properly approached, in part, as works of literature, and works of literature are properly categorized as art, this suggests that it's appropriate to approach at least some comics as artworks.

The considerations raised by art exhibitions and literary studies indicate that there is overlap between the comics world and the artworld. Comics have become the sorts of things that one can find in the right context for artwork status (in the classificatory, modern sense). But, to reinforce an earlier point, this does not entail that all comics have penetrated that context, nor that the place of comics in the artworld is settled and secure.

1.5. Conclusions

We started this chapter with a list of exemplars, works that are uncontroversial to categorize as comics. I offered the standard history, which more or less encapsulates the development of comics in America. The exemplars (at least those of American origin) fit handily into that history. That's why we've got no problem thinking of them as comics, or at least, would have a problem with anybody who claimed that they are not comics.

Still, not all components of the standard history are comics. In particular, we need to be careful to differentiate the category of comics from the category of cartoons, even though comics can be rendered in a cartoon style. I argued that the explanations for the dominance of that style in comics stem from facts about the production of comics, rather than efforts to increase reader identification.

The category of comics has stylistic overlaps with other categories that are not comics, and it also overlaps with art. This overlap is complex, and its exact nature depends on the notion of art that you're deploying at the moment. In the evaluative sense, and the premodern sense in which art is contrasted with natural objects, it's pretty clear that a lot of comics (maybe even all of them) turn out to be art. But in the classificatory sense, understood as standing in opposition to mere craft, fewer comics are artworks. Some, indeed, now occupy the right kind of contexts for artworks, but the comics world and artworld frequently stand apart. Looking forward, it's because of these conclusions about the artistic status of comics that I'll frequently refer to the category of comics as an art form. Not only is comics the sort of thing that supplies examples of artworks, but the similarities that comics bears to more renowned art forms like literature, painting, music, and film will be increasingly important as this book goes on.

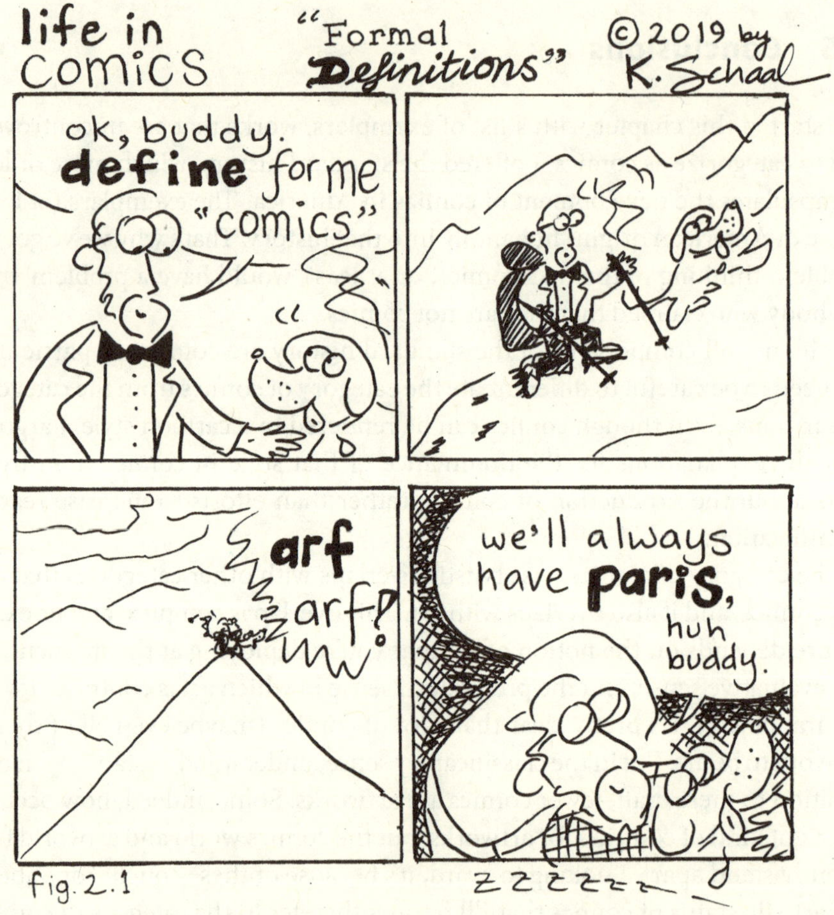

life in comics
"Formal Definitions"
© 2019 by K. Schaal
ok, buddy. define for me "comics"
arf
arf!
we'll always have paris, huh buddy.
zzzzzzz

fig. 2.1

2

Formal Definitions of Comics

Pictures, Panels, and Words

2.1. Can Comics Be Defined?

Here's where we find ourselves after Chapter 1: We have exemplars of comics. We've learned about the standard history—the account that typically gets told about how comics came to be, which helps us understand the central fittingness of the exemplars into the comics category. We've seen that comics and cartoons are different categories, though we have an explanation of why they're sometimes conflated, and why comics are most often cartoons in style. And we have a grasp of whether, when, and which comics are properly classified as artworks.

All this without any definition of the category of comics. So do we need a definition? Is there any point to trying to find one?

When philosophers consider a category like comics for the first time, they tend to try their hand at what we'll call an *essentialist definition* (sometimes also called a *real definition*)—an attempt to capture what it is to be a comic by using necessary and sufficient conditions. Together with Greg Hayman, I attempted such a definition myself. It was fun and worthwhile (though potentially futile, as we'll see as this chapter develops).

In case you haven't encountered the format before, let's get a better sense of what an essentialist definition is. It's supposed to capture all and only the things that fall under the concept you're trying to define. For comics, any essentialist definition can be translated into the following format:

> x is a comic if and only if x has properties $p_1 \ldots p_n$.

Here x refers to any potential candidate for status as a comic, and $p_1 \ldots p_n$ are the property or properties that all comics share (the necessary feature or features) and that, when combined, entail that something is a comic (the jointly sufficient feature or features).[1]

The Philosophy of Comics. Henry John Pratt, Oxford University Press. © Oxford University Press 2023.
DOI: 10.1093/oso/9780190845445.003.0002

Fitting a definition into the essentialist format is simple enough, but it's not so simple to find one that works. Consider, for example:

> x is a comic if and only if x has been placed on the bookshelves where I keep all my comics.

This one won't do for some fairly obvious reasons. First, not everything that's a comic is on those bookshelves: for better or worse, I don't personally own every comic. Second, there are objects on there that are not comics, including my *Return of the Jedi* lunchbox, a hand-carved moose, and a Moss Man Masters of the Universe action figure with a tiny reproduction of my head substituted for Moss Man's own.

To show that an essentialist definition is incorrect, it's enough to find a counterexample in either direction. That's what I did in the previous paragraph: find something that's an x but doesn't have one or more of $p_1 \ldots p_n$, or find something that has all of $p_1 \ldots p_n$, but that isn't a comic.

The counterexample game is all too easy to play, and not just with definitions of comics. Try to formulate a counterexample-proof definition for the concept *chair* some time and you'll quickly see what I mean. It might be that counterexamples are so easy to find because essentialist definitions of categories like comics or concepts like *chair* are actually impossible.

Compare the project of defining comics to that of defining art. Famously, Morris Weitz argues that art is the wrong kind of concept for essentialist definitions. Art is what he calls an "open" concept (1956, 31–32). It can't be defined using necessary and sufficient conditions. Unlike a "closed" concept like prime number, Weitz claims, definitions of open concepts are always subject to revision: there aren't any new numbers that we can find that will cause us to change our concept of what a prime number is, but there will always be new artworks that challenge our extant ideas about art. Essentialist definitions of art foreclose on the possibility of these creative and original challenges, and so are not only metaphysically, but also *normatively* problematic: one ought not to endorse them. The best we can do is to recognize that artworks bear family resemblances to each other—that there are strands of similarities between artworks that allow us to recognize that they are art. And the utility of these family resemblances renders any definition moot.

While Weitz is interested primarily in the overall category of art, Aaron Meskin has argued that his general approach is appropriately applied to more specific, finer-grained categories of art like literature, film, poetry, dance, and (most relevant for our purposes) comics—in short, as Meskin puts it, all "non-logical/non-mathematical/non-technical concepts," which cannot be defined nonarbitrarily (2008, 136). The concept or category of comics is presumably not logical, mathematical, or technical, and so falls squarely under the umbrella of Weitz's view. Like the project of giving an essentialist definition of art, the project of giving an essentialist definition of comics reflects a fundamental misunderstanding about the kind of category that comics is.

Moreover, for Meskin, like Weitz, defining comics presents a normative difficulty (2008, 140–42). It's not that essentialist definitions foreclose on the possibility of creativity—which Meskin recognizes is often abetted, rather than hindered, by arbitrary restrictions. Rather, Meskin thinks that there is a range of different understandings of comics present in critical and cultural practice. Essentialist definitions prioritize some of these understandings over others, which leads to a significant problem in evaluation and interpretation of comics. Evaluation and interpretation of any given comic depends crucially on judgments about whether that comic is typical of the category or something of an outlier. Essentialist definitions eliminate outliers from the category entirely, rather than allowing for a spectrum of typicality to atypicality, and that risks serious critical error.

Meskin proposes shifting the debate away from classificatory, essentialist definitions of comics. Such definitions aren't required for identifying or evaluating comics, which we appear to do quite well antecedent to any theorizing about them (2007, 375–76). That's why we could go about our business in Chapter 1 without having already formulated any essentialist definition. Instead of casting about for necessary and sufficient conditions, we could think about comics in the terms laid out by Kendall Walton in his highly influential article "Categories of Art" (1970, 338–40). What are the *standard features* for the category of comics, which tend to qualify works as members of that category? What are the *variable features* of the category comics, which might be aesthetically significant in individual works, but which are irrelevant to category membership? And what are the *contrastandard features* of the category of comics, which tend to disqualify (though do not always guarantee disqualification of) works as members of that category? Addressing comics from this perspective would help us take the turn that Meskin recommends: to concentrate on "the normative question—and ask what concept of comics will pay off critically and appreciatively" (2008, 142).

I mentioned earlier that, together with Greg Hayman, I've tried my hand at an essentialist definition. If Meskin is right, then our definition—one that has (much to my surprise) acquired something of a canonical status—was part of an ill-conceived project. Is it worth revisiting? What justification, if any, could there be for the remainder of the present chapter?

One possibility is that Meskin is just wrong about the indefinability of comics, for reasons that are, at present, not entirely understood. Perhaps it's possible to give a good essentialist definition of comics, for which there are no counterexamples, and that Meskin's arguments appear convincing because nobody has managed to do it yet. It's easy to say that something (e.g., running a four-minute mile) is impossible until somebody (Roger Bannister) comes along and does it.

But to use this case to motivate the definitional project appears to rely on an unwarranted degree of optimism, particularly since there isn't exactly a trajectory of essentialist definitions of comics getting better and better (in the way that world records in timed sporting events tend to get faster and faster). Furthermore, even if an essentialist definition, contra Meskin, were possible, his point remains that we don't *need* one for any practical purpose, and such definitions might even hinder proper comics criticism.

Fans of essentialist definitions might offer a reply: just because we have no practical need for something doesn't entail we shouldn't pursue it. There are values other than the practical, and I, for one, think the definitional project affords some. Having undertaken it myself, I can attest to the fact that my understanding of comics—both the category itself and the rich variety of particular comics that are found in it—is considerably better and deeper. Even if we grant to Meskin that the *goal* is impossible, I expect that even he would agree that the *journey* toward it can be worthwhile, at least in theory. Arguably, the bulk of philosophy is like this. Will we ever achieve the correct answers to philosophical problems? Probably not—because of the nature of the problems themselves.[2] Are they worth investigating anyway? Yes.

So, boldly, the rest of this chapter immerses us in potential candidates for essential properties of comics. It's likely that we won't be successful. Maybe all we'll end up doing is roughing out some standard features of the category. But regardless of the outcome, we'll learn a lot, I hope, and along the way, we'll set the stage for the discussion of medium specificity that's to come.

2.2. Extant Definitions

The project of defining comics has been tried before and nothing that happens in this book will stop it from being tried again. Notable attempts include the following, in chronological order:

- Coulton Waugh: "(1) A continuing character who becomes the reader's dear friend, whom he looks forward to meeting day after day or Sunday after Sunday; (2) a sequence of pictures, which may be funny or thrilling, complete in themselves or part of a larger story; (3) speech in the drawing, usually in blocks of lettering surrounded by 'balloon' lines." (1947, 14)

- David Kunzle: "1 / There must be a sequence of separate images; 2 / There must be a preponderance of image over text; 3 / The medium in which the strip appears and for which it was originally intended must be reproductive, that is, in printed form, a mass medium; 4 / The sequence must tell a story which is both moral and topical." (1973, 2)
- M. Thomas Inge: "An open-ended dramatic narrative about a recurring set of characters, told in a series of drawings, often including dialogue in balloons and narrative text, and published serially in newspapers." (1990, xi)
- Scott McCloud: "Juxtaposed pictorial and other images in deliberate sequence, intended to convey information and/or produce an aesthetic response in the viewer." (1993, 9)
- Bill Blackbeard and Dean Crain: "A serial sequential narrative in drawn panels featuring recurrent characters in an open-ended series of stories, told by explanatory dialogue balloons *within* the story panels with little or no narrative text." (1995, 10)
- David Carrier: "the speech balloon, the closely linked narrative, and the book-size scale." (2000, 74)
- Robert Harvey: "Pictorial narrative or expositions in which words (often lettered into the picture area within speech balloons) usually contribute to the meaning of the pictures and vice versa." (2001, 76)
- Greg Hayman and Henry John Pratt: "A sequence of discrete, juxtaposed pictures that comprise a narrative, either in their own right or when combined with text." (2005, 423)
- Thierry Groensteen: "The central element of comics, the first criteria in the foundational order, is *iconic solidarity*. I define this as interdependent images that, participating in a series, present the double characteristic of being separated . . . and which are plastically and semantically overdetermined by the fact of their co-existence *in praesentia*." (2007, 18)
- Will Eisner: "An art and literary form that deals with the arrangement of pictures or images and words to narrate a story or dramatize an idea." (2008, xi)
- Karin Kukkonen: "A medium that communicates through images, words, and sequence." (2013, 4)

It's important to recognize that not all of these theorists are trying to offer necessary and sufficient conditions for the category of comics. Many of them are just trying to capture a significant subcategory of comics, to give a rough jumping-off point for further inquiry, to valorize the category, or to situate comics within a larger social discourse. Nonetheless, these definitions contain notable kernels of insight about comics, many of which recur across definitional attempts. Rather than analyzing each individually, a more efficient process will be to extract from them notable and promising candidates for necessary conditions (which might prove to be jointly sufficient). These include the following:

- Created with the intention of entertaining, provoking an aesthetic response, or conveying information.
- A moral or topical story.
- Recurring characters or a cast of characters.
- An open-ended serial narrative.
- Book-size scale.
- Presented in a mass-media format.
- A preponderance of picture over text.
- A visual-verbal blend.
- The presence of word balloons or the equivalent.
- Pictorial.
- Narrative.
- A sequence of spatially juxtaposed panels.

Some of these conditions more plausible than others. In Section 2.3, we'll examine those that I think can be dismissed from consideration without too much effort, at least when construed as necessary conditions. That is, we'll find that there are significant comics and subgenres of comics that fail to have the properties to which these conditions refer. In Section 2.4, we'll turn our attention to the better conditions, for which counterexamples are more difficult to raise. Once we've gone through this work, we'll investigate the merits of combining the best of the conditions, to see if we might be able to find some that are individually necessary and jointly sufficient.

2.3. Less Plausible Necessary Conditions

While I'll have a bit to say about the appeal of each of the conditions considered in this section, I'm going to argue that none of them should be included in an essentialist definition. Here are the conditions and the reasons why they're not very plausible.

- Created with the intention of entertaining, provoking an aesthetic response, or conveying information.

The intentions cited in this condition, generally, do reflect the most prevalent purposes of comics. But because the intended effects of comics, both historical and contemporary, come in a tremendous range, a condition that restricts their scope is arbitrary, at best. Comics can be intended to provoke any response that their creators can envision an audience having. Or, indeed, they can be created with no particular response, type of response, or range of responses in mind whatsoever.

Consider two intended responses not listed above. First, pornographic comics can be created primarily for the purpose of sexual arousal. It's hard to see how this purpose falls under any of the three intentions above. While sexual arousal might overlap with entertainment, it need not. Some pornographic comics might convey information about the sex acts contained therein, or various anatomical facts, but the only way to support the claim that they *all* convey information is to construe "information" broadly enough to encompass any representation whatsoever. At that point, one might just as well argue that comics are all representational (about which more in the next section). And there's a significant strand of philosophical theory according to which sexual arousal is the polar opposite of an aesthetic response.[3] There's also a significant strand of philosophy according to which the notion of an aesthetic response isn't even something that can be reasonably understood at all.[4]

Second, there is a burgeoning genre of graphic medicine, in which comics play a central role. Comics can be created for therapeutic purposes. If such works entertain, provoke an aesthetic response, or convey information, they do so only incidentally, and not as part of the purpose for which they're intended. I'll have more to say about graphic medicine and why comics are well suited for it in Chapter 3.

- A moral or topical story.

Similarly, restricting the type of story that can be told in comics, even to the vague and flexible degree afforded by "moral and topical," fails to encompass the sheer variety of inventiveness found in the category. "Moral" can be interpreted two ways that I can think of. First, it can indicate that the story contains elements that are morally evaluable or significant—to some degree, it's morally good or morally bad, right or wrong. If that's the claim, then it's rendered implausible by comics that have no moral content whatsoever—at least not without stretching the notion of "morally evaluable" in such a way

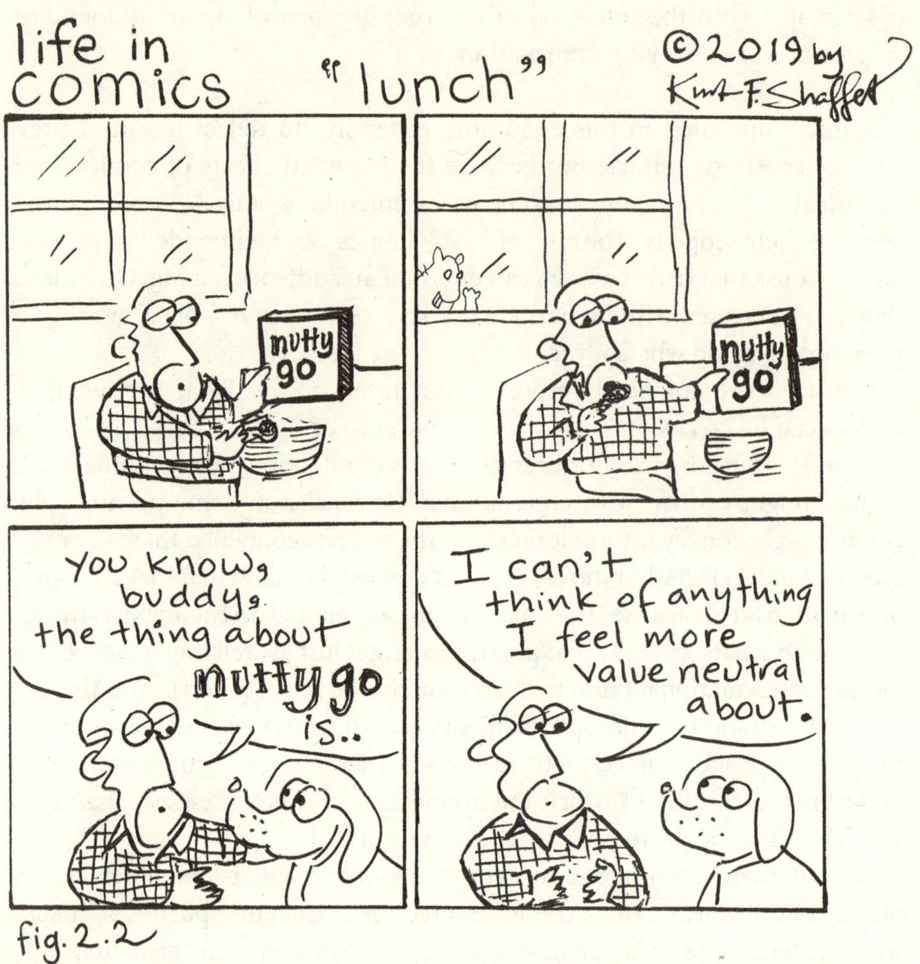

fig. 2.2

as to apply to everything at all times. Figure 2.2 is a representative example of what I mean. It's just a quotidian scene of a guy and some cereal. He's not doing anything that smacks of being right or wrong, good or bad.

Second, "moral" could mean "morally good." The idea here would be that the stories comics tell have positive moral value. That's just plain false. As we'll see in our final chapter, there are plenty of individual comics that are immoral (have overall negative moral value)—though I'll argue that the category of comics itself is morally neutral.

"Topical" suggests immediate relevance to contemporaneous events. Fantasy comics, historical comics, literary adaptations, talking animal comics for kids, and many other subcategories gain at least some of their appeal because of their escapist elements—they're the polar opposite of topical. So "moral or topical" won't do as a necessary condition.

- Recurring characters or a cast of characters.

This condition is ambiguous. Does it mean that a recurring comic (that is, created or published in more than one installment) must have at least some recurring characters, or that each individual comic (whether that comic recurs or not) must have at least some recurring characters in it? While the majority of comics have recurring characters in at least one of these senses, neither is necessary for comics.

With respect to the first interpretation of the condition, authors could use different characters for each installment of a recurring comic. Would this make it difficult to count it as the same comic through time? Not necessarily: there are ways to unify a comic other than recurring characters, such as theme, style, authorship, and even something as mundane as the title. With respect to the second interpretation, it seems possible for there to be unique or "one-off" comics with nothing that's plausibly counted as a character that appears in more than one panel. Consider, for example, Figure 2.3. There's a common theme here (obviously, a play on different usages of "duck"), but no repetition of characters.

- An open-ended serial narrative.

Following ideas developed by Roy T. Cook (2013), I have characterized a *serial narrative* (previously) as follows:

> At least two proper, nonoverlapping subnarratives that are ordered both diegetically and nondiegetically. This results in multiple episodes set in the same storyworld, where narrative threads persist across episodes. Diegetic changes—alterations in truths internal to the storyworld—made in one episode affect the next, and each episode represents a progression of the overall narrative rather than a return to equilibrium. (Pratt 2013, 266)

Fancy talk aside, what this means is that serial narratives tell stories that persist across installments—like *Game of Thrones*, but unlike (more or less) *Law & Order*. If there's no planned end-point, then the serial narrative is open-ended.

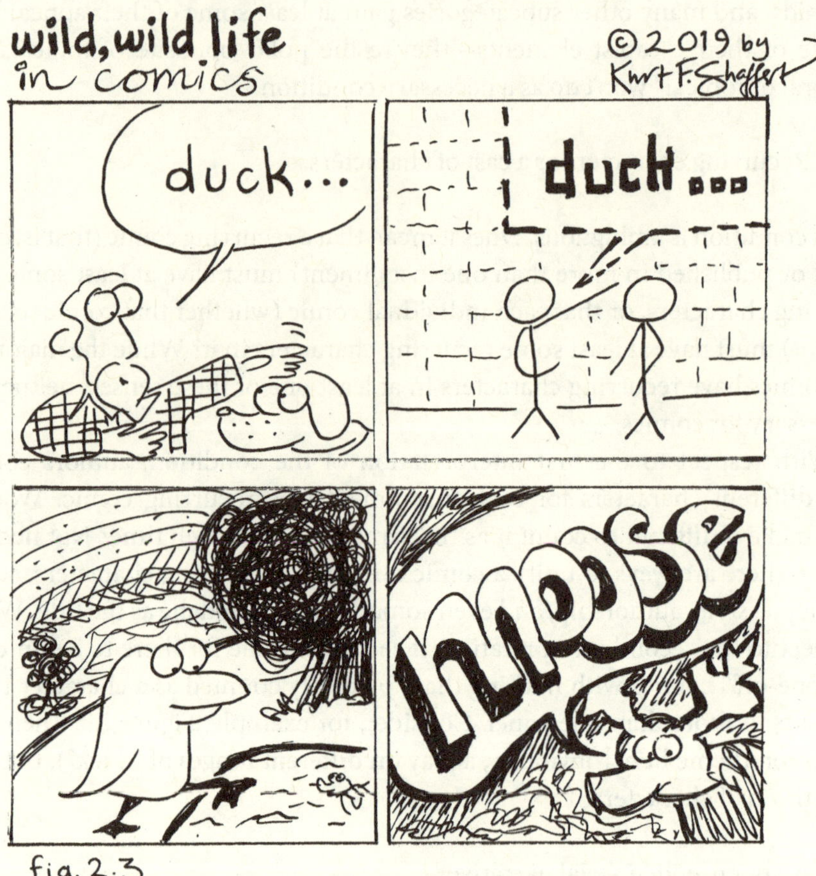

fig. 2.3

Lots of comics—including the vast majority of superhero comics—are open-ended serials. But lots of them aren't. While released in multiple installments, gag strips like *Garfield* are almost never serialized. Plenty of graphic novels are one-offs that come in a single installment. And there can be comics like Figure 2.4. You won't see this frog show up in any other comic, unless for some reason you start making Figure 2.4 fanfic. (I can confidently say that Shaffert and I would be rather excited if you did.)

These are what I've called "stand-alone" narratives, in which "sub-narratives occur in a common storyworld that does not reset after each, but [where] they comprise a single unit that is released, when complete, in its entirety" (Pratt 2013, 266). Because there are lots of comics like this, serialization shouldn't be part of an essentialist definition.

- Book-size scale.

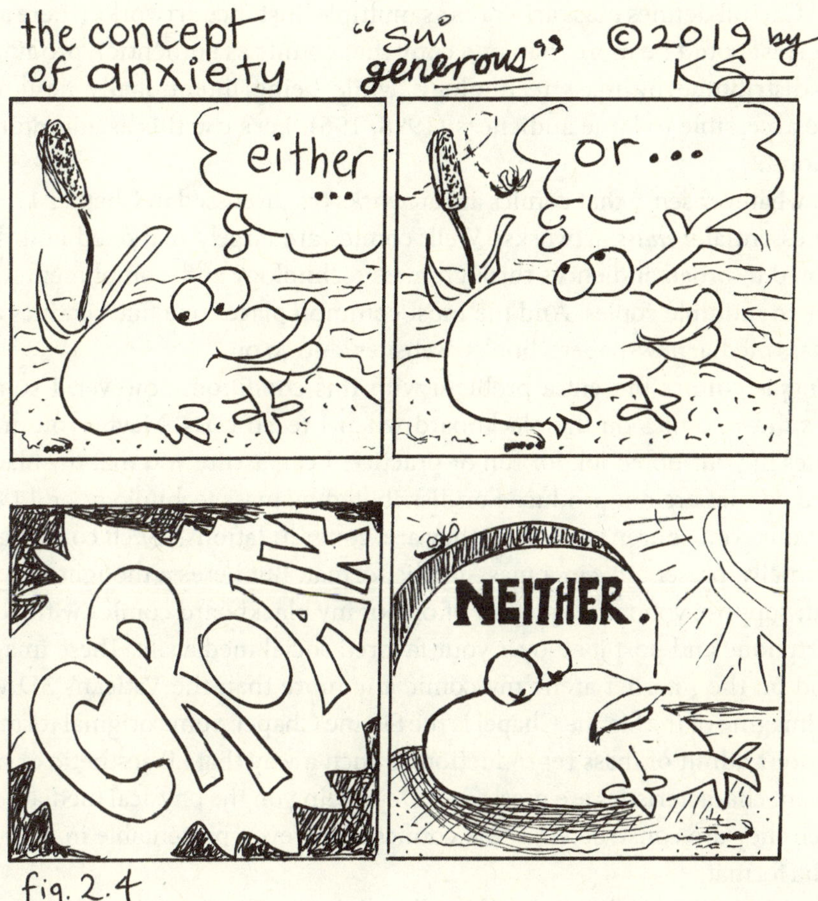

fig. 2.4

When you read comics, you probably read a lot of them in comic books, or book reprints of newspaper comics. But you might also read them in the newspaper. Is this book-size scale? Maybe—one could print a book that big. What if an issue of *Batman* was released in a scale that only worked on smartphones? Would that stop being a comic? No. Could a comic be made from a careful arrangement of nanoparticles, visible only with a powerful microscope? Could a comic be released only as an image projected on an IMAX screen? Yes and yes. Could a comic be carved into a wheatfield? Yes. If any of these answers are right (and I think they are), then we shouldn't hold that any particular scale is necessary for comics.

- Presented in a mass-media format.

Noël Carroll defines mass artworks as multiple-instance artworks (there are, or at least could be more than one copy that counts as authentic), produced and distributed by mass technology, while being intentionally designed to be accessible to large audiences (1998, 196). Let's use this as a jumping-off point.

In whatever sense that comics are artworks (as discussed in Chapter 1), are they essentially *mass* artworks? Well, comics are largely marketed and distributed to broad audiences through mass technology and, complimentarily, come in multiple copies. And the most common places one finds comics are in mass media: newspapers, books, websites, and so on.

Unique comics present a problem with this condition, however. I sometimes draw comics on the blackboard when I teach class. Maybe you draw comics in your notebook for fun or practice. I can assure you that my blackboard comics are not produced or distributed by mass technology, and I bet that your comics aren't either. (If they are, congratulations!) Such comics are, potentially, present*able* in a mass-media format. But here's a thought experiment: suppose you take a picture of one of my blackboard comics with your smartphone and post it all over your favored social media site. These images found on the internet aren't my comic any more than the Vatican's 3D virtual imaging of the Sistine Chapel is the Sistine Chapel. Some original formats just don't admit of mass reproduction in such a way that all aesthetic or art-relevant characteristics are preserved. Depending on the physical media from which they are constructed, some comics aren't even presentable in a mass-media format.

Rejecting this condition, incidentally, allows for the possibility that painterly works from the likes of Roy Lichtenstein can still be comics. That's not to say that Lichtenstein's paintings ought necessarily to be counted as comics, but only that there's no in-principle reason to rule them out simply because genuine instances of those paintings can't be created through mass reproduction.

For the record, comics aren't all intentionally designed for accessibility either. If you don't believe me, just have a look at Gary Panter's *Jimbo in Purgatory*.

- A preponderance of picture over text.

Pictures are *very* important in comics, as I'll argue in the next section. But even on the most plausible interpretations of the term, it's difficult to support the claim that they preponder—dominate or outnumber—text in all comics.

"Preponderance" isn't feasibly understood in this context as literally having a higher *number* of pictures than—what: texts? It has to be about either the comparative amount of space that pictures take up or the comparative burden that pictures bear in conveying the comic's content.

Two examples show why it's odd to require that pictures take up more space than text. In Figure 2.5, the text takes up more space because there's a lot of it. In Figure 2.6, the word balloons are just plain big. Both of these are pretty clearly still comics.

So do pictures have to do more "work" in comics—carry more of the narrative burden? They don't in Figure 2.7.

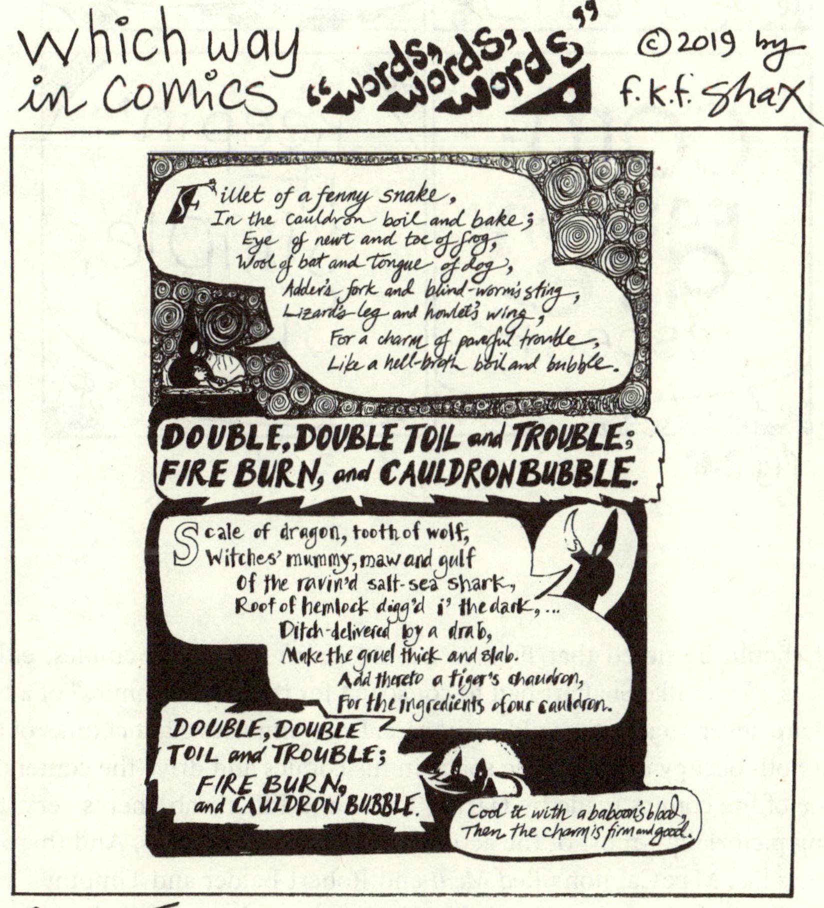

fig. 2.5

fig. 2.6

It should be noted that Figures 2.5–2.7 aren't esoteric examples, either. That is, it's not like Shaffert had to construct for this book "comics" of a type that are never seen in the wild, as it were. Dave Sim uses giant chunks of text that both occupy considerable space in his comics and drive the content. In some of the comics made by Harvey Pekar and R. Crumb, there's very little going pictorially—most of the action is in the word balloons. And there are comics like Max Cannon's *Red Meat* and Robert Balder and Timothy Crist's *PartiallyClips* where the picture doesn't change at all from panel to panel—only the word balloons and narrative text shifts. It's hard to think of any way in which the picture could preponder in these comics.

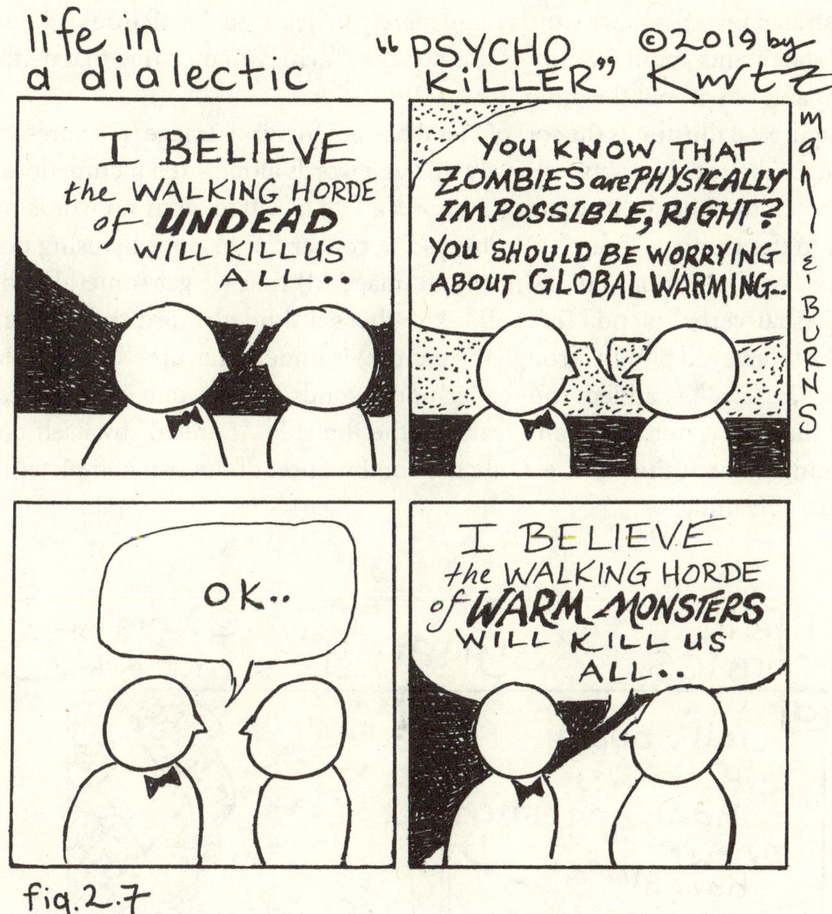

fig. 2.7

2.4. More Plausible Necessary Conditions

Let's move on now to conditions that are better candidates for inclusion in an essentialist definition.

- A visual-verbal blend
- The presence of word balloons or the equivalent.

I'm lumping discussion of these two conditions together because they're closely related. The first might be Harvey's most notable contribution to the literature on comics. What he has in mind is that in comics, text and images function together. Pictures aren't there merely to supplement words (as in illustrated texts), nor are words there merely to describe the pictures (like artists' statements about paintings). Rather, they "achieve a meaning that neither is capable of without the other" (2009, 38).

Figure 2.8 illustrates the sort of blend he's got in mind. Image (a) expresses a thought that can be captured easily through words alone—the picture doesn't do much to enhance it. Image (b) shows a kite in a tree, with no words that add to the content. Image (c) conveys the concept of balance by using nonverbal symbolization, but it's not until image (d) that we get something like the visual-verbal blend. There, the kite-flier's attitude toward the lightning strike (conveyed purely through the picture) is underdetermined visually, but once "Eureka!" is added, the reader understands that it's one of excitement and discovery, not shock and fear. On the flip side, "Eureka!" by itself does nothing without the picture. Only the combination of the two completes the image's meaning.

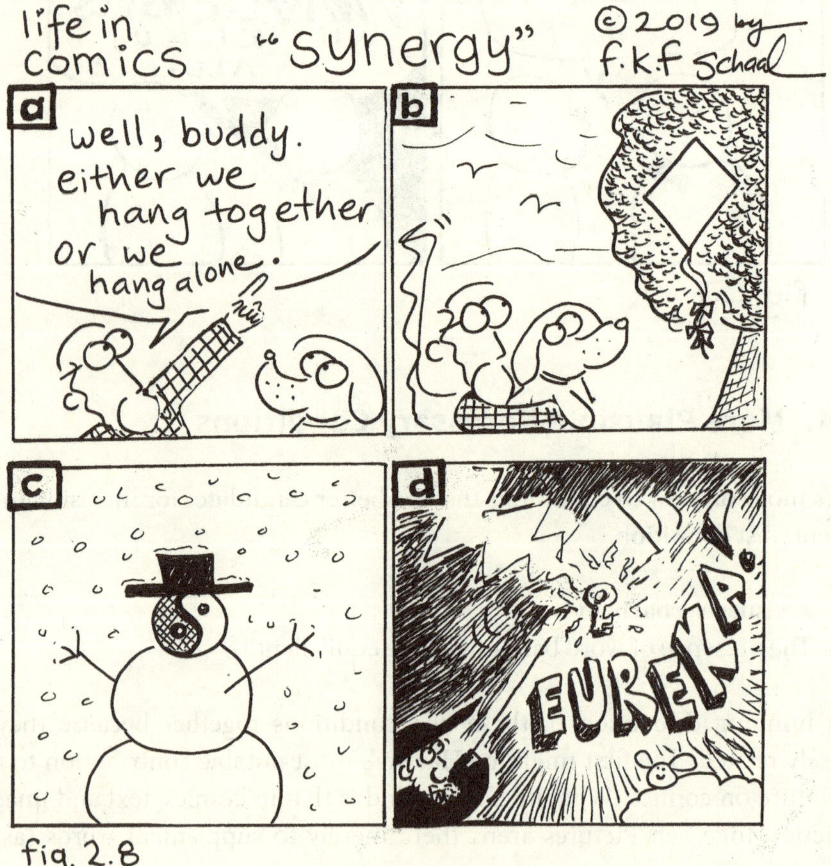

fig. 2.8

One major problem with Harvey's proposal also plagues the relatively common suggestion that comics necessarily feature word balloons, so I'll move on to that and get back to Harvey shortly. What word balloons are should be fairly obvious to anybody familiar with comics, but we might as well loosely describe them as follows: figures or shapes within a panel containing text that is taken to be the thoughts or utterances of the comic's characters. Sometimes word balloons aren't enclosed (as in the style employed in G. B. Trudeau's *Doonesbury* or Berke Breathed's *Bloom County*), but their borders are more or less implied by the white space that surrounds them. Word balloons, unless something has gone horribly awry, also feature some type of directional "tails" between them and the character with which they're associated.

Word balloons, of course, aren't the only form of text that comics feature. Other types include narration (sometimes placed in boxes or equivalent devices), sound effects, and captions (which typically occur below panels). But the word balloon might be the most striking text delivery method. Other art forms involving either text or images seem to have no real equivalent. Literary works are generally composed exclusively of text (I'll often call these "paradigmatic literature" or "nongraphic literature" as we go forward). In illustrated literature, readers already know what the author wants us to know about what the characters are thinking and saying: their speech and thoughts have already been conveyed through the text itself and need not be duplicated in an illustration. Paintings, by way of contrast, do not usually need or use word balloons because they generally depict the appearance of a moment in a sequence rather than that sequence itself. (That's a medium specific claim akin to the pioneering theorizing of Gotthold Lessing—I'll have much more to say about it in the next chapter.) Depictions of speech are not required in order to capture a moment, and although it may be important to reveal the thoughts of a painting's subject, these are usually inferred from the subject's appearance, body language, facial expression, and so on.

Word balloons are often very important in particular comics, because they contribute to the stories that the comics are trying to tell. They're an incredibly useful and easy way to convey thoughts and speech. In fact, one might think that there's no other way to tell a story in a comic. One might think that, but one would be wrong. What's the alternative? Pantomime, as in Figure 2.9.[5]

Meaning, narrative and otherwise, can be imparted without any text or words. You do that if you ever play charades. While pantomime comics don't exactly dominate the category, they aren't weird aberrations either. Once you start looking for them, you find them everywhere. If you read newspaper comics regularly, you'll see prominent features (*Peanuts*, *Garfield*, *Doonesbury*, *Zits*, and so on) omitting word balloons occasionally. On the days when this

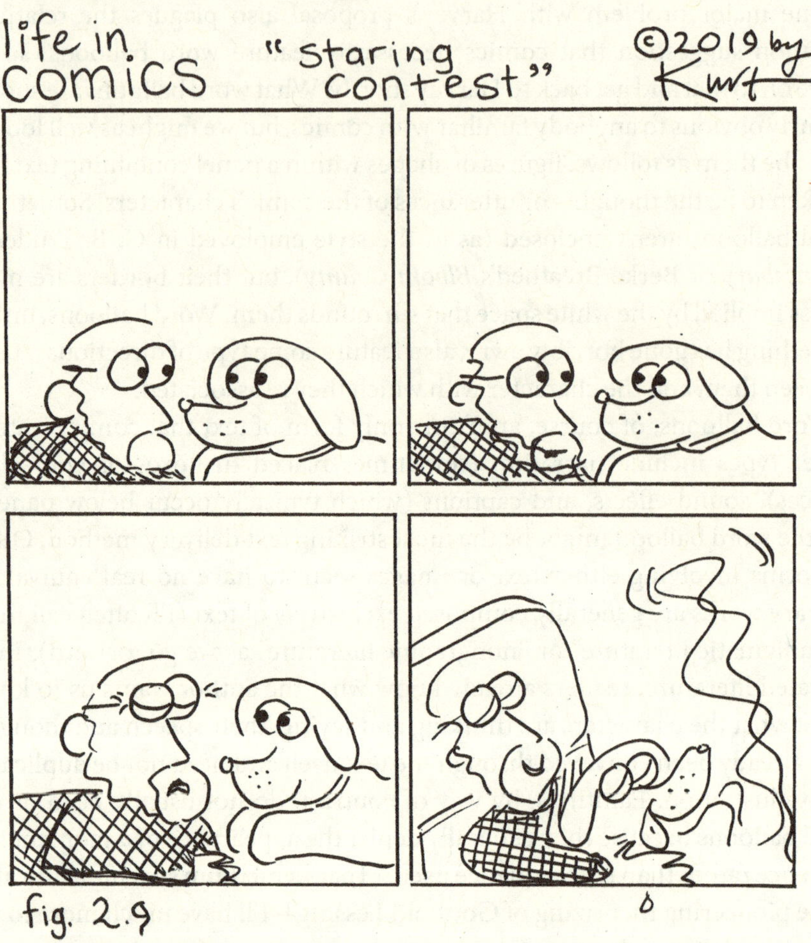

happens, you're obviously still reading comics. There are newspaper comics whose entire run occurs in pantomime, such as Otto Soglow's *The Little King* (which also ran occasionally in the *New Yorker*) and Al Jaffee's *Tall Tales*. And there are plenty of pantomime comic books. These include particular issues like Marvel's *G.I. Joe* #21 ("Silent Interlude") and Will Eisner's *Spirit* story "Hoagy the Yogi." They also include stand-alone works like Jim Woodring's *Frank* comics and Shaun Tan's *The Arrival*. Nor are pantomime comics exclusively American, as the work of Norwegian artist Jason attests.

Now, it's open to anybody who wants to advance the presence of word balloons as a necessary condition just to deny that these are comics. My intuitions go against that move (and yours might too), for a simple reason: within the comics world (a notion of Beaty's that we considered in Chapter 1), pantomime works are unproblematically understood as comics.

These works are naturally placed right alongside comics that feature word balloons.

If comics don't necessarily feature word balloons, or indeed can omit all text whatsoever, then Harvey's proposal about the visual-verbal blend is a nonstarter for a necessary condition. There won't always be something verbal to blend the visual with! But maybe not all is lost for Harvey. He writes: "In the very best examples of the art, the words (or the pictures) taken by themselves are . . . virtually meaningless because the best comic strips exploit fully the dramatic economy of which the verbal-visual blend is capable" (2009, 38). By itself, this isn't a claim about which works ought to be classified as comics—it's an *evaluative criterion*. That is, Harvey is advancing a theory about what makes comics good. Perhaps there's something to the idea that the integration of the verbal and visual is evaluatively important—a topic we'll take up at some length in Chapter 6.

- Pictorial

Let's think of pictures roughly as a kind of symbol, where what that symbol refers to can be recognized by looking at it, because of some resemblance between the picture and the object to which it refers.[6] Being made of or containing pictures seems like it should be an uncontroversial requirement for being a comic. Certainly, all of the exemplars that I raised in Chapter 1 are pictorial. And think of the comics you know: while they might not all contain text, they all contain pictures, I'd guess.

Like most things in philosophy, it's not that simple. Roy T. Cook has raised interesting doubts about the pictorial condition, arguing that the most we ought to claim is that comics *involve* (rather than consist of or contain) pictures (2011, 286). Cook's argument is driven by examples of pictureless comics. By this, he doesn't mean comics that consist of pictures of nothing. A picture can literally represent nothing. In some panels of DC's *Crisis on Infinite Earths*, the aftermath of the Anti-Monitor's consumption of a universe is depicted as blank whiteness—this is a picture of nothing (the absence of a universe), whereas there had previously been something (a universe). Rather, Cook has in mind a rather peculiar issue of *Batman* (#663, collected in Morrison 2014), which consists exclusively in passages of prose accompanied by illustrations that do nothing in themselves to advance the narrative. A bit like Figure 2.10.

Cook's intuition about *Batman* #663 (shared, he attests, by his students) is that it's a comic. A version that had no pictures at all, he thinks, would still be a comic. However, if it were not part of a larger *Batman* series that does

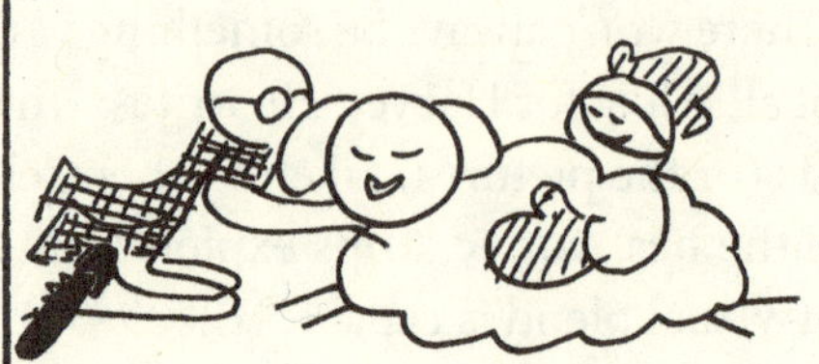

life in comics
"type"-cast
©2019 by Kwt
'Type'-cast
"Sheep is scared," said Fig. "Scared of the future. But mostly scared of clones."
"Baa-aa," said Sheep.
"Oh, I see. I heard about the cloning of Dolly," said Stig.
"They cloned Dali?!" screamed Fig. "Mustaches and all?!"
"Well, I wouldn't worry about the mustaches," said Stig.
"Baa-aa," said Sheep.
"I mean, the choice about mustaches is really up to the individual," Stig reasoned.
Fig quivered. "But think of what could happen! Clocks melting in the street? Jesus flying out of a hypercube? Freaky horses carrying houses around on stilts? Miscreants in capes running amok?"
"This all seems very unlikely to me." Stig continued. "I mean, clones really don't actually take on all of the properties of their genetic originals, do they? They look the same, but nurture has a fundamental role to play as well. If the genes are expressed differently, the resulting organism could be quite different as well."
Sheep, by this point, had figured out the misunderstanding, and bumped strongly into Stig, who toppled over into Fig, who toppled over in relief. It was time to hug.
"BAA-AA!" said Sheep.

fig. 2.10

contain pictures (and is itself a comic), then *Batman* #663 wouldn't be a comic (2011, 290). Being part of the larger, pictorial series isn't *sufficient* for making *Batman* #663 a comic. But since it *is* part of that series, its lack of pictures isn't enough to disqualify *Batman* #663 from being a comic. As long as it *involves* pictures—which Cook explains as being a part of something that consists in or contains a sequence of pictures (2011, 293)—it can still be a comic even though it's pictureless itself.[7]

There's a substantial debate in philosophy about whether intuitions ought to be treated as evidence for or against a position. Let's temporarily grant for the sake of argument that they should be. Are the intuitions Cook cites decisive? Well, I've got the opposite intuitions about *Batman* #663. I think it's not a comic. For the record, so do *my* students, at least most of them. (There's probably a lesson to be drawn here about ways in which professors' views affect those whom they teach, though I try to poll my students on this issue before revealing to them my own perspective.)

Furthermore, intuitions about *Batman* #663 diverge among comics critics. Let me cite a representative sample of those. Marc Sobel writes that the issue "looks and feels like no *other* Batman comic that has ever been published" (2007, n.p., emphasis added). To say that it's like no other comic is to imply that it's a comic, so he's with Cook on this one. However, while Tucker Stone judges that it's a "rare prose-style comic," he also thinks that "*Batman #663* is closer to, and resembles, *The Cat In The Hat* a hell of a lot more than it resembles, say, *Batman #664*" (2007, n.p.). Mononymous critic Jog says, somewhat confusingly, that it's "a comic that's so obviously not actually a comic" (2007, n.p.). Don MacPherson straightforwardly claims that "This issue of the Dark Knight's adventures is not a comic book. I know . . . it looks like a comic and feels like a comic, but it ain't a comic. Writer Grant Morrison offers up a prose short story, accompanied by illustrations by John Van Fleet" (2007, n.p.). And Joe Louis states, "For those of you who didn't have the extreme displeasure of reading Batman #663, don't bother. It is not a comic book, it is a novella, and a badly written one at that. Yep, that's right I said it: Grant Morrison wrote a terrible short story and it got shoved in to the pages of Batman #663 with some horrible art by John Van Fleet" (2007, n.p.).

At the very least, it appears that intuitions about this particular case appear to be much less tilted toward Cook's perspective than he lets on, even among readers whose familiarity with comics is intimate and extensive. So let's just say that the status of *Batman* #663 is unsettled, and probably can't drive an argument for pictureless comics all by itself. Moving forward, let's consider another case that I think tilts intuitions against Cook.

What if, after *Batman* #1, every issue to date had contained no pictures whatsoever? Imagine as well that DC has assured fans that the final issue of *Batman*, whenever it may be, will contain pictures in the same format as #1, neatly bookending the series. Apparently, the lack of pictures in *Batman* #999, or any arbitrarily selected issue after #1, doesn't disqualify it from being a comic, any more than the (comparative) lack of pictures in the actual *Batman* #663 does. The works in our imaginary scenario are all part of a series of comics—*Batman*—that consists in or contains a sequence of pictures, and so they can be comics as well.

Something has gone wrong here. My intuitions indicate strongly that the works after *Batman* #1 not only aren't comics, but they can't be, and I bet yours do too, even if you're one of Cook's students. Now, Cook could reply that since few of the works in this hypothetical series consist in or contain pictures, the series itself isn't a comic. And if the series isn't a comic, then the pictureless works in it aren't either. However, there's a significant cost to this move. It looks like we're determining whether something is a comic based on how heavily the series in which it is embedded is pictorial. Since *Batman*, both my hypothetical version and the real thing, is an open-ended series, we don't know the comparative proportions of it that are and are not pictureless. It could be the case that the (imagined pictureless) issues #2–#999 represent a thousandth of the total run of the series, and all the other issues have pictures. (The proportion of pictureless comics is similar in the actual series.) So not only do we not know whether any particular pictureless issue of *Batman* is a comic—we *can't* know, until the series concludes!

This should strike you as extremely odd. But there's a way to fix it. If we commit to a stronger pictorial thesis, on which a necessary condition for comics is that they consist of pictures, we can rightly disqualify not only the actual *Batman* #663 from being a comic, but also the hypothetical *Batman* issues #2–#999. Sure, these issues might be part of series that contains comics (the *Batman* series). But just as comics can contain parts that aren't comics, like the fake ads integrated in issues of *The Goon*, a series (e.g., *Batman*) that contains comics can have parts that aren't themselves comics, like, well, the actual *Batman* #663.

Before moving on, it would be a good idea to see if we can explain why Cook and others feel like *Batman* #663 is a comic, even though speculating about the mental states of others and the reasons for them is risky business. One source of what I, at least, believe to be a confusion might be Cook's impression of the comic, reflected in his description: "Although every page contains at least one small illustration, fully seven of the twenty-two pages contain just one, and only the final page contains more than four illustrations" (2001, 289). To my mind, the illustrations are much more significant that Cook lets on, taking up considerable space (I would describe few of them as "small") and prominence in the layout. The words are clearly arranged as part of the overall graphic compositions of the page, deliberately placed, with careful attention to font and color. If they appeared in the narrative boxes typical of comics, I have no doubt that #663 would be consistently identified as a comic. It's possible that this accounts for the intuitions that ground Cook's argument—#663 is close enough to a conventional comic that it's easy to mistake for one. I conjecture that without the example of #663 in the background, if readers were presented with Cook's thought experiment of an issue of *Batman* with no pictures whatsoever, they wouldn't even be tempted to say it's a comic.

Cook's position is intriguing, and I expect I won't have convinced all readers—or Cook himself—that it's wrong. But pending more robust arguments to the contrary, I do think that we still have no good reasons for claiming that pictures aren't necessary for comics.

It might have occurred to some readers that there's another way that comics could be other than pictorial. They could be comprised of images that are neither words nor pictures, but are instead completely abstract—visual arrays that don't refer to any object, real or imagined. This is a possibility we'll grapple with in considering the next two criteria.

- Narrative
- A sequence of spatially juxtaposed panels

We've now considered the importance of words and pictures for comics. On the view I've endorsed, the former aren't essential, whereas the latter quite probably are. Along with these two putative necessary conditions, we should think about how words and pictures are *organized* in comics—whether there are any restrictions on the ways in which they can be combined.

A work's property of narrativity—telling a story—is determined by the content of that work (or, possibly, the intended content). Hence, a truly content-neutral definition of comics would also be neutral about whether comics must be narrative. And as we saw in the discussion of the first three conditions that were rejected in the previous section, there's at least some reason to think that definitions of comics should be content-neutral.

Meskin (2007, 371–72) has raised two arguments in favor of excluding a narrativity condition. First, he compares comics to film and literature. Though our most common experiences of works in these categories are of narratives, both have significant nonnarrative subgenres, mainly in the avant-garde. Even if the familiar comics (including our exemplars in Chapter 1) are narrative, shouldn't comics admit of a nonnarrative avant-garde as well? The panels of comics have to be organized somehow ("deliberately," is the word McCloud uses in his definition cited in Section 2.2 above), but the organization, Meskin thinks, doesn't have to be narrative. Second, Meskin raises examples of what he considers to be actual nonnarrative comics, by R. Crumb, Renee French, and Stefan J. H. Van Dinther. Other examples cordial to Meskin's view might include the various works anthologized in *Abstract Comics* (Molotiu 2009), where panels are typically organized by theme, style, or graphic design. It's because the images in these works aren't pictorial that they aren't narrative.[8]

Should we include works like Figure 2.11 under the umbrella of comics? I used to favor using a narrativity condition to exclude them: Hayman and

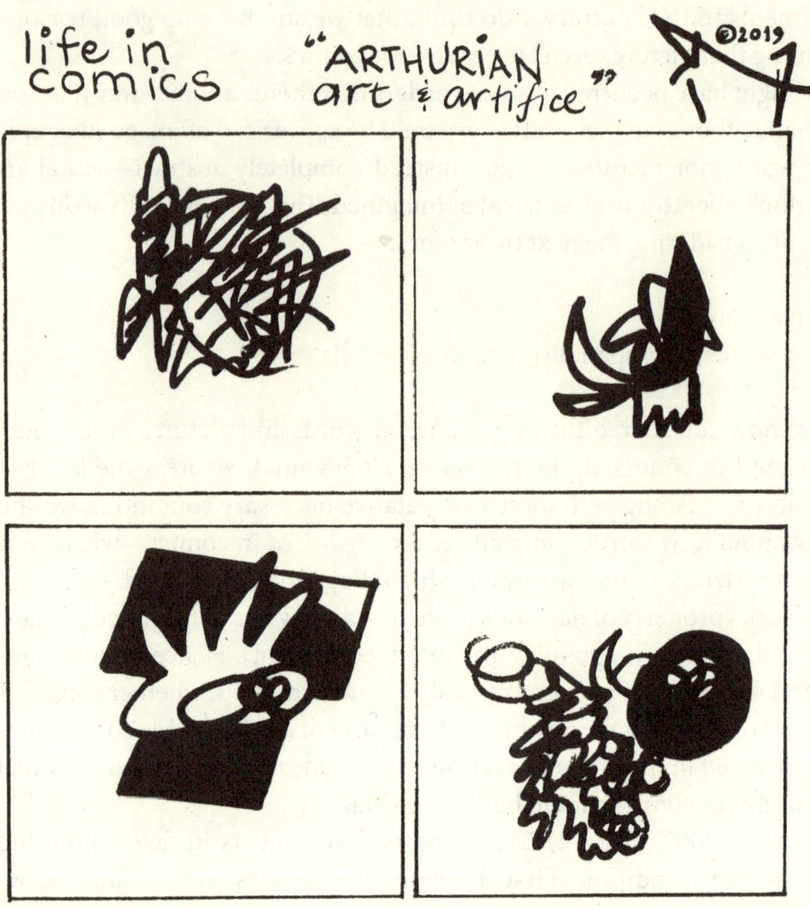

fig. 2.11

I held that the pictures in comics must "comprise a narrative, either in their own right or when combined with text" (2005, 423). Now I'm less sure. I'm still convinced that the default mechanism that readers use for the *understanding* of comics is to try to fit them into a narrative structure. This is how I find myself approaching even the abstract works collected in Molotiu's anthology—thinking about things like what is happening to a particular abstract squiggle and whether that's good or bad for it. Molotiu himself refers to works that "chronicle the movement or metamorphosis of one or more shapes from panel to panel, thereby effectively still focusing on 'characters' (no matter how abstracted)" (2017, 124). Note that this basically treats abstract images as pictures—they refer to things that can be recognized by looking at them, but the things they refer to are abstract designs or patterns.

My own inclinations, however, might just be because narrative comics are pretty much the only kind I read regularly. Readers with less conventional tastes might default to different ways of understanding comics. And different abstract works might demand different ways of understanding. As Molotiu continues, immediately following the passage quoted above, "Others foreground the sheer graphic drama of mark-making, or else the power of sequential dynamism—arising from the compositional lines and energy in each panel and their juxtaposition within the layout—to carry the viewer from first page to last" (2017, 124). Furthermore, Meskin is pretty convincing in his point that comics should be able to be just as radical as other kinds of art. So I want to retract my previous view: we should put narrativity aside as a necessary condition, though we should recognize how important it is in most comics. (We'll investigate narrativity in comics extensively in Chapters 4 and 5.)

This leaves us with one more way in which we might claim comics to be organized essentially: in a sequence of spatially juxtaposed panels. Something like this condition is present in nine out of the eleven definitions cited earlier in this chapter—it's clear that a lot of theorists who have turned their attention to comics think it's pretty important. The exemplars raised in Chapter 1 all have this property, and most (all?) other familiar comics do as well.

Before evaluating its plausibility, let me explain the proposed condition further. Let's use "panel" loosely, to describe individual images separated in some discernible way, whether through the traditional border line or otherwise. When objects are juxtaposed, they're located next to each other. The panels in comics are spatially juxtaposed, meaning that they're located next to each other in space. This contrasts with temporal juxtaposition, which is a feature of the images that constitute films. A sloppy but intuitive way of explaining the difference is that comics panels are located at the same time in different spaces, and film images are located in (e.g., projected on) the same space at different times. Spatial juxtaposition, then, is a property that differentiates comics from film.

There can't be juxtaposition without multiple objects to be juxtaposed, so the notion carries with it a commitment to a sequence of more than one. Technically speaking, as Holbo points out (2012, 6), there are sequences of one, or even none, but let's just restrict our inquiry to sequences of two or more, since discussion around this condition has centered on those. If we endorse such a sequence of spatially juxtaposed panels as a necessary condition, we're eliminating the possibility of single-panel comics. *That* I'm willing to do this should be evident from Chapter 1, in which I argued that the category of cartoons is distinct from that of comics. Here's *why* I'm willing to do this.

Granted, one-panel features like *The Family Circus*, *Dennis the Menace*, and *Marmaduke* (the daily versions, not the Sunday ones) are often found in the same context as multiple-panel comics—newspapers haven't historically differentiated the two. (Nor, for the record, have they differentiated one-panel works or multiple-panel works from noncomic features like the *Junior Jumble* or *Uncle Art's Funland*.) However, a necessary condition that requires panels to be in a sequence has a very important function. If we don't use one, we need some other necessary condition or conditions in place in order to exclude from the comics category all the other single pictures that aren't comics. Without such a condition or conditions, we'd have to count as comics stand-alone caricatures—distorted or exaggerated pictures of either famous individuals or a stereotypical individual, usually created for the purpose of lampooning or denigrating those individuals or an idea they represent. And we'd have to count as comics any representational painting.

Worryingly, we've already rejected the two most promising necessary conditions for eliminating mere caricatures and representational paintings from the category of comics. Adverting to word balloons is unsuitable. Not only are there wordless comics (as we saw earlier), but there are paintings that aren't comics that have word balloons. A good example is Roy Lichtenstein's *The Engagement Ring* (1961): a necessary condition requiring comics to have word balloons wouldn't rule this out. And so we return to narrativity.

In fact, this was one reason why Hayman and I included narrativity in our definition. We figured that works comprised only of a single picture generally aren't narratives in their own right: they can only be parts of a narrative insofar as viewers have information available to them not contained in the picture that allows them to identify it as part of that narrative. We also reasoned that the few single pictures that *are* narratives in their own right are actually multiple-panel works in disguise, like Figure 2.12. This is a narrative, but only because we can mentally separate it into multiple panels by attending to the complex timing involved.[9]

The upshot: narrativity and the spatially juxtaposed sequence both seem central to mainstream understandings of comics. Either, or both, have useful functions as necessary conditions, such as the exclusion of paintings from the category of comics. But the costs might be too high: again, endorsement of either of these conditions will lead to the exclusion of single-panel cartoons (which might or might not bother you), and using narrativity is going to foreclose on the possibility of avant-garde abstract comics.

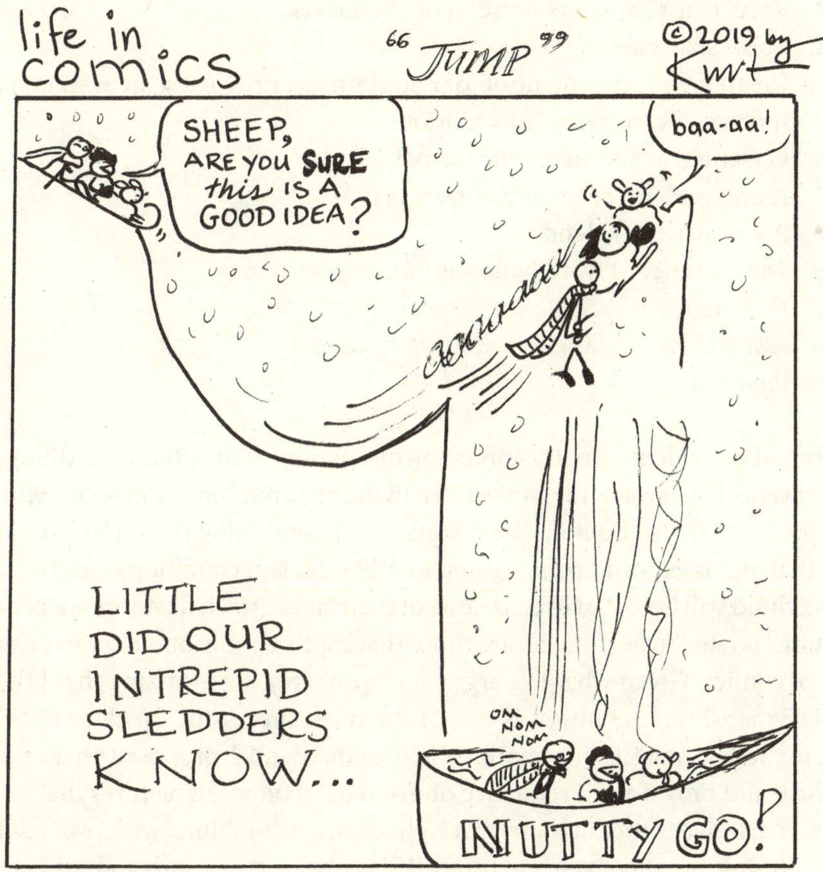

fig. 2.12

2.5. Conclusions

So where do we stand? In Section 2.1 of this chapter, we considered Meskin's suggestion that comics can't be defined and that it's better to think of the category in terms of Walton's standard conditions—features that tend to qualify works as comics. That might well be the way to go, if none of the conditions we've considered so far are defensible as necessary. That said, as we've seen, some seem to be more defensible than others. I'd rank the conditions we've discussed in the following order from less standard and less defensible to more standard and more defensible:

1. An open-ended serial narrative
2. A moral or topical story

3. Recurring characters or a cast of characters
4. Book-size scale
5. Created with the intention of entertaining, provoking an aesthetic response, or conveying information
6. Presented in a mass-media format
7. A preponderance of picture over text
8. A visual-verbal blend
9. The presence of word balloons or the equivalent
10. Narrative
11. A sequence of spatially juxtaposed panels
12. Pictorial

As should be evident from the foregoing discussion, each of these conditions is controversial in its own way. Some form of the pictorial condition seems widely accepted, but that's about it. The prospects for combining them into a definition that provides both necessary *and* jointly sufficient conditions seem dim.

We could still hold that even if none of them are perfect, the more successful definitions cited in Section 2.2 are those that capture more of the central elements of comics. Given what I've argued, it's probably unsurprising that I think the Hayman/Pratt definition is one of the most successful. To close out this chapter, let's look at it one more time. Hayman and I proposed that "x is a comic if and only if x is a sequence of discrete, juxtaposed pictures that comprise a narrative, either in their own right or when combined with text" (2005, 423). I think we effectively captured the pictorial and sequential aspects of comics, while leaving open the role of word balloons. We remained content-neutral except for the narrativity requirement. And we managed to exclude paintings and works of film from the category of comics.

But our definition doesn't allow for the existence of one-panel, nonnarrative, or abstract comics. It might be too exclusionary in that regard. It's also arguably *too* inclusionary—it classifies as comics works that shouldn't be so classified. As Meskin has pointed out (2007, 372–73), we have a real problem with children's literature, wherever pictures combine with text to form the narrative. A subnarrative in Dr. Seuss's *Hop on Pop* provides an example: the pictures are vital because without them, you can't tell whether we all, who are tall, are different people from we all, who are small.

Another way in which the Hayman/Pratt definition might be too inclusionary is also frequently held to be a problem with McCloud's definition. Since Hayman and I, like McCloud, are working in purely formal terms, our definitions are ahistorical. There are no references, vague or otherwise, to when comics began. According to the standard history I related in

Chapter 1, comics started in the late nineteenth century. It's compatible with the Hayman/Pratt and McCloud definitions that there were comics *way* before that. McCloud even states explicitly that ancient Egyptian paintings, a pre-Columbian picture fold from Mexico, and the Bayeux Tapestry (from eleventh-century Europe) are comics (1993, 10–15). Meskin claims that it's "perverse" to call these comics, and that McCloud does so mainly to validate comics as an art form (2007, 373–74).

Should a historical condition be added to the Hayman/Pratt definition to fix this problem? Something like "which became a category in its own right in the late nineteenth century"? I'm not sure. Its plausibility depends on whether comics could have evolved at any other time. On one hand, it does seem odd, as Holbo points out (2012, 4–5) to think that comics are *essentially* rooted in the nineteenth century. And there's a way in which ahistoricism can be mitigated: works like the Bayeux Tapestry, one might claim, are properly classified as *both* comics and some other form of art. While most people see them through the lens of that other form of art, it's interesting and interpretively productive to see them as comics as well. On the other hand, Meskin reminds us that there are significant arguments in favor of the position that comics, like everything else, couldn't possibly have existed much before they actually did (2007, 374). As Danto puts it, Andy Warhol's *Brillo Boxes* (from 1964) couldn't have been art in 1914, just as "there could not have been, everything being equal, flight insurance in the Middle Ages, or Etruscan typewriter erasers" (1964, 581).

Even if difficulties about the historical condition are themselves resolved, problems with essentialist definitions remain. Perhaps these can be resolved too—I encourage readers to try. Regardless, engaging in the definitional project has revealed much about the category of comics and its scope. With this knowledge in the background, we're now well situated for investigating how comics work, and what that has to do with the media from which they are constituted.

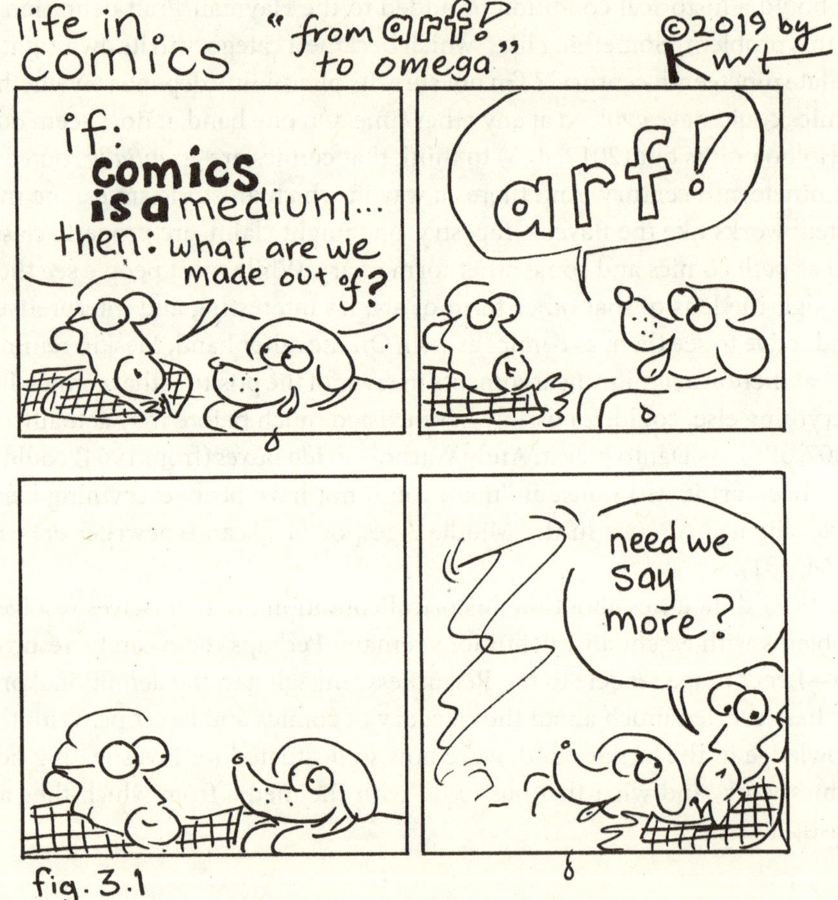
life in comics
"from arf! to omega"
©2019 by Kwt
if: comics is a medium...
then: what are we made out of?
arf!
need we say more?

fig. 3.1

3
The Media of Comics

3.1. An Introduction to Medium Specificity

Alan Moore, famed writer of comics like *Watchmen*, *Batman: The Killing Joke*, and *The League of Extraordinary Gentlemen*, also has written a book offering advice to those aspiring to follow in his footsteps. In it, he laments a tendency to write for comics as one might write for film: "Rather than dwelling upon film techniques that comics can duplicate, shouldn't we perhaps consider comic techniques that films *can't* duplicate?" (2008b, 4). This recommendation invites important questions about the relations between comics and film, an issue to which we'll return in some detail in Chapter 5. For now, however, I want to point out another interesting aspect of Moore's claim: that there are things that comics can do that film can't.

In our last chapter, we explored the possibility of defining comics. We unearthed some relatively promising necessary conditions—the best of which are stubbornly content-neutral. Or so it seems. Could it be the case that something about fulfilling even formal criteria produces tendencies in the direction of certain content? Could comics, in virtue of what they are and how they work, operate differently from other art forms? Do comics, as Moore suggests, have capabilities that other art forms simply don't?

These are issues of *medium specificity*, and the focus of this chapter. There is a wide variety of medium-specific views and associated arguments pro and con. Some, I'll show, are definitely not reasonably applied to comics. But others are—to the extent that a moderate, defensible version of medium specificity will be a driving force in significant remaining portions of this book.

Debates about medium specificity go back at least to Plato, but most commentators on the subject emphasize its modern roots in Gotthold Lessing's *Laocoön: An Essay upon the Limits of Painting and Poetry* (originally published in German in 1766). In this text, Lessing is attempting to refute some of his contemporaries who believed that the arts can be understood systematically—that the creation, interpretation, and evaluation of any artwork whatsoever has little or nothing to do with its category. Lessing's focus is on painting—by which he means "the visual arts in general" (1962, 6)—and poetry. The domain of the former, on his view, is to depict bodies as

The Philosophy of Comics. Henry John Pratt, Oxford University Press. © Oxford University Press 2023.
DOI: 10.1093/oso/9780190845445.003.0003

they appear at a single moment of time, whereas the domain of the latter is to describe actions—events that unfold over time (1962, 91–92). Violations of these domains are artistic flaws. Hence, we have in Lessing the seeds for the most common components of medium specificity: a claim about the particular effects of each medium, and a claim about the need for artists to pursue those (and only those) effects.

In more contemporary times, medium specificity has loomed large in two contexts. First, in the 1960s, the influential art critic Clement Greenberg advocated forcefully for the medium-specific view that painting is supposed to achieve separation from the other arts through self-consciously drawing attention to its two-dimensional media (see Greenberg 1982). On his view, the best paintings (i.e., those Greenberg favored—note that he could have gotten this wrong) are modernist works that lead viewers to contemplate the flatness of the painted surface. Second, medium specificity found purchase in classical film theory. Rudolf Arnheim argues (1957) that the art of film lies in its capacity to diverge from reality through the editing techniques that the medium permits, such as montage. By way of contrast, André Bazin contends (1967) that since the media of film are photographic, and photography gives us access to reality, the art form is suited for realistic depictions above all else, and filmmakers should aim for as much.[1]

How is all this relevant to comics? In the twentieth century in particular, medium specificity tended to be used in service of validating the status of new or otherwise suspect art forms like modernist painting and film. After all, if there are things that these art forms can offer that other art forms cannot—unique capabilities afforded by the media that compose them—then that justifies the existence of these art forms. They give us a mode of access to a distinct type of excellence. As noted in the preface to this book, comics have struggled, historically, to find social esteem. Medium specificity offers promise as a way to carry on the process of legitimating comics. Combine it with McCloud's ahistoricism and you've got an ancient art form with abilities that no other has—and that's undoubtedly worthy of attention!

Moreover, medium specificity used as a guide to both what artists ought to attempt and how to evaluate their attempts has two promising aspects when applied to an art form, comics included. First, it opens the door for teaching the techniques of comics as a practice and profession: if there's something that comics are good at, then expertise in comics would presumably consist in having learned to do whatever that thing is. Second, it generates evaluative standards, providing a framework for a critical discourse surrounding comics (a feature, hearkening back to Chapter 1, Section 1.4, that Dutton argues is characteristic of art forms in general). We'll return to the connections between medium specificity and value in Chapter 6.

Supposing, reasonably, that medium specificity is interestingly pertinent to comics, we need to investigate further. We need to see if anything can sensibly be identified as the medium of comics. In Section 3.2 of this chapter, I develop an instrumental account of media and apply it to comics. We also need to see if there's any *defensible* version of medium specificity that can help us understand comics. In Section 3.3, I argue that there is. And, finally, we need to explore how the media of comics make them effective for certain purposes. That's Section 3.4.

3.2. What Comics Are Made Of

It's vital to think a bit more about the term "medium," particularly because whatever we hold a medium to be will have significant effects on the acceptability of medium specificity. I'm going to offer a definition of "medium" here, but it's of a rather different type than the sorts of essentialist definitions for the category of comics that we explored earlier in this book. I'm not looking for an account of all and only media, or even an account that encompasses the central or prototypical aspects of applications of the term in contemporary practice. What I'm looking for is an instrumental definition—something that I can use as a device that will be productive as we dig deeper into medium specificity a bit later on. Accordingly, I want to stress that other ideas about media also have important functions. When it might appear that I'm disagreeing with other theories of media, what I'm really doing is showing how they won't serve the function to which I want to put them. That's fully compatible with those alternative theories serving different aims than mine perfectly well, in a different context.

"Media" is often used to refer to the *materials* out of which artworks are made. It's this use you have in mind if you ask a painter what media she prefers to work with and get an answer like "gouache." It's this use as well that could create confusion if you were to ask a violinist the same question, since music doesn't seem to be material in the same way that paint is.

If we're going to think methodically about the media of comics going forward, I don't think it's going to be a good idea to concentrate on materials, for the same reason that it's not generally a good idea for contemporary film theorists to concentrate on the material constitution of film. For film, historically, thinking about materials might have made sense at one time. Most films used to be made out of *film*—a technology consisting of a flexible base of transparent nitrate, acetate, or polyester supporting a photographic emulsion. Now they usually aren't. They're digital. In part, that's why Carroll recommends rebranding film as "the moving image" (2008, 63), a category that he means to encompass visual displays that give the impression of movement, regardless of whatever material they're made out of. (Carroll's proposal probably isn't going to be taken up widely: "film" is too deeply entrenched in use.)

In contrast to film, comics never had any one type of material uniformly associated with it, even historically. There is, and never has been, any characteristic *stuff* of comics.[2] Presumably, this explains why none of the definitions we looked at in Chapter 2 and none of the putative necessary conditions we extracted from them focus on the material constitution of comics. Comics have been made on all kinds of stuff, ranging from paper to blackboards to photographs to computer code and beyond, and they can be drawn with pencils or pens, painted, chalked, etched, compiled, collaged, and so on. Anything that can realize a spatially juxtaposed sequence of pictures is going to be able to ground a comic metaphysically. This is why I've been trying so far in this book (and will continue to try) to avoid talk of comics *as* a medium. Instead, I've been favoring the idea that comics is an art form with particular formal features, one that, like other art forms, *uses* media in its construction.[3]

So if comics isn't a medium, and it's not useful for us straightforwardly to identify media with materials, what *is* a medium? One prominent place we might start is with Marshall McLuhan's influential book *Understanding Media*. McLuhan's conception of media is not fixated on materials: a medium is any "extension of ourselves" that can be used as a conduit of information (1964, 23).[4] Effectively, any technology or product of human activity is a medium, including not only familiar candidates like comics, film, television, radio, and literature, but also such things as speech, writing, electric light, clocks, the wheel, clothes, the bicycle, and the automobile.

For us, the chief merit of McLuhan's view is that it allows for discussion of the commonalities and connections among many types of objects and practices. Just as some philosophers hold that (nearly) everything is the proper subject of philosophy, McLuhan holds that (nearly) everything is the proper subject of media studies. By thinking about media so broadly, he's able to theorize about all human activity. We'll see later how this is useful when we compare comics to other art forms—in particular, when we try to understand how comics tell stories in ways that contrast with literature and film.

Unfortunately, to the extent that McLuhan analyzes the media of comics, he does so in terms of the printing technologies of the 1960s and earlier. Perhaps these technologies produce medium-specific implications, but what

I'm interested in goes beyond that. Comics, as I pointed out earlier, can be reproduced in lots of ways. Does the art form of comics itself have medium-specific implications apart from the particular technology used to reproduce individual comics or the materials from which they're constructed? Can different comics use different media? I think we should answer both these questions in the affirmative, in contrast to McLuhan's perspective.

Here I turn to a theory about media identity—what it is that qualifies works as using the same media—developed by Dominic Lopes in the context of computer art. "Artworks," Lopes writes, "standardly belong to the same art medium when and only when they are produced in accordance with a set of practices for working with some materials, whether physical, as in sculpture, or symbolic, as in literature" (2004, 110).[5] It isn't materials or technologies that differentiate media from each other, but the way materials or technologies are *treated*.

With Lopes's notion in mind, let's bring practices into the picture, so as to broaden our definition of media beyond materials and technologies. Bear with me here—this is going to be fairly formal, but I'll follow it up with an explanation of the media of comics in "plain English." Let's stipulate that from here forward, we'll be using "media" as follows:

> The media $M_1 \ldots M_n$ of any work W that is a member of art form A are (a) any of the resources (e.g., materials, technologies, symbolic or formal elements) that are (b) used in the production of W, where (c) there is a sufficiently robust set of practices associated with A that guide the appropriate use of $M_1 \ldots M_n$ in the creation of W.

What does this definition do? It allows different works within an art form to be comprised of different (though potentially overlapping) sets of media: art forms aren't necessarily tied to one medium or one set of media. (So some works in the art form of film, for example, can be made out of celluloid while others can be made out of digital code.) In the first clause, the scope of media is expanded beyond materials and technologies, which we'll see is very useful. In the second clause, media are associated with the work's coming to be—what makes it what it is. And the third clause is a bit of a restriction according to which in order to be a medium, it's got to have some norms that govern how it can be used within that art form.

I want to emphasize again that I'm not claiming that this is the one true definition of media. There are many alternatives, each of which offers its own payoffs. The virtues of this definition are that it allows new, hybrid art forms (like comics) to develop their own characteristic sets of media without requiring the existence or use of new materials or technologies (as long as the art forms develop new norms); and, most importantly, that it provides a convenient way both to describe the media of comics and assess the specific tendencies of those media.

Filling out the definition in its application to comics, the result is:

> The media $M_1 \ldots M_n$ of any work that is a member of the category of comics are (a) any of the resources (e.g., materials, technologies, symbolic or formal elements) that are (b) used in the production of that work, where (c) there is a sufficiently robust set of practices associated with the category of comics that guide the appropriate use of $M_1 \ldots M_n$ in the creation of that work.

Here's the basic idea, less formally. Comics can be made from practically any materials (as we discussed earlier), and their creation isn't restricted to the use of any particular technologies. They do have a set of practices surrounding them that govern how things that are used to make them are to be used. Whatever it is that those practices cover, those are the media of comics.

So what are those practices, and what *do* they cover? Happily, in previous chapters, we have encountered and developed a theoretical framework that allows us to answer these questions with a little less fuss. Return to the comics world, a notion that we got from Beaty in Chapter 1: "the collection of individuals necessary for the production of works that the world defines as comics, [including] writers, pencillers, inkers, colorists, letterers, editors, assistant editors, publishers, marketing and circulation personnel, printers, distributors, retailers, and retail employees" (2012, 37). (I extended this earlier to include comics readers, which I'll do again here.) The practices of the comics world relevant to the media of comics are behavioral norms—more precisely, they're the behavioral norms that guide the creation and reception of comics.

We probably can't give a precise or exhaustive list of those practices. Moreover, they tend change through time and vary across cultures. It's probably wrong to think of the comics world as a single, monolithic entity: better to think of it as a complex of ever-shifting social structures and relationships. However, it is possible to point to some central elements of medium-relevant practices that have been relatively stable within the comics world across time. Not incidentally, we encountered these central elements in Chapter 2—they're exactly the more defensible of the necessary conditions for the category of comics that we considered.

The practices of the comics world contain strong norms about a few of the things that can be used to make comics: pictures (which might even be an essential ingredient, as we've seen) and words (which aren't an essential ingredient, but are a common one). The media of comics are primarily pictorial and secondarily verbal: aside from what constitutes them materially and the technologies used to produce them, most comics are made out of pictures and words.

There are also strong norms about the appropriate *use* of the media of pictures and words. These include but are not limited to the following:

- Pictures are to be organized in panels.
- Panels are to be spatially juxtaposed in such a way as to form a narrative.
- Words are to be incorporated in speech and thought balloons, narrative boxes, or captions outside panels.
- Words and pictures are to be blended or interact to a certain degree.

At the most basic level of comics, materials (and technologies used to manipulate those materials) are irrelevant to these norms I've just listed, though as we'll see, materials and technologies do have effects on how the pictures and words turn out. Generally, you can use whatever physical stuff you want to in order to make a comic, as long as it allows for the creation of a juxtaposed sequence of pictures.

I don't want to give the impression that these norms are inviolable. Plenty of comics authors have tried successfully and will continue to try to transcend or subvert them. When individual comics *are* produced in accordance with these norms, however, there are, I'll try to show, medium-specific results. And when individual comics are *not* produced in accordance with these norms, or when they're produced in contexts where additional norms apply (e.g., those imposed by the restrictions of various conventionally determined technologies for publishing comics), we get medium-specific results there as well.

Before moving on to medium specificity, it's worth pausing to consider an objection to the view that media can be understood as anything other than other than physical materials. Carroll (1985b, 8; 2003, 6) argues that if we think of media in such a way as to include nonphysical design elements like juxtaposition, symbolic elements like words, or representational elements such as pictures, then medium specificity is a nonstarter.[6] Such elements are used in the creation of many different types of art forms. For instance, comics and film both use juxtaposition, comics and poetry both use words, and comics and painting both use pictures. If multiple art forms use the same media, then each art form won't have distinctive effects or distinctive evaluative criteria that apply only to it. And so, it appears, medium specificity will be untenable.

Carroll's objection will only succeed if two assumptions are in place.[7] First is the assumption that medium specificity is limited to a focus on media and not the art form-relevant norms that govern the use of those media. If such norms are distinctive for each art form (as they are, I believe, for comics), then even when art forms use the same media (where "media" is construed as I've done above), the effects will be characteristic for each art form. That would be enough to get medium specificity started. Second is the assumption that medium-specificity theorists are restricted to the particular kind of view that Carroll targets. They aren't, and once we see how a moderate, defensible version of medium specificity can be developed, we'll see that there's something to it after all.

3.3. Defensible Medium Specificity

Earlier in this chapter, I mentioned that medium specificity generally involves two kinds of claims. First, it involves claims about the particular effects of any given medium. Second, it involves claims that tie the value of artworks to the media with which those artworks are made. In the literature on medium specificity, it hasn't much been recognized that there are multiple ways to spell out to what degree the medium-specificity theorist is committed to each of those kinds of claims.

In this section, I'll take some steps to remedy that by contrasting what I'll call *strong medium specificity* with what I'll call *moderate medium specificity*. I'll agree with Carroll that strong medium specificity is deeply flawed, but argue that his objections don't really affect moderate medium specificity. Moderate medium specificity, unlike strong medium specificity, is aptly applied to comics, and will ultimately provide us with plenty of ammunition for understanding both the relations comics bear to other art forms and the value of comics.

Strong medium specificity is the view described (and, I want to underscore, rejected) by Carroll (1985b, 5–7; 2003, 3). I'm going to characterize it this way:

> *Strong Medium Specificity*: For any art form A, (a) A has a set of media unique to it, from which works in A are made, where (b) these media produce a specific set of ends or effects that A alone is best at, so (c) artists working in A should focus on and limit themselves to perfecting those ends or effects: (d) violating this rule results in artistic flaws.

Let's apply this to our context:

> *Strong Medium Specificity (Comics)*: The category of comics has (a) a set of media unique to it, from which individual comics are made, where (b) these media produce a specific set of ends or effects that comics alone is best at, so (c) artists working in comics should focus on and limit themselves to perfecting those ends or effects: (d) violating this rule results in artistic flaws.

We're now, finally, in a position to be able to assess a version of medium specificity as it applies to comics.

Given the account of media developed in the previous section, clause (a) appears problematic. Individual comics don't all share the same media, since their production can involve different materials, technologies, and symbolic and formal elements. Moreover, some of the media that comics use are obviously shared by works in other art forms.

In response, an advocate for strong medium specificity could claim that the *combination* of media used by the art form of comics is unique to it, as are the normative practices that govern the use of those media. No other art form, one might argue, juxtaposes pictures and incorporates words in the specific way that comics does. Whether you think that's plausible will probably track the degree to which you think that one or more of the definitions raised in Chapter 2 captures what's essential to comics and nothing else. If the elements of comics can be given a specification narrow enough to differentiate comics from all other art forms, and those elements, together with the norms that govern their use, are indeed unique to comics, then clause (a) will be satisfied. But if kindred art forms like children's literature, printmaking, film, and graphic narrative use many of the same ingredients, and their authors are required to combine them in much the same ways, then we should be skeptical about (a).

Let's just suppose for the sake of argument that something like (a) can be maintained with respect to comics. This supposition is worth making because it allows us to move on to (b) through (d), the clauses that are really doing the heavy lifting within strong medium specificity. Once we do that, we'll discover that strong medium specificity is just *too* strong.

The key word in (b) is "alone": do the media that comics use really lead to specific effects that comics *alone* is best at? This seems unlikely. Think of some of the things that comics can do. A quick list would include ends and effects such as telling stories, showing appearances, giving a sense of spatial relationships and motion, relating speech, revealing characters' thoughts, conveying other types of propositional and nonpropositional information, creating beauty and other aesthetic features, prompting emotional responses, and so on. Each of these is done by other art forms as well, and sometimes done better. Take the examples of music and film. While the precise relation between music and the emotions is a matter of extensive philosophical debate, there's a pretty significant connection between the two: at the least, music seems to excel at triggering emotional states. The media used in the creation of music are not shared by comics, but the effect (triggering emotions) is. Film shares even more effects with comics—maybe even *all* of those listed above—and again, the media are different. It's hard, and maybe even impossible, to find something that comics can do that can't be done by any other medium.

It's similarly hard to find something that comics, among all art forms, is best at. Even individual comics that use exactly the same resources and are governed by the same norms for the use of those resources can have very different ends and excellences. Ryan North and Erica Henderson's run on *The Unbeatable Squirrel Girl* is medium-identical to Rick Remender and Jerome Opeña's *Uncanny X-Force*. But a primary end of the former is to produce cheerful amusement, at which it excels; any shred of humor in the latter, by way of contrast, could only be described as "dark," used only to throw the dominant themes of horror and sadness into relief. A medium, as Carroll puts it, "does not select a unique purpose, or even a delimited range of purposes, for an art form" (1985b, 9).

The least feasible of the three clauses of strong medium specificity is (c), that comics artists should devote their attention to producing that single best effect for which comics are suited, and that if they don't achieve this, their work will suffer. If (b) is wrong, there's no single best effect, so (c) is a nonstarter. Even worse, strong medium specificity restricts the scope of artistic creativity. The idea that artists should concentrate on the supposed unique ends of their art form and avoid any ends that are shared by other media ignores the inspiration afforded by attempts to transgress and transcend limitations. It's true that plenty of artists have found success by working within the framework of very definite, and sometimes completely arbitrary restrictions, whether imposed by others or the artists themselves. Strong medium specificity produces norms for using media, and that can be useful for artists working in the category to which the norms apply. But the problem is that strong medium specificity treats the norms as inviolable and eliminates the possibility of exploring alternative norms and alternative styles through the use of the very same media.

A short example before moving on. One of the effects that comics media afford, which we'll dwell on at some length in the next chapter, is the ability to depict simultaneous events and actions coherently. In Figure 3.2, we see two

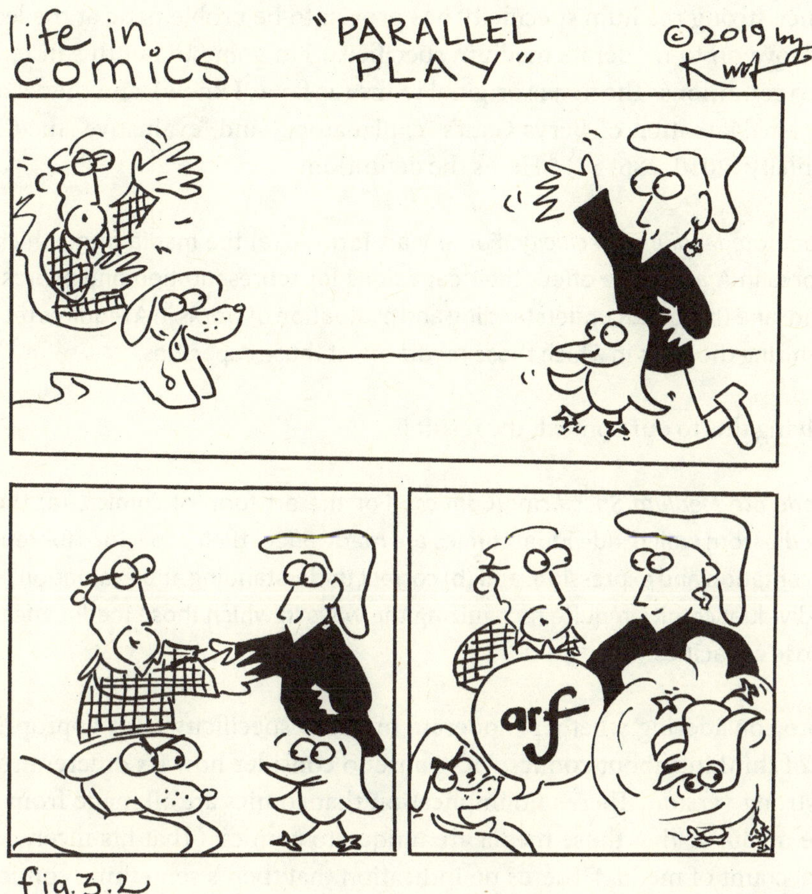

fig. 3.2

parallel narratives: two humans meet happily, while at the same time the dog and the duck don't get along nearly as well.

While this is a very simple example, it can get a lot more complex, and it's something comics is quite good for achieving. Later, I'll argue that comics does it a lot better than film.

But does this mean that comics artists *should* make comics that depict simultaneous events and actions, or that a comic is bad if it *doesn't* do so? No. There are plenty of great comics that wouldn't be improved by the addition of this effect and aren't diminished by its exclusion. Whether to employ a specific effect that comics media enable one to use is a stylistic choice, and there will be stylistic reasons to avoid any given effect in various contexts.

Since strong medium specificity has proven to be problematic at the least, let's move on to moderate medium specificity. I'm going to put this in terms of two conditions. The first is original to me (as far as I know), and the second is an amalgamation of Berys Gaut's "explanatory" and "evaluative" medium specificity (2010, 286–87).[8] Here's the definition:

> *Moderate Medium Specificity*: For any art form A, (a) the media from which works in A are made affect their capacities for representation and expression, and (b) correct understanding and evaluation of works in A requires recognizing the ways in which those media affect those capacities.

Applying this to our context, the result is:

> *Moderate Medium Specificity (Comics)*: For the art form of comics, (a) the media from which individual comics are made affect their capacities for representation and expression, and (b) correct understanding and evaluation of individual comics require recognizing the ways in which those media affect those capacities.

Before considering whether moderate medium specificity is an appropriate way of thinking about comics, let's pause to consider how it's different from the strong version. There's no implication that comics are all made from the same media or that those media are unique to comics. (That fits nicely with our account of media.) There's no indication that there's something comics is best at that can't be done by any other art form. And there's no generation of a set of specific and inviolable norms for making comics that are determined by comics media. To put it more positively, moderate medium specificity allows for the media from which comics are constructed to be shared by other art forms, for comics and other art forms to at least sometimes excel in the same ways, and for artists to be stylistically flexible in how they use the media of comics to achieve their particular goals. These are all good results: moderate medium specificity is not subject to the difficulties that plague its strong cousin.

So should we endorse moderate medium specificity? I think so, though I'll concentrate in this chapter on clause (a) and leave (b) mostly for later. With respect to that first clause, it's hard to comprehend how the media of comics and of other art forms could *fail* to influence what can be done and how it can be done. The notion of media with which we're working encompasses formal and symbolic resources used in the production of a comic—including pictures and words. We're going to spend a lot of time on this in the next chapter, but to foreshadow a bit, think about what the use of pictures and words in comics enables (and doesn't enable, for that matter). Pictures offer the capacity to represent the world easily in ways that nonpictorial art forms can't. The pictures used in comics resemble objects visually in ways that other symbols don't and, accordingly, can *show* us how things look, rather than merely *telling* us. Correspondingly, there's information that's much easier to convey by using words than otherwise—anybody who's ever played Pictionary can attest to that. Just think of how hard it would be to introduce a character's *name* without using words.

The symbolic and formal media used to create comics also produce limitations. Consider "stink lines" of the type depicted in Figure 3.3.

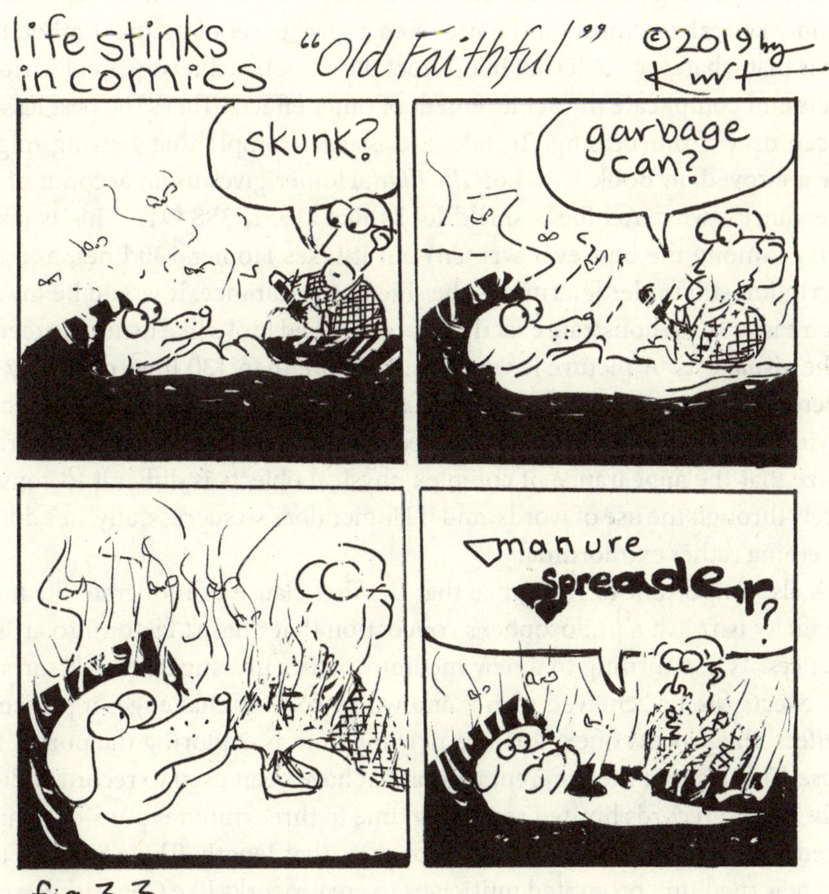

fig. 3.3

We know the dog in Figure 3.3 is intensely stinky, but the picture by itself can't convey exactly what the dog smells like. The man is trying to guess, but he never quite figures it out, and the reader's knowledge of the source and qualities of the stink is even more lacking.

Word balloons have their limitations too. They can tell us what characters are saying, but underdetermine the precise sounds that their voices make (in ways that audio recording technologies don't—at least not to the same degree). In Figure 3.3, what's the man's voice sound like? High or low? Raspy? Melodic? We could describe it, or the illustrator could vary the way in which the words are written to narrow it down a bit. (This, by the way, is a very cool thing that comics can do—convert words into pictures.) But until such time as this book gets an audio supplement, you'll never know exactly what the voice sounds like.

I'm not claiming here that the functions that the media of comics serve can't possibly be realized through the use of an alternate set of media. Rather, the idea is that whatever media are in use abet the smooth achievement of various effects and complicate the achievement of other effects. That's the best lesson we can draw from Lessing. To take a classical example that Lessing might have approved, in Book XVIII of *The Iliad*, Homer gives us an account of an appearance—what Achilles's shield looks like (1951, 388–91). This is great poetry (among the best ever written) but it takes Homer 130 lines, and his description still underdetermines the shield's appearance. It would be much, much easier to demonstrate exactly what the shield looks like using the media of the visual arts. A picture is worth much more than 130 lines of poetry, as it were. (For the record, the second clause of moderate medium specificity provides us with a means of better appreciating Homer's achievement. We recognize that the appearance of complex physical objects is difficult to convey merely through the use of words, and if Homer does so successfully, he's doing something rather extraordinary.)

It's also important to recognize that the first clause of moderate medium specificity isn't just a philosopher's concoction that doesn't factor into artist's practices. When turning to a new medium, artists investigate which sorts of new effects can be achieved with it and which sorts of challenges it presents. In effect, the process of exploring a new medium is exploring the norms for its use. Think about the different media that have been used to record audio.[9] Early 78 rpm records limited recording time to three minutes per side, which forced musicians to concentrate on songs of that length. The advent of the LP, a new medium, prompted musicians to create works like Genesis's *Foxtrot* (1972), featuring the nearly twenty-three-minute track "Supper's Ready." The revolution to digital media produced different capacities to exploit. Brian

Eno's *Reflection* (2017) consists in a single fifty-four-minute ambient track the constituent parts of which are continually rearranged by an app that Eno also issued. One probably could produce musical events equivalent to "Supper's Ready" or *Reflection* with a lot of 78 records and an extraordinarily complex apparatus for regulating their speed, volume, and succession, but this would be difficult at the least.

This point about the evolution of music recording technologies finds a parallel in the evolution of the materials and technologies (remember that these can count as media—they're just not all there is to it) that go into producing comics. In Chapter 1, we encountered the way that printing format affects artistic style, contrasting Windsor McCay's *Little Nemo in Slumberland* with Scott Adams's *Dilbert*. Whether a comic is printed with its vertical dimension longer than its horizontal (as in traditional comic books) or vice versa also makes certain panel layouts—and hence, what they can easily depict—more or less achievable.[10] Additionally, which tools are used to draw comics is significant. Whether one is working in pencils, paints, inks, markers, digital media, appropriated images, combinations thereof, or something else entirely is going to alter one's representational and expressive capacities, as Figure 3.4 shows. Each panel is drawn with a different technology, which you can see described in the gutters.

The advent of the digital revolution was just as significant for comics as it was for music. Aside from speeding certain processes (lettering! coloring!), digital tools expanded—or, at least, massively abetted—possibilities for image construction and manipulation. McCloud's *Reinventing Comics* is a book that hasn't aged well, unfortunately, since it concentrates on some technologies that have become obsolete and makes predictions that haven't come to pass. But he does nicely describe some ways in which comics artists can take (and have taken) advantage of digital's potential: twirling backgrounds, using "emboss" effects, blurring, adding noise and motion blurs, pixelating, using custom brush effects, and so on. As McCloud puts it, "While a bewildering variety of traditional tools would have been necessary [to produce these effects], digital tools can now put all of these possibilities in a single location: Right at the artist's fingertips" (2000, 147–48). To finish our parallel to music recording: using the technology of the 1970s, it might be possible to make comics that look just like those of the 2010s (and vice versa), but it would be *difficult*.[11] Media, as the first condition of moderate medium specificity has it, matter.

If, contra moderate medium specificity, the technological and material aspects of media were to have no influence on an art form's capacities for representation and expression, we'd expect a rather different situation. Neither

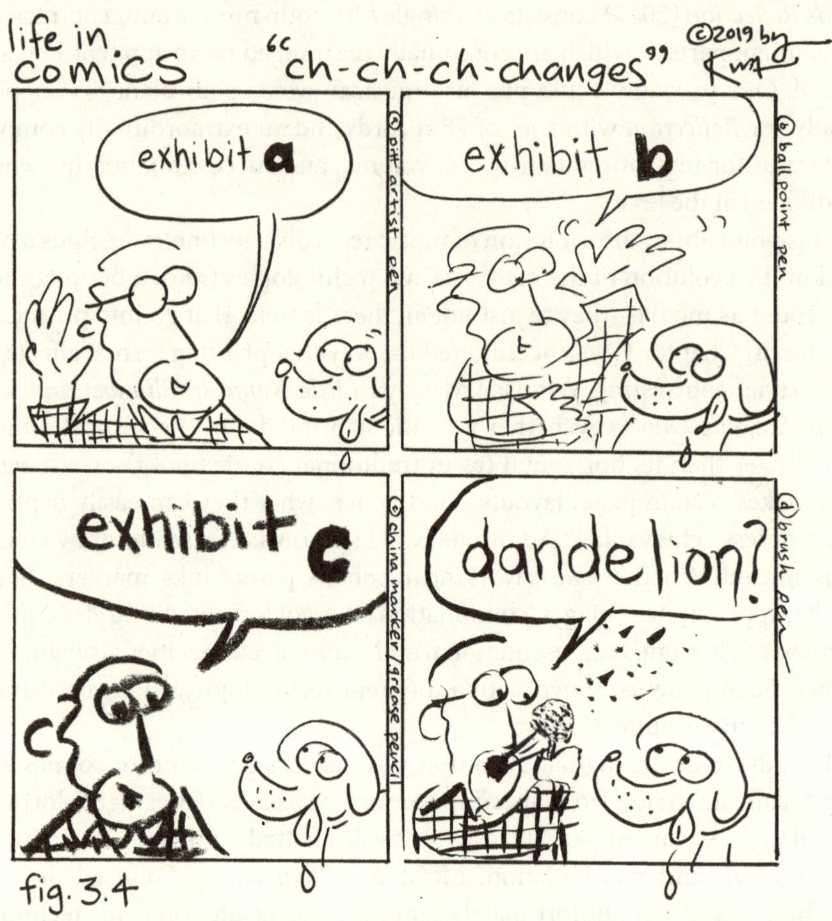

fig. 3.4

music nor comics would have evolved along with technological developments. Each recording medium would be equally apt for capturing the same musical events; each printing or creation technology would be equally apt for producing the same images.

Incidentally, even Carroll, a vocal critic of medium specificity, appears to recognize the plausibility of its moderate variant. In the context of arguing that photography, qua medium, is capable of being used to make art, Carroll points out that no art-making medium (photography included) gives artists complete control of their final product. What's interesting in our current context are his claims to the effect that "most artists have to negotiate compromises with their medium—to adjust to the material at hand" and that "virtually every particular artistic element comes with limitations" (2008, 24). On Carroll's view, writers are restricted by the language they use, composers by their chosen instrumentation, architects and sculptors by their materials, and painters by available types of paint. This sounds a lot like moderate medium specificity: to say that materials and artistic elements (i.e., media) limit artists is just to affirm that the media used contribute negatively to representational and expressive capacities.

In closing, the first clause of moderate medium specificity has a good deal of explanatory power. It allows us to understand why comics from different eras and different artists look different.[12] It helps us to recognize what comics, as an art form, is particularly good at—and what it isn't. The ideas we're developing here are going to drive significant portions of the rest of this book, starting with the next section, and the degree to which moderate medium specificity is plausible will hinge at least somewhat on how successful and productive this project turns out to be—so as you go forward, feel free to refer back to this section to see whether its promise has been fulfilled.

I need to address a glaring omission before moving on. What of the second clause of moderate medium specificity—the idea that understanding and evaluating individual comics depends on a recognition of their medium-specific capacities? Well, that's the subject of Chapter 6. At that point, I'll show that moderate medium specificity provides important background for determining the value of particular comics.

3.4. Tendencies of Comics Media in Practice

I've argued that medium-specific considerations can help provide us with explanations of what comics is good at. In this section, I'll give some examples of what I mean. The media from which comics are made, I propose, account for their effectiveness when used for instructional and educational purposes, as well as in the burgeoning field of graphic medicine.

As a culture, the United States has gone through times when the prevailing view of comics was that they were the opposite of educational—that their main effect was to degrade and pervert young minds. That was one of the attitudes dominant during the 1950s hysteria about comics spurred by Frederick Wertham (mentioned in the standard history I offered in Chapter 1, and which we'll revisit in the final chapter). It hasn't always been like that, though. Comics have a long history not only of condemnation, but also of use in education, promoting literacy, and for general instruction.

In "Teaching and Learning with Comics" (2017), Carol L. Tilley and Robert G. Weiner give a detailed overview of the ways in which comics have been incorporated into educational and instructional contexts going back at least to the 1920s. According to Tilley and Weiner, comics have been used to teach a wide variety of common subjects: history, math, management, science, social studies, medicine, English, philosophy, library mastery, and many more. They've been deployed to develop vocabulary and language skills, encourage reading, and introduce young readers to classic literature. Will Eisner even did a long-running series for the US Army that used comics to demonstrate how to do important tasks like oiling a machine gun and changing wheel bearings. If you buy into McCloud's broad definition (which we encountered in Chapter 2), you might notice comics teaching you how to do things like use your seat cushion as a flotation device in case of a water landing. If McCloud is right, then, historically, people have also used comics to teach and learn about such subjects as Christian doctrine, the Roman emperor Trajan, and the Norman Conquest of England.

Tilley and Weiner approvingly cite ample research according to which comics have positive effects when used for these various purposes. Similarly, when it comes to science education, Matteo Farinella claims that recent studies have reached the conclusion that "comics were consistently more effective [than mere text] at improving students['] engagement and motivation" (2018, 3). Agreement about the data referenced by Tilly and Weiner, as well as Farinella, seems widespread, at least judging from the ways in which comics have increasingly infiltrated the classroom. There's even an anthology now (edited by Stephen Tabachnick) called *Teaching the Graphic Novel* (2009), devoted to offering advice for teachers who aim to maximize the potential of comics for instruction. (It focuses on the graphic novel, but as you know, that's just a marketing term for comics.) Given that you're reading this book, I'm guessing you're inclined to think about the role of comics in instruction favorably: comics, you might figure, are awesome and fun and make learning anything better. Let's just assume the studies are reliable and this is generally a well-supported result. What could explain it—that is, what could the causal mechanism be for the effectiveness of comics in education and instruction?

The power of comics for education and instruction shouldn't just be explained just by talking about the value of individual comics. While it's true that contemporary research tends to focus on the use of good comics (whatever that means—we'll try out some options later) like *Watchmen*, *March*, *Persepolis*, *Maus*, the *Tintin* series, and so on, it's not the individual comic so much that seems to matter, but rather the fact that it's a *comic* rather than a work in a different category (e.g., nongraphic literature or animation). And thinking about comics itself gets us into the medium-specific explanations that we'll explore after a brief discussion of another practical application of comics: graphic medicine.

As described in the introduction to *The Graphic Medicine Manifesto* (cowritten by M. K. Czerwiec et al.), "Graphic medicine combines the principles of narrative medicine with an exploration of the visual systems of comic art, interrogating the representation of the physical and emotional signs and symptoms within the medium" (2015, 1). Within the practice of graphic medicine, comics have an educational role, as tools to train medical professionals. But they're also used to allow medical providers/caregivers and patients alike to explore their perceptions of medicine and their own experiences through the processes of comics creation and reception.

Some of the resulting works—like David B.'s *Epileptic*; Kaisa Leka's *I Am Not These Feet*; Harvey Pekar, Joyce Brabner, and Frank Stack's *Our Cancer Year*; and Ian Williams's *The Bad Doctor*—are done by professional artists and published in the usual manners, often to critical acclaim. But many more are done just by and for their amateur creators and won't be shared widely, if at all. For example, the illustrator whose work graces this book, Kurt Shaffert, has used comics in several ways in collaboration with amateurs. In a therapeutic technique that he calls "process cartooning," Shaffert serves as a facilitator who draws graphic narratives in response to "stage directions" given by patients (he's done extensive work in with traumatized war veterans) who take the role of narrator/directors. This process empowers the narrator/directors to explore, witness, and reflect on "the things on their hearts." The result might look something like the images inserted into each frame of Figure 3.5 (although keep in mind that it's the process that matters here, not the product).

Together with other artists, writers, and collaborators, Shaffert has been involved in projects that bring together the White River Junction VA Medical Center (in Vermont) with the Center for Cartoon Studies. As part of the latter's mission of "applied cartooning," they have initiated the Cartoonist Veteran Project, resulting in books like *A Whole Lifetime of Firsts* (2018), which gives voice to the experiences of women veterans.

There really seems to be something to graphic medicine. Practitioners, if the articles and comics in *The Graphic Medicine Manifesto* are given credence, believe that comics are effective tools in the medical milieu. Let's take this at face value and try to explain it. Again, medium-specific claims are going to come to the fore.

Just how do the media of comics make them well suited for instruction and in graphic medicine? For starters, because comics are made of pictures, they're ideally built for reader uptake. Pictorial literacy—recognizing and identifying what one sees in a picture—might be a learned skill, but it's one that people

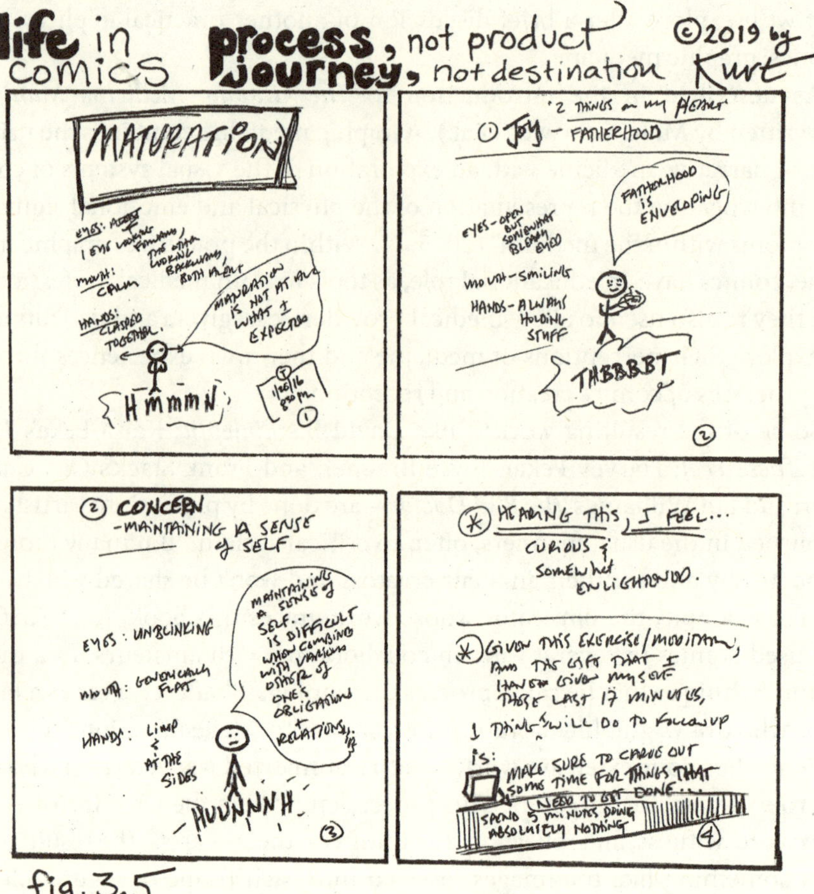

fig. 3.5

across cultures are very quick to acquire (and, notably, precedes verbal literacy in children). Unlike works made exclusively out of words, comics have a nearly instant and universal appeal, even for those who don't read the language (if any) in which the comic is written. Understanding the pictures in a comic written in an unknown tongue goes a long way toward being able to derive the contextual meaning of the words. That's why the kindred art form of children's literature is heavily pictorial, and why comics are excellent for language acquisition. (In my experience, reading *Tintin* and *Asterix* definitely helped my education in French.) In the graphic medicine context, the pictorial media of comics contribute to the comfort level of caregivers and patients: participants are not being asked to engage with a symbol system that is unfamiliar or difficult to grasp. Comics, more than nonpictorial art forms, is eminently available to those who have trouble reading or otherwise feel daunted by the demand to engage with or produce the written word.

In addition, the spatial (rather than temporal) juxtaposition of comics panels lends itself to educational purposes. The kind of access to panels that readers have allows them to easily to reinvestigate and reassess the content of panels with respect to each other. Farinella claims that this kind of processing is deeply involved in the adoption of a scientific outlook. "Science," he writes, "often requires readers to make connections between multiple scales and domains of knowledge, not necessarily arranged in a hierarchical, linear order" (2018, 6). Note that such connections aren't just hallmarks of acquiring scientific knowledge, but any knowledge that requires other than perfect, linear thinking (perhaps all of it!).

These explanations for the power of comics apply to all of them, if all of them are pictorial and all of them consist in spatially juxtaposed panels. But lots of comics use words as well, and the incorporation of words into the pictures produces other important medium-specific effects. When comics use verbal media, they can convey nearly every aspect of lived experience. Pictures by themselves can show us what objects and persons look like (or perhaps more importantly, in graphic medicine, how the artist *thinks* they look); reveal spatial relationships among objects and persons; portray body language, facial expressions, and reactions; and give us a sense of position, motion, and speed. But the addition of words also allows for the straightforward representation of speech, thought, and narration, which enhances reader comprehension of the mental states of those depicted—their thoughts and feelings. It should be evident how this is important in the processes of therapy and giving and receiving care.

Tilley and Weiner gesture at the medium-specific effects of comics when they raise dual-coding theory, which has the potential to reveal how the engagement of different types of mental processing enhances instruction (2017, 363–64). According to proponents of dual-coding theory, the brain processes (codes) information delivered by different symbol systems (i.e., part of our account of comics media) in different ways. We encode the information we receive from the words in comics in the form of sequential narratives, whereas pictures of comics are encoded nonsequentially. That these encodings combine synergistically produces mutually enforcing learning channels along avenues not readily available through the use of other media.

The combination of pictures and words has proven to be effective as well in the related art form of children's picture books. Pediatric scientist John Hutton and his coauthors have done research that measures children's brain activity, using fMRI machinery, when the children are exposed to stories told using different media.[13] Hutton et al. compared the effects of the same picture book when read and seen in the normal way, when listened to in an audio-only version, and when presented as an animated cartoon (the works they compared were all by popular children's author Robert Munsch, who conveniently has posted audio and animated versions of his stories on his website). According to their results, picture books are more effective than the alternatives when it comes to language learning, actively imagining, and promoting self-reflection. The authors speculate that this is because of a "Goldilocks effect": picture books engage the brain neither too much nor too little.

Now, as we discussed earlier, picture books and comics aren't exactly the same thing. However, it's difficult to come up with an essentialist definition that differentiates them clearly. They deliver content in very similar ways—through pictures and (generally) words. So I'm willing to bet that if picture books are better for language learning and so forth than the alternatives, comics are better than those same alternatives, for the same reasons (i.e., through optimization of the mechanisms that encourage brain development).

The tie-in with children's picture books brings up an important qualification: I'm not advancing any arguments that support Alan Moore's claim with which we opened this chapter—that other art forms *cannot* represent and express the things that comics can. That would be the verdict of strong medium specificity, which I think we should reject. Rather, the idea is only that comics lend themselves particularly well to certain representational and expressive applications. (For literacy applications, other art forms—e.g., picture books—might be equally well suited.) For example, to pursue and apply one of Lessing's thoughts, art therapy that makes use of sculpture engages participants in a tactile and creative way, but does not allow them easily to produce narratives. Purely written arts like poetry excel at enabling participants to articulate their internal lives and feelings, as well as the psychological states they believe are to be attributed to others. But the lack of pictures makes it very hard to show rather than to tell. The media used in graphic medicine like process cartooning help facilitators collaboratively to produce works that show (and not just tell) visually and viscerally how narrator/directors conceive of their subject.

When the pictorial media that comprise a comic are rendered in a cartoon style, there are medium-specific effects as well. Cartoons are eminently legible, as we discussed in Chapter 1. As Ed Tan has argued (2001), this makes it comparatively easy to discern which emotions characters depicted in that style are feeling. In the instructional context, this is a positive effect: emotional legibility precedes literacy and emotional resonance (sympathy or empathy, or, if you buy McCloud's arguments, identification). That resonance has the potential to engage readers who might be put off by media that provide less of an emotional connection. Likewise, in the medical context, one important goal is to promote emotional clarity, or at least clarity about the murkiness of one's occurrent emotional states. Cartoons are well suited for providing this clarity.

And when comics are cartooned, they're playful and easy to draw. Anybody can make a comic with anything that will make a mark. (Not incidentally, since comics have a historically lowbrow reputation—perhaps as a partial result of the cartooning style—they're not an intimidating art form to take up.) The result is that comics, unlike something like opera, doesn't demand that we take it with the utmost seriousness and commitment. That can make comics comparatively more fun for students to learn from. Furthermore, in situations like those fostered by practitioners of graphic medicine, the pressure to produce a work of objective excellence or genius is removed. As M. K. Czerwiec points out (2015, 145–46), working in comics avoids a troubling tendency in our society to select at a very early age only certain persons (i.e., those with an affinity for realistic drawing) as artists.[14] In virtue of their media, comics are excellent for use in therapy and other medical aims because of their accessibility to all, even those without artistic skills that meet conventional norms and attitudes.

3.5. Conclusions

I hope the discussion in the previous section has been enough to demonstrate convincingly that there are reasonable medium-specific explanations for the power of comics in instruction and medicine. If comics are good at meeting the goals to which they are put for instructive and medical purposes, and the reasons why have to do with their media, then it's got to be true that media affect what can be done with comics. And that, in turn, lends credence to the first clause of moderate medium specificity.

The way we got here, of course, has to do with the way in which I'm understanding media—the broad idea that media aren't merely the materials and technologies that go into the production of works in an art form, but also the symbolic and formal elements that they bring to bear in that production. I want to stress again that this isn't the only way of thinking about media, but just one that I've found to be especially fecund. Defining media otherwise, e.g., more narrowly, would have different implications for medium specificity in general and for medium specificity applied to comics in particular.

Bearing in mind everything I've claimed about the suitability of comics for various purposes, one might get the impression that comics is in some way superior to other art forms. I don't actually think that's the case—it's just that comics is good at some things that are more difficult to achieve in other art forms, given the media from which comics and those other art forms are respectively composed. Comics is also bad at some things that are comparatively easy to achieve in other media. I've gestured at a few of these earlier, but want to close with an example that connects us back to the instructional and medical contexts.

Comics are pictorial: they use pictures as a medium. As such, accessing comics requires pictorial literacy. I argued earlier that this is easily acquired, but that's a bit too quick. Pictorial literacy requires the use of sight. Pictures, and hence comics, aren't readily accessible for those who have visual impairments. So using comics to instruct those with visual impairments (or even those without visual impairments, in situations where it's dark!) is going to be ineffective. Similarly, because of the limitations of comics, graphic medicine probably isn't the best tool for those dealing with vision issues—at least in comparison to, say, art forms that incorporate auditory or tactile media.

But once more, just like it isn't impossible to use nongraphic literature to convey appearances (according to moderate medium specificity, it's possible but difficult), it isn't impossible to use comics with the visually impaired, for either instructional or medical purposes. For example, Shaffert believes (as he's conveyed to me in conversation) that process cartooning can be done in such a way that the comics that are part of it are realized only in the imagination.

There are very interesting and complex philosophical and scientific questions having to do with the connections between experiences and the imagination, and I don't want to wade in too deeply. Nonetheless, the reasonable default position seems to be that somebody who has never seen a comic (or at least the constituent ingredients of comics, like pictures, panels, and written words) is not going to be able to imagine one. But somebody who has seen a comic in the past, or at least its constituent ingredients, and is no longer able to see ought to be able to imagine a comic. For those in that particular situation, comics could be used for instruction or therapeutically, if not as easily as some other art forms.

And this raises one last point for this chapter. If the visually impaired can use comics by means of imagining them, does that mean that the media of comics aren't necessarily mind-independent? Can there be comics that are just made of *mental* "media"? Well, the account of media developed in this chapter leaves open that possibility, as long as the notion of mental materials, technologies, symbols, or formal elements makes sense. However, a potential complication emerges from something we considered during the previous chapter. Suppose that it's plausible to hold that, minimally, comics consist in a sequence of spatially juxtaposed pictures. In what sense are mental images spatially juxtaposed, given that they have no actual spatial position or orientation? Maybe being imagined as juxtaposed is enough to satisfy this necessary condition on comics—I'll leave that up to you to decide. Or maybe the better alternative is to say that even though comics can be imagined (which makes even imagined comics possible to use in instruction or therapy), imagined comics aren't *really* comics, any more than an imagined muffin is *really* a muffin.

Interestingly, even merely imagined comics, if such things exist, appear to involve medium-specific constraints. To the extent that comics are pictorial, imagining a comic requires imagining pictures. Imaginary pictures are representatively and expressively different in their capacities and capabilities than, e.g., imagined sounds, textures, or movements. And so even merely imagined comics, should such objects be possible, would be more or less easily applied to various purposes than imagined works in other art forms.

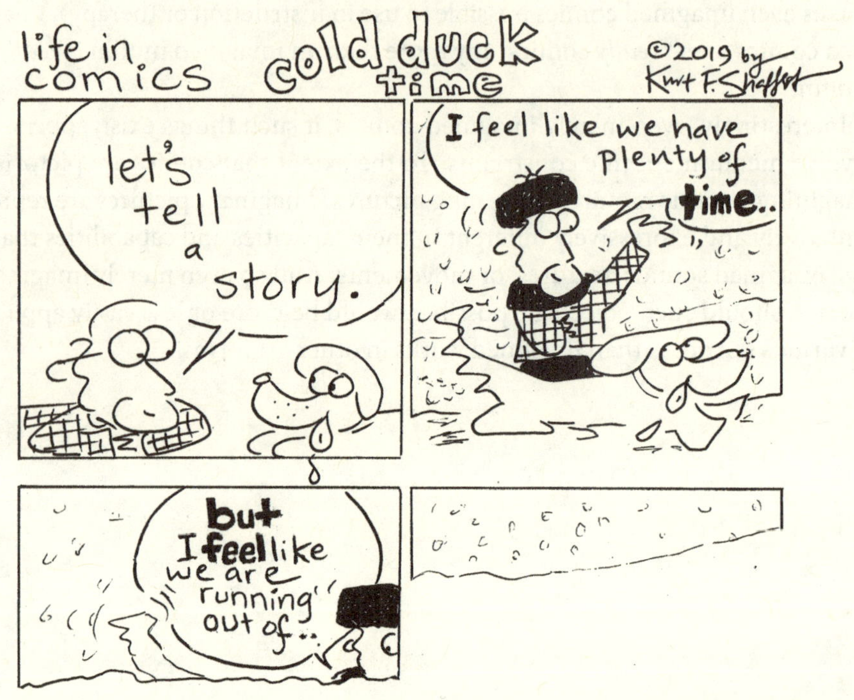
life in comics
cold duck time
©2019 by Kurt F. Shaffert
let's tell a story.
I feel like we have plenty of time..
but I feel like we are running out of..

fig. 4.1

4

Narrative, Time, and Space

4.1. Narrativity

We encountered the putative importance of narrative considerations in Chapter 2 when we inquired whether narrativity should be a necessary condition for comics. The conclusion reached there, to remind ourselves, was that on the one hand, including narrativity in the definition would have useful results, by allowing us, for example, to rule out paintings as comics. But on the other hand, including narrativity also risks ruling out single-panel works as comics. Moreover, we encountered Meskin's argument that a narrative condition threatens to foreclose on the possibility of nonnarrative, avant-garde strategies for organizing panels. Not only that, but there might be good reasons to think that comics can't be given either necessary or sufficient conditions in the first place.

Nonetheless, there does seem to be a strand of narrativity that runs deeply in comics—the *vast* majority of comics produced are narrative. And this is reflected in the fact that many prominent commentators on comics stress the role of narrativity. Out of the eleven definitions I quoted in Section 2.2 of Chapter 2, eight contain some version of a narrative requirement.[1] Even if narrative isn't essential to comics, it's obviously an incredibly significant feature to notice.

At the very least (as I also argued in Chapter 2—see Section 2.4), even if some comics are not narrative, the process of reading a comic still requires us to cast about for some kind of a unifying device. Because the vast majority of ordinary readers of comics typically encounter them exclusively in narrative form, the default way that most of us have for processing a comic at a macro level involves casting about for the story that it's telling.

For these reasons, I think it should be uncontroversial to hold that comics is a *predominantly* (if not essentially) narrative art form. This chapter is about understanding how comics work narratively. Before plunging in, I should offer a brief remark about what narratives are. Unsurprisingly, this issue has attracted considerable controversy.[2] On the most minimal definitions, there can be narratives that portray just one event. I think this only makes sense for events that involve a temporal sequence.[3] If "The NIH declared that alcohol is

The Philosophy of Comics. Henry John Pratt, Oxford University Press. © Oxford University Press 2023.
DOI: 10.1093/oso/9780190845445.003.0004

a carcinogen"[4] is an event, then, to my mind, not all representations of events are narratives.

To be a narrative, it would have to include something further: "The NIH declared that alcohol is a carcinogen, and so, in my efforts to ensure a prolonged and painful death, I decided to drink heavily." This is a sentence that represents a causal connection between at least two events. That's what I think narratives are (following Bordwell 1985). However, if you think narratives are something different, don't worry—most of what I have to say below will be compatible with most reasonable views. The only import thing that hinges on requiring narratives to represent a causal sequence of events is that if no time elapses in a comic (or a work that is professed to be a comic), then it's not a narrative, and what I have to say in this chapter will be largely irrelevant to it.

We say that we "read" comics, but what does this amount to? At a certain level, the notion makes plenty of sense. While there are wordless comics, we've seen that most comics do employ words (among other media), in the form of word balloons, captions, and/or sound effects. The words in comics provide what I'll call the *verbal dimension* of narrative: the narrative features of comics are constructed (at least in part) in the same way as nongraphic works of literature.

The verbal dimension is clearly not all there is to comics, however. Comics, I've argued, are pictorial, perhaps even essentially so—that is, without pictures, a work isn't a comic. The pictures (as we will see) are crucial to the narrative construction of comics. Words alone will not do all the narrative work. This suggests that comics have both verbal and *pictorial* dimensions of narrative. Narratively, comics is a hybrid art form that employs strategies closely connected to literature, on the one hand, and other pictorial narrative art forms (like film), on the other.

In this chapter, then, we'll think carefully about the verbal and pictorial dimensions of comics. We'll consider the medium-specific ways in which comics construct their narratives out of words and pictures. Of particular interest will be the regulation of reader perceptions of narrative time and space. We'll also think about how the ways in which some comics are published—serially—produce narrative effects.

At the outset, I want to preempt two potential sources of confusion. First, while Eisner might be right that "the psychological processes involved in viewing a word and an image are analogous" (2008, 2), strictly speaking, comics aren't *literally* read. You can't read pictures. Though "reading" may not be the most apt word for the way in which we encounter narrative in comics, it's deeply entrenched. Indeed, as I related in the standard history offered in Chapter 1, the first true comics were published in newspapers, a predominantly verbal medium that it is uncontroversial to think of as "read." And the fact of the matter is that we don't have any better word for our method of processing comics. So that's the term that I'm going to stick to throughout this discussion.[5]

Second, over the course of this chapter, many of the claims I make are going to be pitched at a rather high level of generality. My aim is to investigate the most prominent narrative functions of comics. As always, I think it's worth covering the various genres of newspaper comics, comic books, and webcomics together, though I will explain some differences among these where warranted. Comics are very diverse in style, and many comics artists show no hesitation in exploring, expanding, and rejecting the norms that govern the media with which they work. As always, I don't want to support the implication of strong medium specificity that all and only the narratives of comics have the features upon which I concentrate—merely that this is a cluster of features particularly central to and dominant in the art form.

4.2. The Verbal Dimension

Words are found in comics in four different forms. The most obvious, and the most characteristic of the art form, is the word balloon: the speech or thoughts of a character are presented within the panel with some pictorial indication or implication that connects them directionally to that character. Second, we find text that is not in balloon form, but is often contained in a box or in a caption outside the panel. In general, this sort of text does not convey dialogue, but serves as narration—it's the voice of whoever is telling the story, whether that's one of the characters or an impersonal narrator. In the past few decades, textual narration outside balloons has increasingly replaced thought balloons, at least in American superhero comics. I'm guessing that this is to avoid associations with the campier comics from the 1960s and 1970s. Third, there are sound effects. These usually occur inside the panel (or, dramatically, across panels), and are drawn in a typeface that reflects visually the timbre and volume of the sound that they're supposed to portray. McCloud, typically, gives some excellent examples of how to do this (2006, 147). And finally, pictures of words can occur within a panel, when, for example, a sign or book is depicted. You can see all of these forms of word use in Figure 4.2.

Now that we're dealing with narrative, it's going to be useful to introduce some new terminology (new to us in this book at least—the terms go back to ancient Greece). The *diegesis* is the story world of a narrative that's "real" to, and hence can be experienced by, the characters in that narrative. Elements in this story space are *diegetic*; elements that are not are *nondiegetic*. These are

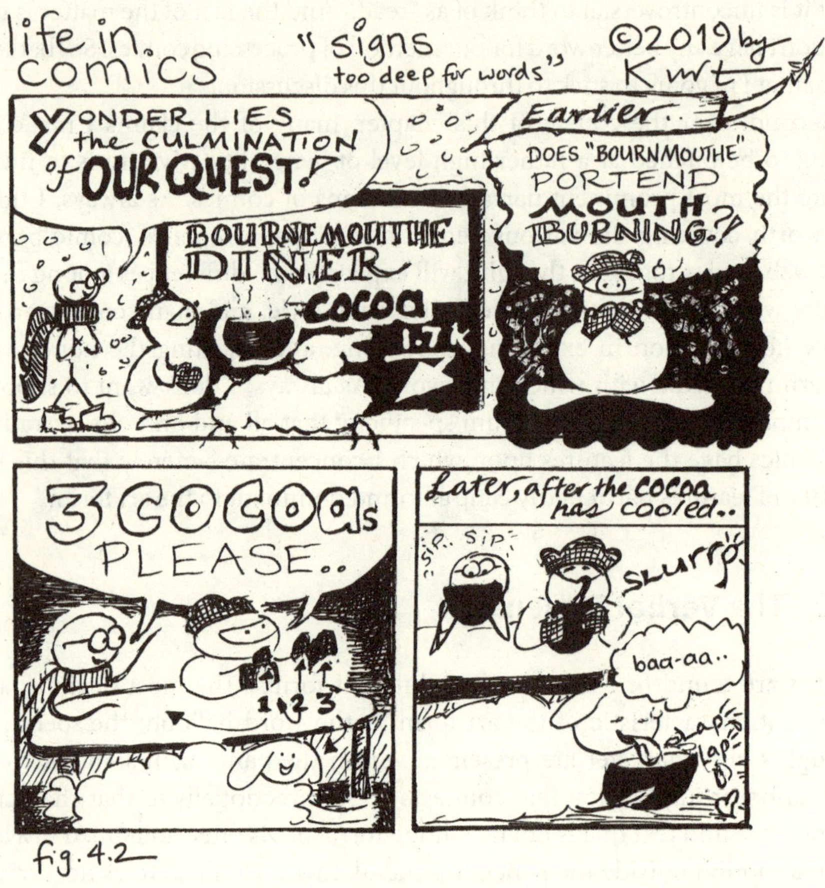

fig. 4.2

terms that can be used during theorization about narratives in any art form, including comics.

The relations of words to a comic's diegesis are interesting. Look again at Figure 4.2. The billboard in panel 1 is diegetic. Not only the reader, but also the characters can see it. However, only the reader can see the other types of words that occur in this. The characters can't see the word balloons, thought balloons, sound effects, or narration in boxes. But some of these features aren't exactly nondiegetic. Though characters can't see speech balloons, they can hear the words in them, and presumably characters are aware of the contents of their own thought balloons (even when the others aren't). The sound effects, like those given for drinking cocoa, can be heard by the characters, though the sounds heard within the diegesis may not be exactly the same as the sounds depicted in words. "Slurrp" may be onomatopoetic, but it can't capture the exact sound of drinking from a mug. In this particular comic, the characters aren't aware of the narration, but in other comics, at least some of them can be, as is the case where characters are narrating their own stories or relating their thought processes.

These are all generalizations, of course. There are plenty of metafictional comics that exploit or otherwise draw attention to their own fictionality or category norms, including the diegetic and nondiegetic placement of words. A great example, helpfully provided by Cook (2012, 177–79) is Editor Girl in Jimmie Robinson's *Bomb Queen*. This character has a magic Sharpie that allows her to alter the content of other characters' word balloons. For Editor Girl, word balloons are fully diegetic, as they are for the characters in Figure 4.3. In similar metafictional scenarios, characters can react directly to an impersonal

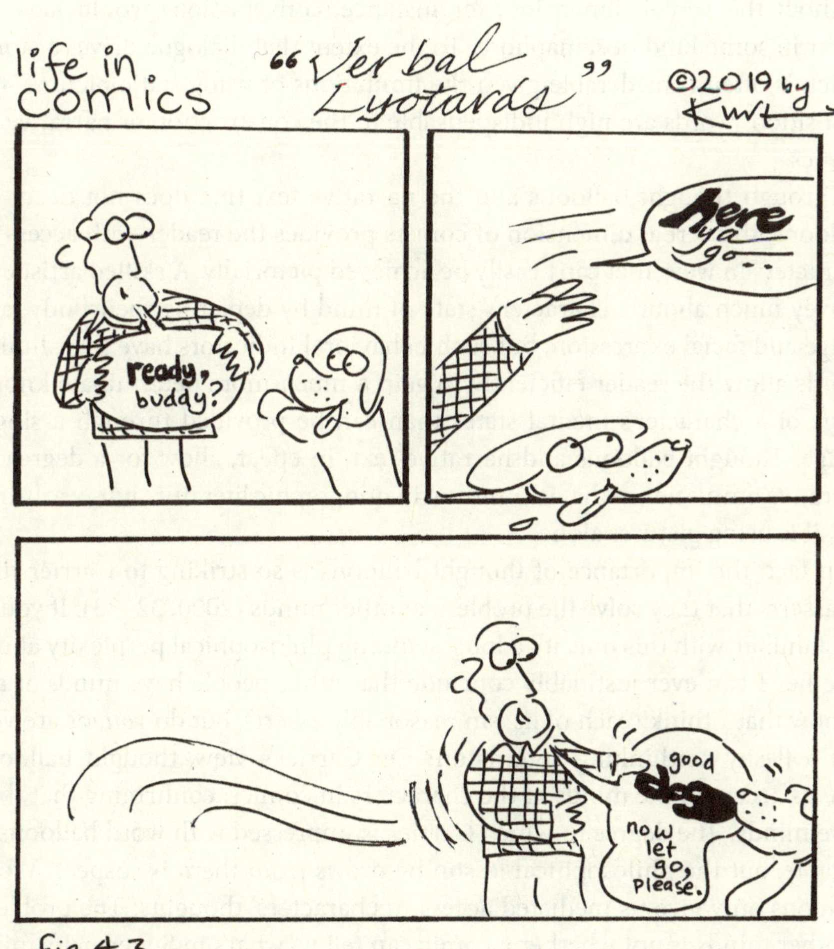

fig. 4.3

narrator or even address the reader (in film and television, it's often called "breaking the fourth wall"). This kind of thing happens in *Deadpool* comics all the time.

Usually, the verbal dimension of comics is nondiegetic *visually.* That is, most of the words found in comics don't determine what the characters in them see. In the case of speech balloons and sound effects, they determine and reflect what the characters hear. In the case of thought balloons or narrative boxes, they determine and reflect what characters (or the narrators, who may or may not be characters within the comic) think. Moreover, because a comic is silent in actuality, the words it contains are the only way the reader has of accessing sounds that are part of the narrative. The presence of words in comics allows us to follow narratives that might otherwise be inaccessible. Without the verbal dimension, for instance, conversations would have to occur in some kind of semaphore. To the extent that dialogue drives a story, which is often considerable given the limitations of using static pictures for exposition, words are nigh indispensable in the construction of narrative in comics.

Through thought balloons and the narrative text that does not occur in balloons, the verbal dimension of comics provides the reader with access to characters in ways that can't easily be achieved pictorially. A skilled artist can convey much about a character's state of mind by depicting their body language and facial expression, but such behavioral indicators have their limits. Words allow the reader efficiently to gain a much more determinate knowledge of a character's mental states than can be provided through a single image. Thought balloons and narrative text, in effect, allow for a degree of narrative omniscience that is common in nongraphic literature but nearly impossible using pictures alone.

In fact, the importance of thought balloons is so striking to Carrier that he asserts that they solve the problem of other minds (2000, 32–33). If you're not familiar with this one, it's a long-standing philosophical perplexity about whether I can ever justifiably conclude that other people have minds at all. I know that *I* think (each of us can reasonably assert), but do *you*, or are you just a fleshy, unthinking automaton? On Carrier's view, thought balloons give us access to the minds of the characters in comics, confirming that they have minds. The degree to which Carrier is impressed with word balloons is notable, but the philosophical lesson he draws from them is suspect. Word balloons only give us mediated access to characters' thoughts. The problem of other minds is not whether a comic can tell us what's in Superman's mind diegetically, but whether anything actual in the nondiegetic universe other than *me* has a mind. There's no extravagant philosophical conclusion to be drawn from comics here: they don't solve the problem of other minds any more than literary works do when written in the first person, or (when in the third person) literary narration attributes mental states to characters.

The verbal dimension is crucial in the governance of the passage of time in comics narratives. As we'll see in the next section, pictures in comics also regulate time. But there are particularly interesting ways in which words can determine the *duration* of a single panel. "Silence," as McCloud notes, "has the effect of removing a panel from any particular span of time" (1993, 164), and for once I agree with him completely. You can see this effect in in Figure 4.4.

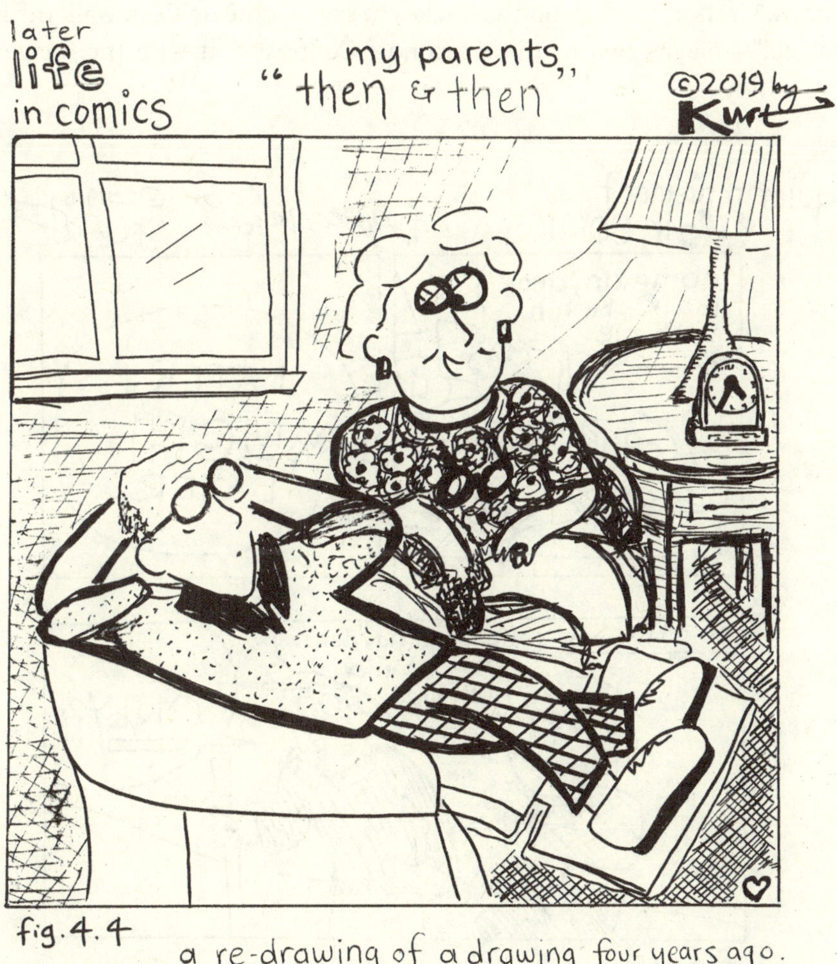

fig. 4. 4
a re-drawing of a drawing four years ago.

Because of the lack of text, this panel is ambiguous. It could represent one instant of a causal sequence. It could represent a long pause in conversation. Or it could even represent an old couple happily frozen in time for all of eternity.

When words are added, however, the passage of time within the part of the narrative encapsulated by a panel is regulated, guiding the reader's attention and interpretation. For sound effects, we extrapolate from our experiences of sounds in the real world. A panel lasts at least as long as the sound to which the effect word refers.

Similarly, when characters fictionally utter the words we find in speech balloons, we get an idea of the duration of their utterances from our experiences of how long it takes to say something. We know that panel 1 of Figure 4.5 lasts at least as long as it takes to say, "Come on dear, walk the hill with me!"—maybe two or three seconds. Contrast that with the image in

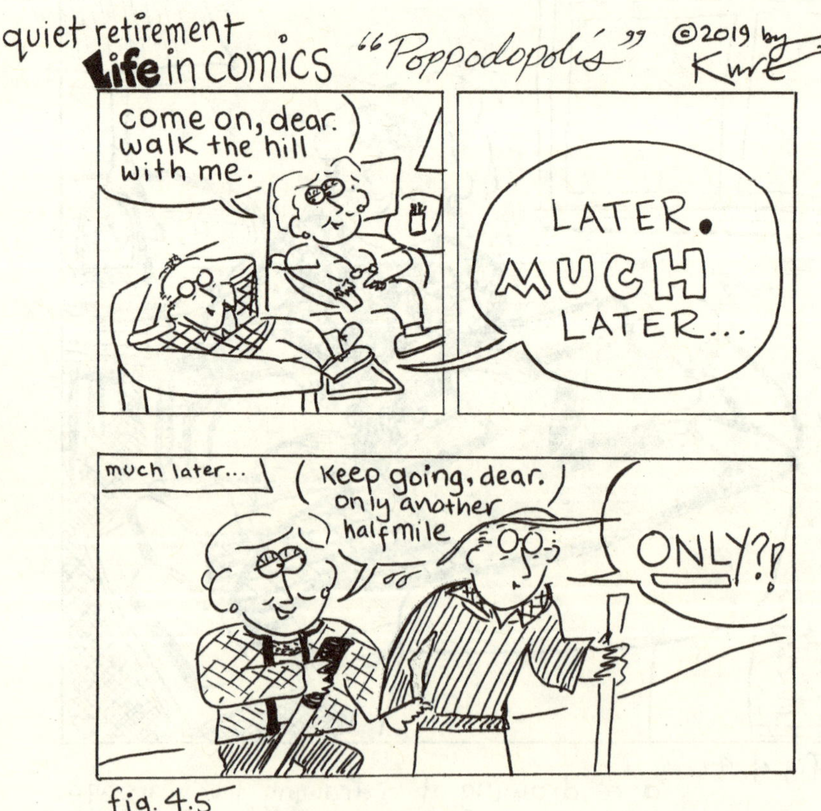

fig. 4.5

Figure 4.4, which has roughly the same pictorial content without any word balloons.

This comic is interestingly complicated by the word balloon that tails into the second panel. Does the man's half of the initial conversation occur temporally within the first panel, or within the second (having a dual role as a temporal bridge to the events of the third panel)? Crossing a panel border isn't necessarily an indication of a different temporal frame. The third panel is easier to parse: its duration is determined by the conversation, though it's a pregnant moment that serves as a microcosm of the walk together.

The regulation of time within a panel by a comic's verbal elements can be very complex indeed. Human thoughts can be more or less instantaneous, so in comics we find what might seem like a strange phenomenon: a character can undergo a very complicated thought process while experiencing an event of very short duration, e.g., falling over. In effect, thought balloons and narration might take much more time for the viewer to read through than occurs in the panel in which they are located. We're supposed to understand that thought balloons generally occur *faster* than speech balloons. And we're supposed to understand that narrative text outside balloons is often in some way removed from the time frame of the panel. Such text does not usually determine panel duration because it's a take on the actions of that panel from another temporal perspective. How long does the panel in Figure 4.6 take? A pie is being eaten, a complex thought had, and a conceptual introduction is placed in a narrative box.

There are other curious temporal features associated with speech balloons. Speech balloons routinely indicate a conversation between two or more people, each one speaking after the next, and our experience of actual conversations tells us roughly how long this would take. But a panel can also represent a number of simultaneous utterances, multiple conversations occurring simultaneously, or even separate conversations one of which is supposed to transpire after the other. We've already considered this possibility in an illustration—see Figure 2.12.[6]

The diegetic exchange represented by the words in a panel might even take much more time than is possible given the physical activity depicted in the panel. In American superhero comics, it's not uncommon for characters to have full conversations while the picture only depicts the delivery of a single punch. The only way the reader has of making sense of these possibilities is through the visual skill of the artist, who needs to guide our perception of the verbal dimension through the pictorial placement of each balloon.

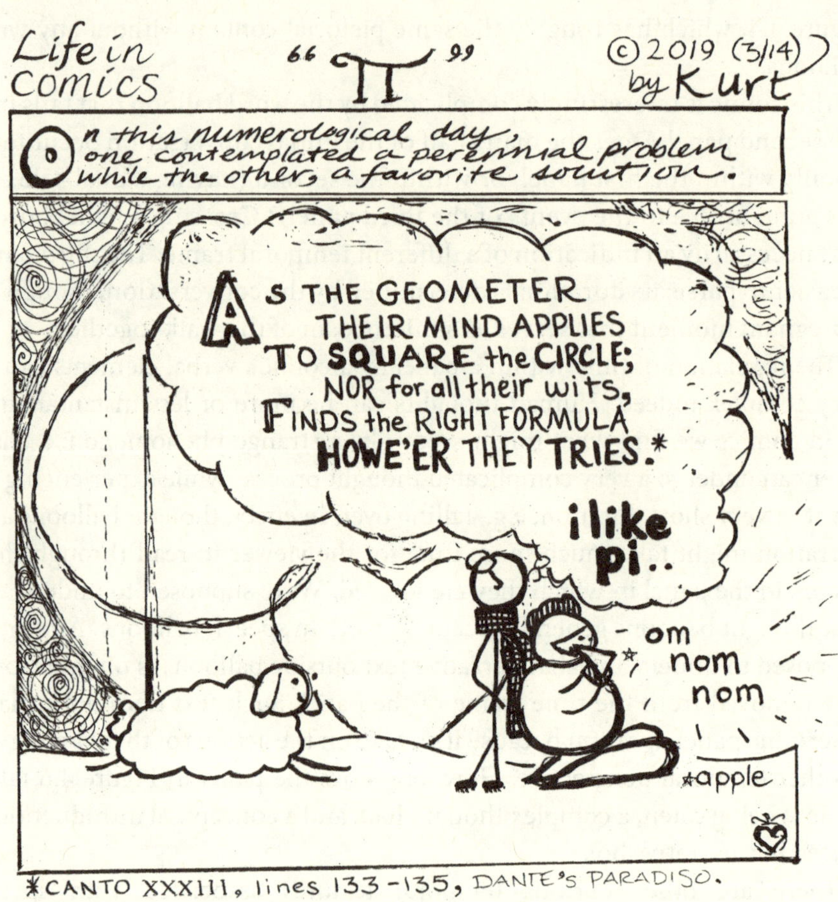

*CANTO XXXIII, lines 133-135, DANTE's PARADISO.

fig. 4.6

The prominence of word balloons shapes the reader's experience of the narrative in ways that exceed management of diegetic time frames. I hope you're convinced by now that the most essential media of comics are the pictures. Even so, when comics contain verbal media, those are quite frequently the reader's *primary* focus of attention. Lawrence Abbott argues that the reader's eyes typically play first over the words of a comic, then pass quickly over the pictures (often just to see which character a word balloon is associated with) before moving on to the next panel (1986, 161). That's typical of my own reading practices, especially on a first reading, but you'll have to consult your own experience to support or disconfirm whether that's how you read comics.[7] There are certainly other ways of appreciating and understanding comics: pictures, for instance, can be savored indefinitely. On a second reading or later, when one is familiar with the narrative, the pictures might be the primary focus of attention. Nonetheless, the words of a comic do seem to play a crucial role—maybe even the primary role—in determining the pace at which we can read comics and the efficiency with which this is possible.

Attention to the pace of narrative comprehension of comics also points to the great extent to which comics that use verbal media are akin to nongraphic literature. Comics are temporally static: while the words place constraints on the time it takes to read comics, these constraints are largely equivalent to those we find in other art forms like novels. The pace of reading a comic, wherein one's eyes and mind play over the succession of panels, is literary. It's constructed by readers, some of whom read faster or slower than others. That's really different from the way in which we process another art form that's dominated by pictorial narratives: film. We'll look at the relation of comics and film much more closely later, but for now, it's worth remarking that there are no slower or faster viewers of films. The rate at which a film *must* be processed is determined mechanically, not by the viewers themselves.

The verbal aspects of narrative in comics are, as we've now seen, crucial to our ways of understanding characters and the narratives in which they are embedded, particularly temporal relations within the story. And the verbal dimension shapes our reading processes. One might wonder, then, what function the pictures serve narratively, if anything. Given that the verbal elements are already in place, are the pictures of comics just narratively inert but charming accessories, like John Tenniel's drawings for *Alice in Wonderland*? Abbott seems to claim as much: "The subordination of the pictorial to the literary is one of the subtlest realities of the medium. . . . the comic art drawing, as a narrative element, must conform to an order of perception that is essentially literary" (1986, 156). I think that such views are misplaced; to see why, we must delve more deeply into the roles the pictures actually *do* play in comics.

4.3. The Pictorial Dimension

I've already tried to establish that without pictures, there are no comics. That's crucial for working out the narrative functions of the pictorial dimension of comics: it would be quite odd indeed if comics was essentially pictorial but the pictures played no significant role in comic narratives. If the story of a comic could be told just with words, there would be no point in making it a comic in the first place. McCloud even goes so far as to claim that "if the prose is independent of the pictures . . . if the written story could exist without any pictures and still be a continuous whole," it's not a comic at all (1995, 75).[8]

The pictures of comics add *something* to their narratives, but what is it, exactly? Since we've already thought some about word balloons, let's consider their pictorial narrative properties first. While verbal, word balloons are also part of a picture, a part whose placement is very deliberately selected by the artist. With a few exceptions, the words themselves won't allow the reader to determine who is speaking. Instead, the proximity of word balloons to the characters to whose utterances they correspond, together with the pictorial directionality implied by a balloon's "tail," cue us in to the identity of the speaker. The graphic properties of word balloons provide an elegant pictorial equivalent of the device for attributing utterances familiar in nongraphic literature: "She said . . ."

But there is a bit more to it than that. As Eisner puts it, in comics, "Lettering (hand-drawn or created with type), treated 'graphically' and in the service of the story, functions as an extension of the imagery" (2008, 2). The shape, borders, and text of word balloons can give pictorial cues to the reader about the mental states, personalities, and attitudes of their utterers. Comics artists convey these cues through how balloon borders are drawn; through the style, size, and emphasis in how the text is rendered; and even through the color used for the balloon or the text it contains.

Walt Kelly was a master of these techniques. By using distinctive word balloon styles for certain characters in *Pogo* (P.T. Bridgeport speaks in circus posters, Deacon Mushrat in old English type, Sarcophagus Macabre in darkly outlined square balloons) Kelly left no doubt what these characters were like (correspondingly: pompous and self-aggrandizing, deeply conservative, gloomy and threatening). Similar narrative impact is made by the use of word balloons that are different colors than white (e.g., when Deadpool's word balloons are yellow or when undersea creatures in Mike Mignola's *Hellboy* talk in purple balloons), or the use of colored type (e.g., when characters in Brian K. Vaughn and Fiona Staples's *Saga* speak in blue). The reader can tell that these characters are or are doing something *different*, merely by how their words are rendered. As moderate medium specificity would have it, this kind of content could be conveyed through other means (i.e., through the use of other media), but it would be a lot more cumbersome to convey it in comics without the pictorial properties of word balloons.

In addition to supplying the reader with the information discussed above, the pictorial aspect of each panel has at least three other straightforward narrative functions.

First, the picture can establish the setting or scene of a story and can guide the reader's perception of spatial relationships within it. Like establishing shots in film, some panels serve to give the reader a sense of the place in which the overall story of the comic will be occurring. And panels can show how characters and other physical objects are arrayed in diegetic space, enabling us to understand that Batman is punching rather than being punched, that Charlie Brown's kite is stuck in a tree, that the train is arriving at the station instead of leaving, and so on.

Second, we acquire narrative information from the artist's pictorial style. The ways in which the word balloons and sound effects are drawn, together with character design, inking, and color choices (if applicable) serve important storytelling purposes. They allow the artist to create a mood, give the emotional context of a scene or story, increase or decrease the drama of a moment, and so on.

Third, as I mentioned earlier in passing, a panel can inform the reader pictorially about the emotional and other mental states of the characters contained in it, without the use of words. We can tell just by looking that the Hulk is angry. Practically speaking, words may be exceedingly awkward in such cases: by and large, it's often better, more subtle, and demonstrates more drawing skill if an artist is able to *show* that the Hulk is angry than it is for the artist to have him say, "HULK ANGRY!" Or at least it's a different way of conveying anger.

Now that we've got a grasp of the role that pictures can play in determining the narrative content of an individual panel, we're in a position to discuss a much more complicated issue: the sequence of panels. In Chapter 2, I argued that the spatial juxtaposition of panels is an important way to differentiate comics from film. That's because while the images of comics take up different spaces on the page simultaneously, the images of film take up the same space—the area on which they are screened—consecutively. Although requiring comics to come in a sequence of panels has the potentially unfortunate consequence of ruling out of existence single-panel works, it should be evident that the sequence is at the very least central to mainstream understandings of comics. Even if it were the case that not all comics are organized in sequences of pictures, the vast majority are. And so it's important to inquire into how readers are able to make sense of a narrative that's displayed in multiple spaces, all of which exist at the same time nondiegetically. More specifically, what is the process that readers use to combine panels to form a continuous narrative, across the gutter (the space that lies between panels)?

Discussion of this problem has focused on what has come to be called, following McCloud, *closure*: the everyday process of "observing the parts but perceiving the whole" (1993, 63). On McCloud's account of how closure works in comics,

> In the limbo of the gutter, human imagination takes two separate images and transforms them into a single idea. Nothing is seen between the two panels, but experience tells you something must be there. . . . Closure allows us to connect [otherwise unconnected] moments and mentally construct a continuous, unified reality. (1993, 66–67)

McCloud's choice of "closure" as a term for connecting panels across the gutter is unfortunate. In narratology, it already has a long history of use to refer to the resolution of narrative tension. In philosophy (not that one would expect McCloud to be aware of this, but still . . .), it's a technical term in epistemology. Nonetheless, I've reluctantly decided to follow McCloud, and perpetuate the use of "closure" when discussing comics.

Why? There's no great alternative. One might attempt to appropriate, from film theory, the notion of suture, wherein the viewer brings order and unity to perception through an unconscious process of mentally "sewing" the film together from disparate elements (see Oudart 1977–78). That's Beaty's preference (1999, 68). But this option imports with it both an abundance of controversial psychoanalytic baggage that many would prefer to avoid and a controversy over the role of the shot/reverse-shot device in film (see Bordwell 1985, 110–13). Moreover, in film theory, "suture" refers primarily to spatial elements. In comics, we're also interested in temporal elements. I could coin an entirely new term, such as "soldering" or "bridging." But because of McCloud's prominence, "closure" has become very standard, and I don't want to confuse the issue by adopting a new term to apply to a concept already in play.

Accordingly, I'll use "closure" to refer to the mental process whereby readers of comics bridge the temporal and spatial incompleteness of the diegesis that occurs in the gutters among panels, thereby participating in the creation of narrative. McCloud thinks closure is a ubiquitous phenomenon, not only in narrative art forms, but in real life. We're going to see later how it works differently across art forms, but in this chapter, we'll concentrate only on how it works in comics.

I've already described some ways in which what's represented within a panel allows for the reader's understanding of temporal and spatial relations. But the sequence of panels that constitute a comic, combined with the reader's ability to use closure, can convey far more narrative information than can be achieved through a single picture. This is a medium-specific result: the fact that comics use sequences of pictures as media explains why they're better suited for narratives than art forms that only use stand-alone pictures (e.g., single paintings or photographs that are meant to be artworks in and of themselves apart from their relations to other images). Because a specific example will be useful, let's focus on Figure 4.7.

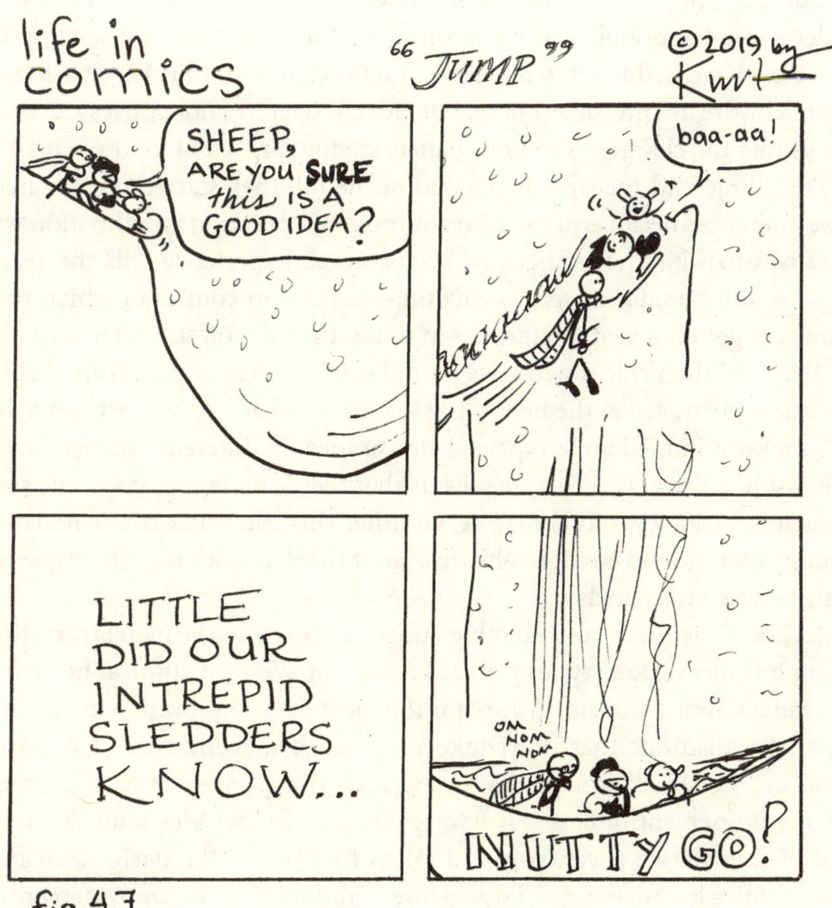

fig. 4.7

Consider again the passage of time within a comic's diegesis. We've seen that a single picture can represent more than an instant of time, especially when there are words involved. In the first panel of Figure 4.7, we know that time elapses—at least as much time as it takes for the speech act to occur. But given the theory of narrative raised earlier in this chapter, the first panel isn't a narrative at all, since it doesn't involve two events in a causal sequence. Since Figure 4.7 is a sequence, though, it can convey a narrative. Now, we saw this done before without multiple panels, back in Figure 2.12. This story can be told in a single panel with only a few components, since it's so simple, and since time can elapse in single panels. A more extensive story would require a much larger and more complex panel.[9]

The comics most readers encounter are dominated (though not exhausted) by sequences of panels in which events or scenes immediately follow their predecessors temporally. In the second panel of Figure 4.7, we see that the characters have sledded down the hill and flown into the air. Very basic abilities of closure are presumed here, but closure operates nonetheless. Closure tells us that the characters in both panels are the same, that it's the same sled they're riding, and that this is the end of the hill they started on. We make these inferences because of the conventions that operate in coordination with narratives to which we've become accustomed. Experience tells the reader that it would be odd indeed to encounter a story in comics in which three characters get on a sled to start down a hill, then get off it, find a very similar sled, and then ride down a very similar hill. It's equally unlikely that the characters portrayed at the beginning (particularly of a very short comic like this one) are immediately replaced by completely different characters that look just like them. No: closure tells us that these are depictions of the same characters, just a few moments later in time. This particular comic makes all of these inferences even more obvious, since the sled ride's trajectory goes directly between the panels.

McCloud has spent considerable effort categorizing the panel transitions of comics into various types (1993, 75–76). In Western comics, he claims, the reader's abilities of closure are for the most part employed to make sense of panel transitions that don't take up a lot of diegetic time. Estimating based on McCloud's rough diagrams, such transitions seem to compose roughly 90 percent of cases. If I were going to follow McCloud down the road of speculative psychology, I'd guess that this is the basic strategy of many comics because of our largely linear and minimally gappy perception of time in the real world.

When a comics author wants to tell a story that spans a significant chunk of diegetic time, there are several options, each of which is at least partially determined by the format in which the comic is published. One option is to produce a vast number of panels that are closely related. This is the strategy we see in continuity comics in newspapers, such as *Mark Trail* and *Mary Worth*. Though parceled out in three- or four-panel increments, these stories stretch on indefinitely, and there is no limit to the number of panels they can consume. Comic books are different from newspapers in this regard, since there's a limit to the space available in each issue. If the authors of these comics want to tell substantial stories that are at least minimally self-contained, they need to allow more than an instant of diegetic time to elapse between panels. Of course, if authors of comic books just want to tell a very short story (or just show a fight), short transitions are just fine. An author might also choose momentary panel transitions to slow down the pace of storytelling in one issue or part thereof, and choose panel transitions with greater gaps in time (and hence, more closure involved) to speed the story up in another issue or part thereof.

One mechanism for coherently cuing readers into significant time elapsing between panels is primarily verbal: narrative text can indicate that a panel happens "later," or "the following day." My favorite example of text indicating large temporal gaps in the diegesis comes from Ruben Bolling's *Tom the Dancing Bug*. The title of one of his "Super-Fun-Pak Comix," which says it all, is "40,000 Years between Panels" (2001). Panels 1 and 3 are depictions of desolate landscapes, while in panel 2, one cartoonish character asks the other, "But why did you bring an extra pair of pants?"

Pictures can also convey significant time between panels without diminishing reader uptake. Look at the final panel of Figure 4.7. Even without the dialogue, the change of scenery indicates clearly that the fate befalling the characters in the second panel comes after the setup from the first, and, similarly, panel 4 comes after panel 2. The narrative box between panels 2 and 4 that reads, "Little did our intrepid sledders know . . ." isn't actually necessary for conveying the temporal gap between their flight through the air and their landing. It's obvious from the pictures that some portion of time has elapsed between panels. Closure allows the reader to construct the time that must have happened in the gutter—enough time for the sled to fly through the air, momentarily stop, and then fall surprisingly into a large bowl of delicious cereal.

Contra Carrier's assertion that only a certain amount of time can elapse between panels (2000, 51–52), the limit here is only the artist's imagination and technique, together with reader's ability to follow temporal changes through the exercise of closure. In general, more diegetic time transpiring in the gutter implies more potential difficulty in following a comic's narrative.

Unless the artist intends the story to be difficult (or, as in the example from *Tom the Dancing Bug* I gave recently, humorous), they are going to have to leave an abundance of pictorial and verbal cues (e.g., establishing shots or narrative text) to make closure successful in such circumstances.

We've seen that the diegetic time that can elapse between panels varies a good deal, but I don't want to give the impression that time *must* elapse. In fact, one of the most intriguing temporal relations between panels is what McCloud calls an "aspect-to-aspect" transition, wherein consecutive panels show simultaneous aspects of the same scene from different perspectives (1993, 72). According to McCloud, aspect-to-aspect transitions are relatively uncommon in Western comics, but very common in manga (1993, 80–83). McCloud's explanation for this difference is that not only are works of manga much longer (thousands of pages) than comics in the Western tradition, but Japanese culture is also more connected to the present and less goal oriented.

McCloud's generalizations might be overblown. Students of mine (most notably, Marty Heck, in my Theorizing Comics and Graphic Novels class at Marist College in Fall 2014) have studied this and have found that when it comes to patterns of transition types, significant differences aren't so much present between Western comics and manga, but between alternative comics and superhero/adventure comics. More research on the topic is probably warranted. But regardless of the accuracy of McCloud's amateur (and potentially Orientalist) sociocultural speculations, the predominant effect of aspect-to-aspect transitions is to give the reader a better sense of the space in which the narrative takes place. Through the ability to perceive what closure tells us is the same scene from multiple viewpoints, we gain a richer understanding of setting, becoming more firmly and profoundly connected to the diegesis than is otherwise possible.

A number of additional techniques have been developed in comics across traditions to give the succession of panels another crucial narrative ability: to portray spatial as well as temporal relationships. A single panel can't easily represent space from more than one perspective. We need a sequence in order to have a narrative that spans different scenes in different spaces. Simply getting characters from one overall location to another must be done through multiple panels, which, again, are woven together by the reader through the process of closure. Readers intuitively understand that when characters are found in front of a different background in different panels, as in Figure 4.7, they have relocated to a different space. Readers mentally rearrange their conception of the narrative to accommodate this spatial transition.

Reader perception of diegetic motion occurs in a similar fashion. The presence of a moving object within a panel of comics is generally signaled by "motion lines" streaming from the object, or blurring of either the object itself or objects in the background.[10] But objects inside a panel can only move so far: after all, they are depicted *within* the panel, and so do not leave its finite boundaries (unless the objects are entering a metapanel or the comic is playing with other metafictional effects). And since the panels of comics are juxtaposed in space and not in time, comics can't literally simulate the illusion of motion provided by the rapid succession of images on a film screen. When you watch a film, your brain tells you that the images are moving, even though they aren't. When you read a comic, you have to imagine all the motion, whether it is within or between panels.

Consider again the first two panels of Figure 4.7. In panel 1, the characters get on a sled. In panel 2, they're partly off of it. By itself, neither panel can give us the information that the characters were *once* on a particular sled and *later* are not quite fully on that very same sled. It's the succession of panels that cues the reader to construct this small part of the narrative. This technique, when iterated throughout the process of reading a comic, contributes to an understanding of the narrative as an entirety.

There's another crucial way in which the pictorial dimension regulates spatial and temporal relations within a narrative. As quite a few theorists of comics have pointed out, comics are organized pictorially in more than one way.[11] One form of organization is sequential: in what order are panels going to follow one another? The other form of organization is *tabular*: how is each page in its entirety going to be arranged graphically?

Tabular organization is very important in comics. As Art Spiegelman puts it, "That architectural [i.e., tabular] notion of the page is, for me, what I'm scanning for. . . . It's the balancing act of trying to get the storytelling elements that have to be communicated balanced with the compositions of individual panels, and even more important the composition of all those panels together that make up the page" (2007, 277).[12] If you talk to people who work in comics that are published in a multipage format, they'll second this observation—tremendous (maybe even primary) attention must be paid to page layout.

The panels of a comic, we have already seen, are spatially juxtaposed, that is, simultaneously present in different spaces. This forces comics artists to make choices about *how* those panels are to be juxtaposed, given the formatting constraints with which they are working. The artist must determine the size, shapc, and position of the panels on the page. These options are severely limited in contemporary newspaper comics (less so in the past), where the standard is three or four panels that are almost always of equal size and in a horizontal arrangement. But artists working in the less restrictive and more sophisticated comic book format (not to mention those working in purely digital media) can use the tabular arrangement as one of their most important narrative tools—one that explains, in part, why comics can carry so much appeal.

Here are just some of the narrative effects that are produced through the construction of the comics page. A panel can be stretched horizontally or vertically to present an aesthetically dynamic image of running or falling. A panel may extend (or "bleed," in printing terminology) all the way through the edges of a page in order to give a sense of vast diegetic space, so big that it spills out of the confines of print. Panels may be nested within each other—a graphic device that allows for close-ups, asides, and focused attention on a particular aspect of a story without detracting from the larger whole represented in the background panel. Word balloons and sound effects may overlap and continue across a page through a number of panels, easing the process of closure by providing unity and a narrative continuity that bridges gutters. Figure 4.7 trades in a very cool effect afforded by the tabular format in which the panel borders divide up a single background image that characters traverse, appearing in the different panels (different locations in the overall background picture) at different times. And the layout of panels can either remain stable from page to page, providing a regular, clockwork rhythm (as in *Watchmen*), or change from page to page, adding variety to the narrative presentation and consequently engaging and maintaining the reader's interest.

Tabular organization factors as well into the overall way in which a comic's narrative is parceled out. While all the pages of a comic could theoretically all be laid out at once next to each other, in practice, the norms for reading comics have it that the reader is only going to have one page (or a two-page spread) visually available at a time. Hence, when comics are printed in multiple pages or screened on multiple web pages, readers have to turn (or click or swipe) from one page (or spread) to another. And that allows comics authors to manipulate the flow of narrative information. Each two-page spread (in conventionally printed comics) or page display (in digital comics) is itself a narrative unit. Which parts of a story are included in or excluded from that unit can make the story more interesting, suspenseful, or surprising, as happens when the payoff of a narrative strand is withheld until after a page turn (or the equivalent).

4.4. Seriality

The form narrative takes in comics is shaped not just by the verbal and pictorial dimensions, but by publication schedule. Some comics are *serialized*. To be serialized, in the sense I mean, involves three aspects. First, multiple issues or other publication units (e.g., daily newspaper strips) are set in the same story world. Second, narrative threads persist across publication units. Third, in the nondiegetic world, publication units are in some way discrete. In comics, discreteness usually amounts to being published or released at different times, with different bindings and covers.[13]

You don't see serialization a lot in newspaper comics any more. The most common newspaper comic genre, "gag strips," aren't serialized, as narratives don't carry over across each daily installment. If Garfield runs off a table and bonks his head in Monday's comic, his owner Jon doesn't rush him to the vet on Tuesday—he's just the same as he always was. Most of the newspaper comics that are serialized—such as *Mark Trail*, *Spiderman*, *Mary Worth*, and *Prince Valiant*—are legacies from a time when comics was the dominant narrative form in popular culture. When comics was supplanted by television and film, serialized comics gradually left the newspapers. However, serialization still rules comic books. As Cook points out (2013, 271), the narrative threads that persist through the DC and Marvel continuities are now so huge that no single person can keep track of or even experience them fully. They're what Cook calls MSCFs: massive serialized collaborative fictions. But even when we go outside the Big Two in American superhero comics, we find serialization all over the place. Again, any comic where a plot spans multiple issues is serialized, and if you read comic books, that's probably what you're used to.

The prevalence of serialization in comic books isn't hard to explain. Some of the explanations are primarily socioeconomic, but deserve brief mention. Serials tend to have lower production costs than stand-alone works. Also, each installment of a serial work serves as an advertisement for the next and, not incidentally, an advertisement for the venue in which it appears. But other explanations are more philosophical, and closely connected to how the serial format affects narrative features.

Reader reception of multiple issues, facilitated by the serial format, has the potential to provide richer and more engaging experiences, and is key to understanding the move away from stand-alone narratives. Multiple issues within the same story framework allow for reader feedback and active involvement. When readers are aware they can engage with comics narratives collaboratively, interest goes up. But that's not all. Membership in fan culture is galvanized by knowledge gained about a narrative's diegetic world, facilitated by specific features of comics that stem from their seriality. The delay in release between issues provides time for audiences to become experts and encourages obsession. Each issue can be discussed and dissected, contributing to a concomitant desire to predict the narrative's future events (and subsequent pleasure taken both in predicting correctly and in being incorrect but surprised).

Readers want to know the outcomes of narrative strands, and this is exploited deliberately through serialized comics by means of what Josh Lambert calls *cliffhanger continuity*: gaps between episodes that generate "a *suspenseful* pause, one [obliging] readers to return for the following episode in order to satisfy their curiosity about the narrative's resolution" (2009, 8). For serial works, the pause is natural. The desire to see narrative strands completed creates a loyal, repeating audience, simultaneously reinforcing and being reinforced by the expertise mentioned above.

Serialized comics also have an edge over stand-alone comics in their ability to sustain suspense. Felt suspense stops whenever a storyline ends: *Garfield* doesn't sustain suspense across daily installments because we know that no matter what happens, everything will be back to normal on the next day. When a comic is serialized and hasn't been completed (where additional issues are forthcoming), it will not be physically possible for readers to access the resolution of a current suspenseful storyline. Even if readers may reasonably infer that the next issue will provide resolution of narrative strands, the unavailability of that issue sustains suspense. Readers will have no way of knowing whether or how their beloved characters will escape harm, and their desires to help those characters will continue to be frustrated because of the time gap.[14] Moreover, the gap between issues allows readers more time to discuss and nurture expectations about the narrative outcome, confirming and reinforcing their feelings of suspense.

The ability of a comic to sustain suspense is blunted when it has been completed and is available to readers in its entirety (say, when it's bound as a trade paperback). At that stage, a comic no longer fully exploits the potentialities of the serial format that stem from the delay between issues. If one of these potentialities has to do with sustaining suspense, then to the extent that this potentiality is lacking, suspense will be as well.

There are pitfalls of serialization as well. Serials carry an added risk of continuity errors—unintended inconsistencies within the diegesis. The more a narrative is drawn out over multiple issues, the more likely it is that continuity problems will arise. Long-running comics serials are particularly prone to this difficulty. Authors may be unable to track or even just forget trivial and even nontrivial aspects of distant prior issues. New authors might take over a comics title and commit continuity errors either in ignorance of the work of previous authors or because they can't be bothered with previous artistic choices. And the diegetic worlds established by the likes of Marvel and DC are now so complex and byzantine that continuity errors become the rule rather than the exception. Such worries can lead to reader frustration as well as periodic efforts to completely reboot narrative continuity (a famous pioneering example being DC's attempt to collapse all divergent storylines into one universe in the 1985 series *Crisis on Infinite Earths*). Even so, relaunches of comics lines never seem to fully take effect, confusingly retaining some elements of the continuity while rejecting others, and soon contain continuity errors of their own.

Now, continuity errors might not always be bad-making features of serialized comics. On one hand, for some or perhaps even most comics readers, the discovery and discussion of continuity errors seems to be a source of great pleasure, "complaints" notwithstanding. On the other hand, creators of narratives generally seem to want to avoid continuity errors, and correct them through ret-conning and altering the canonicity of various fictional parts. It's hard to see why creators would engage in these practices unless they either perceive such errors as flaws or believe that audiences will take them to be flaws. It seems reasonable, then, to conclude that although maximal consistency is neither necessary nor sufficient for being a good narrative, a narrative without continuity errors is going to be better than an inconsistent narrative.

One more hazard of serialization is that long-running comics (including the MSCFs that Cook discusses) can be exceedingly difficult for new audiences to access. The complexity of highly evolved storylines is extremely daunting for those who have not followed a title from its inception. It's so hard to know where to begin reading a comic title without being completely lost that a natural conclusion is that it's not worth the effort. Readers may choose instead to opt for a self-contained title like Simon Spurrier and Jeff Stokely's *The Spire* (2016), which has substantially less serial baggage than, e.g., most superhero comics.

4.5. Conclusions

We've now explored how we use closure for processing the words and pictures out of which comics are made. Readers' understanding of how comics function yields the ability to comprehend the operations of space and time within them, and hence to see how events and actions fit together in order to form narratives. It's likely that you find some of the foregoing discussion to cover points that seem to you to be obvious once you thought about it—but the trick is thinking about it in the first place. It turns out that the mechanisms employed in comics for storytelling are really quite complex, and that's due to the particular mix of media that comics employ.

Not all comics are going to tell stories in exactly all of the ways discussed above. Some comics don't even have a verbal dimension; others aren't serialized. The mechanics of pictorial sequencing are a little different in webcomics—sometimes so different that I'm not even sure they merit classification as comics. And there are plenty of creative people working in comics who keep finding new and interesting ways to tell stories.[15]

There's one more vital set of choices that comics force on their authors, and they're choices that motivate our next topic. A comics panel can only capture a small piece of diegetic time and space: the time that occurs between panels is usually much greater than the time that occurs within them, and the total space available in the world of the story is likely to be much larger than the reader can see in an individual panel. Accordingly, as McCloud advises us, a comics artist must shape the story by "deciding which moments to include in [each panel] and which to leave out," as well as by "choosing the right distance and angle [from which] to view those moments—and where to trim them" (2006, 10).

By selecting one image rather than another, an artist can draw the reader's attention to the particularly salient aspects of the story. An establishing picture, from a distant perspective, provides the reader with a sense of the place in which the scene will occur. But pictures from medium and close perspectives concentrate the reader's attention—on Batman's logo projected into the sky, on Hellboy's stoic facial expression, on Dick Tracy's two-way wrist radio, and so on. An artist can leave irrelevant objects out of the picture, and make the relevant ones stand out to varying degrees by emphasizing their size and placement within the panel.

As we'll see in the following chapter, these aspects of the construction of narrative in comics are virtually identical—unsurprisingly—to some much-discussed techniques in film. The art forms arose at about the same time, both are products of a mass culture and its associated means of reproduction and dissemination, and, most importantly, comics and film alike typically employ a combination of verbal and pictorial media. The techniques of pictorial storytelling used in comics and film are so similar, in fact, that one might well wonder whether comics have anything distinctive to offer as a narrative art form. It might even be noted that many basic and important film techniques like panning, tracking, and zooming are largely unavailable in comics, which are unable to produce the illusion of movement. Are comics basically just cheap, static, deficient films? Is there anything that the media of comics allows it to do that film can't? We'll tackle these issues by considering one of the major things that's been done with comics lately, one that's had a profound effect on popular culture: adapting them for film.

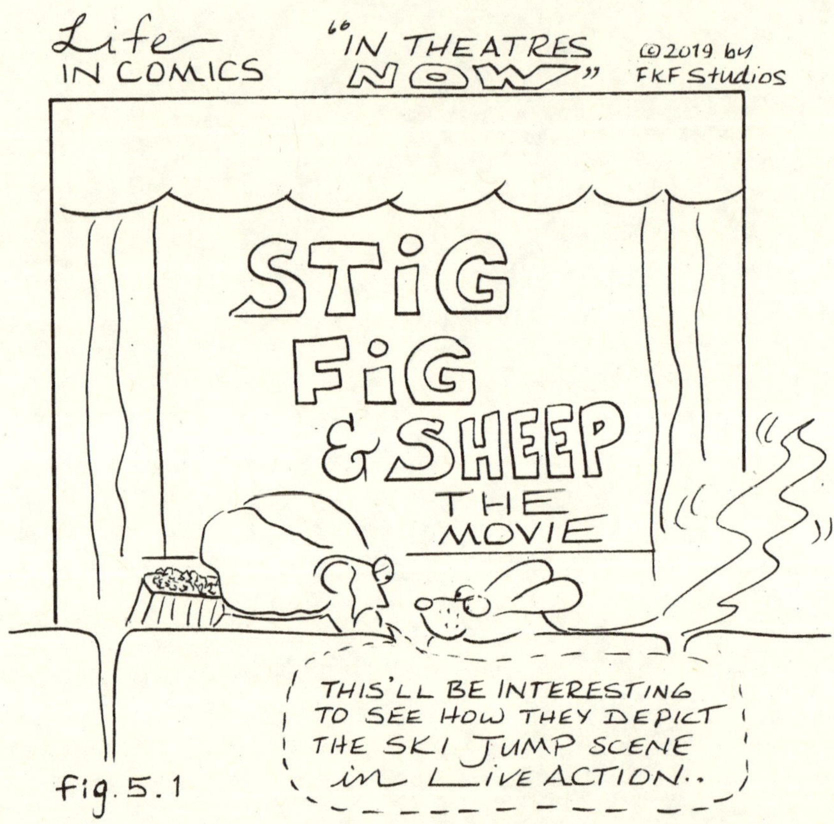
Life IN COMICS
"IN THEATRES NOW"
©2019 by FKF Studios
STIG FIG & SHEEP THE MOVIE
THIS'LL BE INTERESTING TO SEE HOW THEY DEPICT THE SKI JUMP SCENE in LIVE ACTION..
fig. 5.1

5
Adaptation

5.1. Adaptation and Viability

Films adapted from or based on comics have become commonplace. Not long ago, my friends and I were able to sit down and count, with a solid amount of accuracy, films adapted from comics. Now that's too hard—it's way, way over one hundred, and that's just in English.[1] Films based on comics are still coming out at a dizzying pace. While some audience fatigue might be setting in, these films are continuing to be overwhelmingly popular and profitable, and (at the risk of making a claim about the future that in retrospect could be embarrassing to me some day) the trend doesn't appear to be dying down any time soon.

At one level, explaining these facts isn't difficult, and perhaps isn't even philosophically interesting:

- Comics is a mature art form that presents a rich trove of resources for an industry—film—that is starved for original ideas. Plots, characters, and the fictional worlds in which they are embedded are highly developed in comics and present boundless opportunities for adaptation.
- Certain comics, particularly those of the superhero ilk, feature well-known characters such as Batman, Superman, and Spiderman. These characters are highly iconic and highly marketable in films and related licensing opportunities including action figures and video games—as the current business models of large corporate entities like Marvel (owned by Disney) and DC (owned by Time Warner) attest.
- Even films featuring formerly culturally obscure comics characters such as the Guardians of the Galaxy or Morbius retain their marketability, simply because audiences like to see superheroes in epic battles between the forces of good and evil.
- The advent of more sophisticated computer-generated imagery (CGI) has made plausible-looking exercise of superpowers increasingly possible. CGI is allowing films to show viewers practically anything that can

The Philosophy of Comics. Henry John Pratt, Oxford University Press. © Oxford University Press 2023.
DOI: 10.1093/oso/9780190845445.003.0005

be imagined on the comics page, at a relatively low cost, and this couldn't be done convincingly before the digital revolution.

- As an art form, comics is increasingly esteemed, and is beginning to be considered on a par with forms of literature such as the novel. College courses are taught on comics; you're reading an academic text about comics right now. Accordingly, basing a film on a comic doesn't quite carry the social stigma that it once did. Adapting a renowned alternative comic such as *Ghost World* or *Persepolis* is an act that brings critical praise rather than mockery.

In this chapter, we're going to consider some other, more philosophical explanations for why comics are common sources for film adaptations. I'll also argue that comics are the *best* sources for film adaptations (except for film-to-film adaptations, of course). Despite that, however, there are some good reasons to think that comics can't be adapted into film perfectly.

Before getting into these topics more fully, it'll be useful to get a clearer understanding of adaptations and what the relevant issues surrounding them are. For our purposes, let's think of adaptation as a story being made to travel from one place (the *source*) to another place (the *adaptation*). Following narratological precedent, then, "adaptation" will be used to refer both to a process and to the result of that process. The most widely discussed adaptations go across art forms. That is, the source is a work in one category (e.g., comics), and the adaptation is in another (e.g., film). Moreover, the source and adaptation vary in terms of the media out of which they are constructed and the normative constraints that are placed on the use of those media. To take a few quick examples, comics and film both use pictures as media, but only in the latter do those pictures give the appearance of movement; comics and literature both use type, but only in the latter can the choice of typeface be irrelevant to the meaning of the work.

Much of the interest in comics and adaptation so far has rightly focused on comic-to-film adaptations, where comics are the sources and films are the adaptations. While these are currently popular, it might surprise you to learn that they've been made about as long as the two have coexisted, beginning in 1903 with *Happy Hooligan Interferes*. Comics and film have parallel histories. They arose as mass art forms at about the same time. Both are technologically reproducible at a great scale and tend to be designed for popular audiences. At times, each has enjoyed a lowbrow reputation and a prevailing sentiment that it is not art. Both have faced censorship pressures (leading, respectively, to the Comics Code Authority and the Hays Code).

While these similarities between comics and film are intriguing, they pale in significance to their kindred narrativity. There are nonnarrative films, like Peter Kubelka's *Arnuf Rainer* (1960) and Godfrey Reggio's *Koyaanisqatsi* (1983). The existence of nonnarrative comics is more controversial. As we saw in Chapter 2, Meskin holds (perhaps correctly) that comics admit of a nonnarrative avant-garde. At the least, though, comics is *predominantly* narrative. So is film. That is, the vast majority of comics and films that are produced tell stories. Nonnarrative works are unusual exceptions.

The reasons why comics and film alike tend strongly to be narrative are medium-specific. Films are (partially) constituted by images that succeed each other in actual time but appear to the viewer in the same actual space. Comics are (partially) constituted by images that succeed each other in actual space but appear to the reader at the same actual time. While this means that the processes of reading comics and viewing films involve different skills, it's also notable that each art form requires us to make sense of a sequence of images. And the simplest way to do this—to come to terms with a sequence as a unified whole—is through narrative, which I've previously described as the representation of two or more events in a causal relation.

Because comics and film are largely narrative, I'm going to concentrate on cases where both the source and adaptation are narratives. If there are cases of adaptations of nonnarrative works into comics, or nonnarrative comics into other art forms, these are relatively obscure in comparison to adaptations of narratives. Within this framework, I'm going to focus largely on considerations about *viability*: is it possible to adapt into or out of comics while preserving the sources' essential characteristics and particular value?

Viability of adaptations across art forms depends on the degree to which the media used in those art forms place constraints on the stories that can be told using them. Medium specificity looms large here. If strong medium specificity is true, then it's automatically true that no adaptation is viable, since it's impossible to achieve the same effects with different media (even if the media are used to tell narratives). If the media of comics enable authors to present stories in ways that other media are incapable of (and vice versa), then adaptation from other art forms into comics and from comics into other art forms will be problematic. In Chapter 3, I rejected strong medium specificity in favor of moderate medium specificity. If that's the right move, then while media do make certain narrative and expressive effects more or less difficult to achieve, they don't make any effect strictly impossible. Viability of cross-media adaptation then, could perhaps be achieved to some degree, even if not fully. And that's what we're going to explore in this chapter.

While much of the discussion will concern adaptations from comics to film, we shouldn't forget about adaptations where comics are the adaptation rather than the source. Examples include comics of the following kinds:

- Literature-to-comics adaptations, including the *Classics Illustrated* series, EC's *Picture Stories from the Bible*, and the *Marvel Illustrated* series.
- Theater-to-comics adaptations, including Von's *The Illustrated Macbeth* and Alan Moore and Eddie Campbell's *Snakes and Ladders*.
- Film-to-comics adaptations, including DC's *Movie Comics* series and Marvel's adaptation of the *Star Wars* movies.

While not adaptations per se, fictional worlds established in comics have traveled into other art forms (as in the musical *Spiderman: Turn off the Dark* and the television show *Arrow*), and fictional worlds originating in other art forms have traveled into comics (as in comics of *The Simpsons* and *Buffy the Vampire Slayer*). I'll touch on theater and literature occasionally as we go forward.

Despite the historical and narratological similarities between comics and film, there's a certain risk associated with thinking about them in the same terms. Comics theorists like Douglas Wolk have noted this:

> The most thoroughly ingrained error in the language used to discuss comics is treating them as if they were particularly weird, or failed examples of an entirely different medium altogether. Good comics are sometimes described as being "cinematic." . . . It's almost an insult, though, to treat [such claims] as compliments. Using them as praise implies that comics *as a form* aspire (more or less unsuccessfully) to being movies. (2007, 13)

This stance is seconded by some comics authors, like Frank Miller: "The whole reference to comics being movies on paper is a corrupt one, because it makes us sound so inferior" (Eisner and Miller 2005, 87).

The point is well taken. It's troublesome to think of comics as merely inert, static, technologically unsophisticated precursors of films that can be made from them. This is bad for the status of comics as an art form—demoting them to very low level on the totem pole of artistic potential—and can also have negative effects on the creativity of comics creators. For if *they* begin to share the worry that comics are poor imitations of other media, they've got two alternatives. First, they might just give up making comics in favor of a different art form. Or second, they might do whatever they can to make comics most like the art form they're trying to emulate.[2] It might well be detrimental to comics as a whole if creators and readers alike equate success with the cinematic, since, in virtue of the media used, a comic can never fully achieve that which a film can achieve quite easily (such as literal movement and sound).

Does this suggest that nobody should try to adapt comics into other art forms (or vice versa, for that matter)? Perhaps. But we'll need some more thorough argumentation to show that. A good place to begin is with various assertions that certain adaptations are "impossible." Whatever sense of possibility is deployed here must be very weak. Even proponents of strong medium specificity must hold that anything can be adapted into anything else—just not very well. Those who claim that an adaptation is impossible are most plausibly understood to mean that there's something about the original that cannot be *fully* captured in any adaptation of it: perfect viability can't be achieved.

What would perfect viability involve? Minimally, transposition of the story across art forms, causally prompted by the source. Strict story identity seems to be required as well: a perfect adaptation would maintain, in Seymour Chatman's words, "the continuum of events [of the original], presupposing the total set of all conceivable details, that is, those that can be projected by the normal laws of the physical universe" (1978, 28). These points are relatively commonplace in the literature on adaptation, but I want to add something else to them. A perfectly viable adaptation would preserve the style of the original. As Ernst Gombrich argues forcefully in *Art and Illusion* (2000), each artist (or, we might add, collective of artists) has a distinctive temperament or mental set that explains why their works turn out differently than the works made by others (even when all the artists are using the same technology and attempting to represent the same things). If all of the characters and events of a story are captured perfectly by an adaptation, but the style is different, the adaptation has less than perfect viability.

Perfect viability in this sense is too strong a requirement when we are trying merely to determine what counts as an adaptation in the first place. The claim that an adaptation is possible isn't equivalent to the claim that perfect viability can be achieved. Correspondingly, the claim that an adaptation is impossible is not the claim that perfect viability in a particular case can't be achieved. Perfect viability, in short, comes apart from typical claims about the impossibility of adaptation, since it seems pretty well apparent that at least some adaptations are possible even if perfect viability can't be achieved under any circumstances. Better, then, to retreat to a weaker position: when we encounter assertions in what follows that a certain work is impossible to adapt, we'll understand them as the claim that no reasonable degree of viability can be achieved. Generally, as we'll see, such claims have evaluative content: when adaptations are said to be impossible, there's something about the value of the original that is thought to be lost, necessarily, in the adaptation.

So who thinks that comics can't be adapted? It turns out that lots of those who create or theorize about comics have a strong inclination toward this position. Psychologically, perhaps it's because artists and theorists (unsurprisingly) have marked tendencies to believe that the art forms in which they work are notable and distinctive, and that their work invariably loses value when adapted. But there are reasons in play other than the need to feel like one is doing something worthwhile. Here's how Bill Waterson, creator of *Calvin and Hobbes*, puts it: "Different media have different strengths and needs, and when you make a movie, the movie's needs get served. As a comic strip, Calvin and Hobbes works exactly the way I intended it to. There's no upside for me in adapting it" (2013, n.p.). The indication here is that comics just work differently from films. Let's see what could lie behind this claim.

5.2. The "Impossibility" of Adaptation

Some of the reasons given for the impossibility of adapting into and out of comics are better than others. We're going to start with some that aren't terribly strong, then move to others that are more decisive. Let's begin with McCloud. On his view, comics are special because of how the reader uses closure to understand them. (For a fuller discussion of closure, refer back to Chapter 4, Section 4.3.) Though we do need closure to understand film as well as comics, McCloud writes that "the closure of electronic media is continuous, largely involuntary, and virtually imperceptible" (1993, 68). In comics, the exercise of closure is required systematically and necessarily if there are to be time, motion, or any other narrative devices, because there's always a literally perceptible gutter between panels. Because of the intimacy with the narrative produced by the reader's constant exercise of closure, McCloud claims that comics is distinct, not just from film, but from other arts as well: "it's a mistake to see comics as a mere hybrid of the graphic arts and prose fiction. What happens between these panels is a kind of magic only comics can create" (1993, 92).

Like most of his ideas, McCloud's argument has attracted a good deal of controversy. Greg Cwiklik contends that all of McCloud's illustrations of the operation of closure in comics could just as easily be done with film: "Closure is essentially what is referred to in film as montage. . . . the use of these dramatic transitions originated in film and migrated to comics" (1999, 62). Beaty has noticed that McCloud tends to think of closure operating in film only between the individual frames. However, the more salient equivalent to closure in film is between *shots*, "and shots—like panels—are linked by transitions which are 'far from continuous and anything but involuntary.' Indeed, the intimacy which McCloud ascribes to comics as a result of viewer involvement has long been held to be a hallmark of film and television" (1999, 69). And Ng Suat Tong points out that the types of narrative transitions that McCloud finds to occur between panels, which we discussed in the previous chapter, are not unique to comics at all (1999, 77–79). Film excels at portraying the next moment in time in a narrative sequence, but a film can also easily shift between multiple temporal and spatial locations. There are even cases of aspect-to-aspect transitions in film: Tong cites Andrei Tarkovsky's *Zerkalo* (1975) as a prime source of examples.

To galvanize these objections to McCloud's view, we might note that with respect to closure, comics are aptly described by David Bordwell's constructivist theory of narrative in film, wherein "the artwork is necessarily incomplete, needing to be unified and fleshed out by the active participation of the perceiver" (1985, 32). Lots of narratives across art forms are *enthymematic*—that is, they share the feature that the reader (or audience, or viewer) must understand them by supplying missing premises or information.[3] Comics just aren't special in this way, and so closure in comics doesn't provide a reasonable barrier to viable adaptation.

Maybe the use of words in (most, if not all) comics preclude them from viable adaptation into film. Consider Jorge Gracia's statements about film and literature:

> A film cannot do the same things that a written work can do. For example, films need to be relatively short, whereas a written work can have thousands of pages.... Moreover, in films, visual images are directly presented to the audience and take precedence over words, whereas in a written work, images are always mediated through words, the primary medium of meaning. (2007, 200–201)

Gracia isn't writing directly about adaptations of comics, but his ideas are relevant in considering comic-to-film adaptations because comics generally feature printed words (in word balloons, narrative boxes, and so on) and films don't. Incidentally, his point would seem to apply to literature-to-comic adaptations as well. Written works without images (such as most novels) can be hundreds or even thousands of pages long, and one might argue that this format allows for the presentation of a massively complicated and deep story in ways that cannot be achieved adequately using the more limited textual and visual space available in comics. It's almost laughable to consider the *Classics Illustrated* adaptation of *Crime and Punishment*: inevitably, as Delmore Schwartz points out, it will suffer from "serious cuts and omissions" (2004, 54).

Are comics impossible to adapt into film when, like literature, they use the written word as a medium? Is it impossible to adapt nongraphic literature into comics? No—at least, not on Gracia's grounds. While it's true that films usually have a relatively short viewing time, there's no difficulty if the comic to be adapted is also short (as is the case with *Ghost World* and *Sin City*). Longer comics can, in theory, be adapted into longer films (or television shows) that would preserve all of the comics' dialogue and narration. Sheer amount of text is not a problem for adaptation per se. Similarly, there's no reason why a nongraphic work of literature couldn't be adapted into a very long comic. Taken together, serialized comics are among the longest stories available.[4] The problem with the *Classics Illustrated* comics isn't that they can't adapt long, complex works of literature, but that they try to do so within arbitrary length constraints. Perhaps a comic adapting *Crime and Punishment* that ran for several thousand pages (instead of the original forty-eight) would be more to Schwartz's satisfaction.

Another objection to adaptation comes from Wolk, discussing David B's *Epileptic*:

> The book is also a very clear demonstration of what comics can do, as drawn narratives that require the reader's imagination to play along, that nothing else can. And it's impossible to imagine it being adapted into any other medium: to lose the specific work of B.'s drawing hand would be to lose *Epileptic* itself. (2007, 141)

Wolk is making two assertions. First, no other art form can deploy the reader's imagination in the same way as the drawn narrative that constitutes a comic. Presumably, Wolk is referring to the exercise of closure—an echo of McCloud. If so, it's at least unclear that his assertion is correct. Film, we've seen, uses closure in much the same way comics do, and it's entirely possible that the imaginative faculties could well be engaged in the same way by each art form.

Second, Wolk focuses on style. Adaptation of *Epileptic* is impossible, he holds, because B.'s drawings are so distinctive and personal. Any attempted adaptation of *Epileptic* would result in the *loss* of the work, which, since it is a good work, would not maintain value.

Epileptic might be impossible to adapt to film, but it's not evident that this is due to the comic's visual style. The look of B.'s drawings could at least be captured with an *animated* film. Marjane Satrapi's *Persepolis*, heavily influenced by *Epileptic*, was animated in a way that preserved its style. Wolk even compares the style of *Persepolis* directly to that of *Epileptic*: if the style of the former was successfully preserved in adaptation, then it ought to be possible to do so for the latter as well (regardless of whether all the *content* of *Epileptic* can be preserved).

Perhaps it will be responded that we've been thinking about photographically based film adaptations all along, and that bringing animation in at this stage is changing the subject. Very well. Photographs can be made that correspond identifiably with an artist's drawing style. As Guillermo del Toro acknowledges in his director's commentary on the DVD release, his film *Hellboy* (2004) was designed to preserve closely the visual sensibility of the comic's artist, Mike Mignola. (I'd argue that del Toro was relatively successful in this aim, but less successful in preserving the overall atmosphere of Mignola's comics.) So too for *Ghost World*: the events constitutive of the narrative of Dan Clowes's comic are largely vestigial in the film, but Clowes's artistic sensibility is evident throughout. The fact that a comic is drawn just doesn't provide an insurmountable barrier to adaptation into film, even film that's based in photographic media.

Now we're moving on to stronger arguments against viable adaptation. Understandably, a significant test case for a lot of commentators is Alan Moore and Dave Gibbons's *Watchmen* (1987). Wolk writes, "*Watchmen* [the comic], bless its twisted heart, is totally unfilmable—not that people haven't been trying to figure out how to turn it into a movie for twenty years, but it's so heavily invested in *being a comic book* that to take it away from its native medium would be to rip all its bones out" (2007, 241). Moore himself claims:

> There are things that we did with *Watchmen* that could only work in a comic, and were indeed designed to show off things that other media can't. . . . I increasingly fear that nothing good can come of almost any adaptation, and obviously that's sweeping. There are a couple of adaptations that are perhaps as good or better than the original work. But the vast majority of them are pointless. (2008a, 1)

The views of Wolk and Moore, formulated separately, share several salient features. For one, each is ultimately reaching a conclusion about value: an adaptation of *Watchmen* would "rip all its bones out" or be "pointless." Wolk and Moore seem to be grounding their evaluative stances in a basis of medium specificity: there's something about being a comic that *Watchmen* (the comic) exploited to the fullest but which, when adapted for film, would be lost. And *that*, whatever it is, is why adapting *Watchmen* while preserving its value is impossible.

After these comments were published, *Watchmen* was, of course, adapted for film (in 2009, directed by Zach Snyder. The later HBO television series based in the same story world is less of an adaptation than an expansion). Was something lost, and if so, what? One candidate has to do with the sophistication of the content of the *Watchmen* comic, combined with the provocative worldview that it expresses. The comic has a formally complex narrative structure rife with allusion, and presents a great deal of intellectual challenge. In addition, it calls into question the nature of right and wrong and the ultimate significance of humanity in the universe. Heady stuff.

Much of this content is, in fact, lost in the film. In mainstream Hollywood-style cinema, superhero movies like *Watchmen* typically involve beautiful men and women with extravagant superpowers who are engaged in energetic battles with supervillains or other forces of evil, ultimately culminating in a CGI-heavy showdown of property destruction. Plenty of action and excitement is required, but not a lot of thought. The overriding mentality, arguably, is one that prioritizes spectacle and profits. The narrative of the *Watchmen* comic doesn't fit comfortably into this framework. In many ways, its theme is the antithesis of traditional superhero comics. The "costumed heroes" depicted in the comic, save Dr. Manhattan, have no actual superpowers. But the film succumbs to the temptation to show otherwise, as we see right from the initial fight sequence, in which an ostensibly normal human being punches through a cement wall. (This is why seeing Ozymandias catch a bullet with his hand is remarkable in the comic but not in the movie: in the latter but not the former, the audience expects it.)

One "impossibility" in adapting *Watchmen*, then, is that it's extremely unlikely that a mainstream anti-superhero superhero movie can be made. The problem is reminiscent of François Truffaut's famous (apocryphal?) statement that no war movie can be made without portraying war as fun. No mainstream superhero movie can be made without portraying superheroes in action as *awesome*, but that's exactly what an adaptation of *Watchmen* requires. Even Christopher Nolan's much-lauded Batman films succumbed to this temptation. As my friend Ian Hummel once put it, "Batman is the world's greatest detective, not the world's greatest head-puncher." (I hear your protests that Matt Reeves's *The Batman*—loosely an adaptation of *The Long Halloween*—is a detective story. But still . . .) Of course, what this really means is that given the realities of the movie business, a significantly viable adaptation of *Watchmen* is highly unlikely to be made. It doesn't mean that because of *medium-specific* features, a significantly viable adaptation of *Watchmen* is impossible, and that, in part, seems to be what Wolk and Moore are asserting.

One glaring dissimilarity that holds between comics and film, which we've already noted, could interfere with adaptation insurmountably. The images that comprise a comic are juxtaposed in space but are simultaneously present in time. The images that comprise a film are juxtaposed in time but are perceived in a single space. To reiterate a few points from Chapter 4, because of these medium-specific features, comics allows for control that can't be achieved in film, in the processes of both reading and creation. First, reading: film manages "watching time" *for* the viewer. One has no choice but to experience the narrative at the rate of the mechanical succession of the frames. The pace of reading comics, in contrast, is like that of reading literature. Readers of comics are largely responsible for their own rate of processing the narrative, and can freely direct attention back and forth among a comic's images and events.

A comic like *Watchmen* exploits this to the fullest. Consider the sequences it contains of a comic (*The Black Freighter*) within a comic. Here we have two simultaneous narratives running in parallel, each of which continually comments on and enriches the other. It's possible and relatively easy for readers to process this kind of embedding. It's *not* easy to do so in film, and maybe not even possible. While a film can toggle back and forth between different narratives, it can't present them simultaneously (as in a split screen) with any expectation of a reasonable degree of comprehension.

Inclusion of the *Black Freighter* parts in the *Watchmen* film, shown on the screen concurrently with the main narrative, would have made both narratives largely incomprehensible (in notable contrast to the comic). That's presumably why the theatrical release of the film adaptation omitted *The Black Freighter* aspect entirely. If the *Black Freighter* portions were interposed consecutively with the main narrative (as happens in the "ultimate cut" of the DVD release), that disjoints the film and eliminates the subtlety with which the narratives in the comic are intertwined and mutually reinforcing. The only other alternative is to separate the two narratives entirely—*Tales of the Black Freighter* (2009) was originally released as a self-contained, animated feature—but, of course, this brings the adaptation of *Watchmen* farther and farther away from the comic itself.

Moore bears out and expands on this point while being interviewed alongside Dave Gibbons:

> With *Watchmen*, what we tried to do was give it a truly kind of crystalline structure, where it's like this kind of jewel with hundreds and hundreds of facets and almost each of the facets is commenting on all of the other facets and you can kind of look

> at the jewel through any of the facets and still get a coherent reading. Yeah, basically, there are single panels there, single images, that somehow kind of tie up the whole book. (2000, n.p.)

Because comics juxtaposes panels in space, readers have the luxury of being able to process and understand such complex narrative structures. Because film juxtaposes frames in time, viewers don't have that luxury.

Not only can comics display simultaneous and reinforcing narratives, but they can also display simultaneous actions coherently within a scene. Via the word balloon, a number of conversations, speech acts, and/or separate thoughts can occur during the same diegetic time frame (as you can see referring back to Figure 4.7).

A comic that does these things particularly well is Scioli and Barber's *Transformers vs. G.I. Joe* (2017). For example, the two-page splash at the beginning of Chapter 5, overall, depicts the Autobot Metroplex on the surface of the planet Cybertron (now perilously close to the moon), being attacked by a number of Decepticons. However, by means of fourteen (!) inset panels, Scioli and Barber show the readers tiny subnarratives focusing on various members of the comic's huge cast. There's small likelihood (if any) that a film could do that all simultaneously and maintain legibility, coherence, and comprehensibility. Oliver Sava claims that "*Transformers vs. G.I. Joe* is a comic book that takes full advantage of storytelling tricks that are only possible in comics, which makes it impossible to create a faithful movie adaptation" (2017, n.p.). According to moderate medium specificity, that's not quite right, but it's close.

Complex depictions of simultaneous events and the like are relatively normal in comics, and produce comparatively little difficulty for the reader in the process of understanding the narrative structure. By way of contrast, simultaneous events of this sort are almost impossible to capture in film. Words are heard rather than read, and audio media have limitations: viewers will only be able to process overlapping speech and/or voice-over narration as an unintelligible muddle or by focusing attention on one particular aspect of the scene at the expense of others.[5]

Scioli and Barber have some fun with the medium-specific tendencies of comics and film in their *Transformers vs. G.I. Joe: The Movie Adaptation* one-shot (collected in Scioli and Barber 2017). The schtick is that it's a comic book adaptation of a movie (one that doesn't exist, and probably never will). In contrast to the other issues in the series, *Transformers vs. G.I. Joe: The Movie Adaptation* is radically simplified. Each page contains at most four panels (often in an aspect-ratio comparable to film), and almost all panels contain only one or two balloons of dialogue. Part of what they've done is to comment on the Hollywood tendency to produce simple, clichéd, and action-packed narratives and images (a tendency noted earlier in our discussion of the *Watchmen* adaptation). But they're also commenting on the different visual language that comics can employ in comparison to film, and how that affects the particular way in which stories can be delivered.

Of course, these points cut both ways. Film can do easily things comics can't do very well. For instance, since words in comics are read and not heard, we can't ever know exactly what characters sound like, and film-to-comic adaptations necessarily neglect that aspect. Case in point: Kieron Gillen and Salvador Larroca's run on Marvel's *Darth Vader* (starting in 2015) is about as good as comics get in any genre. Nevertheless, it's missing something vital. Given the limitations imposed by comics media, it's extremely difficult to convey the sound of Darth Vader's voice and breathing apparatus. Gillen and Larroca's solution is not even to try.

Not only are comics panels spatially juxtaposed, but they're also organized in tabular fashion, as we discussed in Chapter 4. This is another aspect that can interfere with viable adaptations from one to the other. Tabular organization isn't really a predominant concern in film, again because of the pace at which we process it. You can't put too many moving images on a screen or the audience won't be able to understand what's going on. That's why split-screen effects only awkwardly simulate the experience of comics. Ang Lee tried that in *Hulk* (2003), to my mind unsuccessfully.

The tabular arrangement of *Watchmen* largely takes the form of pages made up of a three-panel by three-panel grid. Even within this rigid framework, graphic choices are made that have vital effects on the reader's experience. We notice how colors, symbols, characters, and motifs recur across the page. Moreover, the grid is occasionally broken up by larger panels. There are many points at which tabular organization is used to maximum effect in *Watchmen*, but perhaps two examples will suffice. First, the entirety of Chapter 5, "Fearful Symmetry," consists of pages that are mirror images of each other in layout, color, overall design, and even narrative event: the last page mirrors the first, the second-to-last mirrors the second, and so on, until they meet in the middle. Without the possibilities afforded by tabular construction, this effect can't be achieved. Second, *Watchmen* contains no splash pages whatsoever until Chapter 12, "A Stronger Loving World," which begins with six of them consecutively. The scenes depicted, not accidentally, are the horrifying climax of a plot that the reader has been gradually becoming aware of throughout the comic. By choosing to withhold the tabular arrangement of the splash page until this part of the story, Moore and Gibbons greatly enhance its impact.

Through such techniques, Moore and Gibbons (not to mention their colorist, John Higgins) not only add depth and variety to the comic, but also draw attention to salient aspects of the narrative in ways not readily available in film, where the tabular possibilities are severely limited. As Groensteen writes, "The flexibility afforded to comics with regard to the form of its frames, the 'elasticity' of the drawn panels, highlights the rigidity of the cinematographic apparatus, which is practically condemned to equip the projected image with a fixed and constant form" (2007, 40). Filmmakers can alter aspect ratios or do split-screen arrangements, but nothing in film can quite duplicate the reader's experience of the spread of panels across a comic's page. Comic-to-film adaptations, then, omit a medium-specific quality of comics, and can only attempt to replace it with a roughly equivalent device.

For the record, nongraphic literature also has no aesthetically relevant tabular organization. It doesn't matter at all where any semantic unit (e.g., word, sentence) is located on the page. Literature-to-comic adaptations have to fabricate a tabular arrangement, which must be done with great care, at the risk of adding aesthetic features where there should be none. Comic-to-literature adaptations, correspondingly, lose all possibility of representing tabular organization of panels.

At least three other medium-specific features of comics complicate adaptations. First, even if different art forms employ closure comparably, the use of different media does seem to require different kinds of imagining. A work of conventional, nongraphic literature can use words to describe the story world it portrays, but the look of this world must be imagined by the reader, as it is not directly shown. Since comics are generally pictorial, literature-to-comic adaptations do too much for the reader.[6] The imaginative activity of picturing is lost; the comics adaptation negates the valuable skill of visualization and might even make the reader incapable of it.[7] In the other direction of adaptation, comics, unlike film, have neither sound nor motion. When a comic-to-film adaptation adds these, it has the same problems as a literature-to-comic adaptation. This is the root of Sava's objection to any film adaptation that contains Doop, the weird, green, potato-shaped X-Man who speaks in symbols that are never translated in the comics (though decoders are possible to find online). Says Sava,

> There's an element of constant interactivity between Doop and his audience; even if people don't want to go to the extra effort for a translation, they're still interacting with the character by using visual context clues to glean meaning from the alien text. [For film,] the character would need to be subtitled in Doopspeak so that the viewer has something to translate, . . . and if Doop is making a sound, there's

> already a restriction being placed on viewers' interpretations that isn't there in a comic. (2014, n.p.)

Second, while all narrative art forms are capable of accommodating metafictional content—calling attention to the fact that they are stories and are employing particular conventions in order to portray those stories—comics admit of distinctive metafictional effects, as Cook has argued (2012). We encountered metafictional comics in the previous chapter. When, as in Figure 4.3, comics contain characters who have an awareness of and are manipulating their own word balloons, Cook claims that they can be understood and analyzed only through attention to the media conventionally used to create them (word balloons, in this case).[8] Although analogous devices can be employed in other art forms, metafictional manipulation of the normative conventions of comics produces different aesthetic effects than metafictional manipulations of the normative conventions guiding the use of media in other art forms. Having characters interact with subtitles in a movie just wouldn't be the same. In cases where metafictional content is present, any adaptation from a comic into another art form will eliminate something that's special to comics. More generally, Cook concludes, you can't correctly read or criticize a comic just because you know how to watch or criticize a film (and vice versa).

Third and finally, comics are like literature in that they're not difficult for one person to produce, independently and inexpensively. Though the mass technologies of printing and distribution generally require many people and complex organization, you can generate a professional quality autograph copy of a comic with little more than Bristol board and some decent pens, or (increasingly) a computer with a drawing tablet and the appropriate software. The illustrator of this book produces his artworks by himself. Steven Spielberg doesn't. While digital camcorders have made it more feasible for films to be made by individuals, filmmaking is generally an art of collaboration on a massive scale—necessarily so for any films requiring actors who are not also the director. Accordingly, a comics author can exert more control over the story than a filmmaker. Narratives told in comics have abundant potential to be expressive of the author's particular point of view. The comparative simplicity of the media involved entails that comics can offer an individual voice and foster an intimacy between artist and reader that meets the level of literature—or even exceeds it, since comics reflect an author's visual as well as verbal sensibility. Close connections between artist and reader in a pictorial narrative art form are hard to come by, and it's with good reason that we value their occurrence in comics.[9]

The considerations raised in this section suggest that perfect viability can't be achieved in adaptations from comics to film. As long as those who claim that such adaptations are "impossible" have an appropriately weak sense of impossibility in mind, their position is more than plausible. Significant aspects of comics can't be preserved in film. Significant aspects of film can't be preserved perfectly in comics either. And the same holds with regard to comic-to-literature or literature-to-comic adaptations.

None of this entails that any of these art forms is superior to any of the others. They're just different, and their differences stem from the media that they use and the conventions that surround the use of those media. Nor does it entail that comics are poor choices for adaptation into film. In fact, I think that comics are an excellent source—perhaps even the *best* source—for film adaptations. And that's the argument I'll explore in the next section.

5.3. The Kindred of Comics and Film

The claim that comics is the best source for adaptation into film is a comparative one, so we'll have to contrast that suitability with other sources for film adaptations. Despite the barriers to adaptation canvassed above, the media used in comics and film produce a lot of similarities between the two. And these similarities aren't shared nearly to the same degree between film and any other art form.

We've already encountered one similarity between comics and film. For both, medium-specific qualities exert a strong pressure toward narrativity. That comes from the sequential ordering of the panels and frames, respectively: a simple and straightforward way to organize pictures in a sequence is to connect them narratively. Accordingly, comics are better sources for film adaptation than art forms that carry with them strong biases *against* narrativity, such as paintings, photographs, and sculpture.

It's true that there are plenty of other art forms (literature and theater, for instance) that tend to be narrative. Comics had better be more closely related to film than these if the thesis that they're the best sources for film adaptations is to be defensible. And, indeed, the relation is close. Consider first the type of narration that's typically employed in comics and film. Narratologists since Aristotle have been aware of a distinction between *mimetic* and *diegetic* narration. Mimetic narration occurs when the storytelling act is one of showing, with no direct narrator (as in *Hamlet*). Diegetic narration occurs when the storytelling act is one of telling, directly by a narrator (as in *Moby Dick*).

Many narratives blend together both types of narration, though some are purely one way or the other. A particular comic or film can employ both mimetic and diegetic narration. In comics, diegetic narration is usually provided in those narrative boxes we discussed in Chapter 4. In film, diegetic narration usually arrives in the form of voice-overs and intertitles. Not all works of comics and film, however, and not all narrative components of individual works—panels, pages, shots, and so on—rely on diegetic narration, as any survey of either will demonstrate. Comics and film alike overwhelmingly employ mimetic narration: in most (if not all) panels and shots, the reader or viewer is directly shown narrative events. Why are comics and film this way?

If you've read through this book in order, you'll probably be unsurprised to find out that I think the explanation is medium-specific. The media that comprise comics and film alike are fundamentally visual, rather than tactile, olfactory, and so on (verbal media, of course, are optional in both). That is, to be experienced properly, they must be perceived through sight. One *watches* a film. And though one *reads* a comic, this is a special kind of reading that requires attention not merely to the words of the comic (if present), but also to the pictorial images that comprise it. If comics turns out to be an essentially pictorial art form, then each comic shows the reader at least something, implying that comics narratives are mimetic essentially.

Comics are highly adaptable into film, then, because the media of both are visual. It's advantageous to adapt from one visual art form into another because the visual produces tendencies toward mimetic narration. Typical literature, in which visual appearances do not have any effect on the narrative, are more awkward than comics to adapt into film because the nonpictorial media that they employ force them to rely predominantly on diegetic narration. To capture the details of a novel coherently in a film, diegetic narration in the form of a voice-over is often shoehorned in, sometimes to disastrous results (as in David Lynch's *Dune* [1984] or the original theatrical cut of *Blade Runner* [1982]). When adapting into a mimetic medium, better to keep everything mimetic, including, if possible, the source narrative.

What about theater? It's an art form where visual appearances are crucial, and lends itself to mimetic narration. Arguably, the media of theater relate it much more closely than comics to film. Theatrically performed narratives show us actual motion; as Carroll argues, the possibility of perceived motion is a crucial characteristic of film (2008, 58–63). Theater has the capacity to engage senses other than sight, since we can hear what the actors have to say. Since the 1920s, synchronized dialogue and other recorded sounds have given film the same capacity: even if sound is not essential to film, it is, at present, expected. Theatrical works take actual time to perform, and the time it takes to perform a scene generally corresponds directly to the diegetic time of that scene (the time that elapses during that scene in the world of the narrative). Just so for film: movies have an actual screening time, and the scenes depicted therein may (and often do) elapse in "real time." Finally, theater provides us with direct perceptual access to real human beings. If photography is transparent, as Kendall Walton famously claims (1984), cinema provides us with the same access. That is, when a film is based in photographic technologies, we literally see the people (actors) and objects (sets) that it depicts, just removed in time—in the same way that we literally see stars through a telescope, just removed in time.

Comics have none of these features. They're engaged exclusively through the process of visually processing still, silent pictures and words. Actual motion and sound are impossibilities in a print medium. While these features may be added in electronic media, the category of comics would be stretched to the breaking point by including works that move and make noise.[10] Furthermore, the time frame in which a comic is read is largely severed entirely from the diegetic time that elapses within its narrative. This is not to say that comics cannot be read in "real time": Jeff Smith's *Bone* (2004), for example, contains a sequence ("Eyes of the Storm") in which reading time and diegetic time are supposed to be identical.[11] In Chapter 4, I argued that our experiences of how long it takes events to occur in the real world informs our knowledge of how time passes within and among comics panels. But we don't *process* events in comics at the same rate that they occur diegetically, as we do in our experiences of theater and film. Comics is also prototypically nontransparent. Though there are photographic comics (which are more common in Europe than in America), the dominant form of comics is drawn by hand or on a computer. Such comics, unlike theater and film, do not provide us with perceptual access to any real people or objects.

Theater and film appear to be closely related, and adaptations from the former to the latter are not unusual. However, adapting theater to film can be awkward and difficult. To do so generally requires more than merely placing a camera in front of a theatrical performance, which risks accusations of not being "cinematic." In some ways, there's a disconnect between the media of film and theater, a source of difference that presents challenges to the task of adaptation. Understanding how this could be so provides further support for the claim that comics are the best sources for adaptation into film.

Think about how theatrical works are organized. Typically, each work consists of one or more scenes, each of which, as previously noted, takes place in real time. That is, within each scene, diegetic time is largely identical to performance time. Temporal gaps—jumps in diegetic time—conventionally occur only between scenes.

The spatial organization of theatrical works is managed in much the same way. The viewer's relationships to the diegetic space represented in each scene are stable, in virtue of relatively stationary positioning vis-à-vis the actors and set. The spatial relations between viewer and diegetic space generally change only when there are scene changes, which may toggle the viewer between, for instance, a blasted heath and a Scottish castle.

Film and comics, by way of contrast, are organized in a fashion different from theater. While these art forms also tend to be divided into scenes, each scene typically contains discrete units that may be discontinuous both in diegetic time and diegetic space. Consider film first. Scenes can be composed of only one shot; ordinarily, they are composed of more. With a few exceptions, successive shots are taken from different angles, but viewers understand that they are seeing the same scene—just from a different perspective, at a later time. Accordingly, it's appropriate to say that films are "gappy": the relationship between the viewer and the diegetic time and space is constantly shifting. Some classical film theorists such as Rudolph Arnheim (1957, 87–102) went so far as to locate the essence and the particular value of film in its ability reconstitute reality through the intentional production of gaps, achieved through editing techniques such as montage.

In comics, gutters among panels serve the purpose of separating pictures from each other and require closure to process (see Chapter 4, Section 4.3). The panels of a comic can show the reader the same scene from the same perspective, requiring minimal closure on the part of the reader. More common, however, are transitions whereby the perspective from which the scene is depicted, like a camera angle, varies in the interests of graphic liveliness and to focus the reader's attention. Except for the aspect-to-aspect transitions we encountered earlier, diegetic time elapses in between panels. Readers must reconstruct the events that occur in these temporal and spatial gaps in order to make sense of a comic's narrative.

Panels and the transitions between them are to comics what shots and the transitions between them are to film. The art form of comics, like film, is gappy. Just as classical film theorists were drawn to the idea that the capacity for gaps is essential to film, theorists attempting to come to terms with comics—including many of those we studied in Chapter 2—have been drawn to the idea that gaps and the process of closure are definitive features of comics. Essentialist characterizations of comics that rely on such features are controversial and have attracted a great deal of criticism, and analogous essentialist characterizations of film are correspondingly tendentious. Yet it's uncontroversially true that filmmakers are drawn to the use of editing techniques that exploit gappiness, and in comics, manipulating the gutter and the closure process is the gateway to managing reader perceptions of diegetic time and space.

Theater, in contrast, admits of no readily identifiable organizing device comparable to the shot or the panel. Not even the scene: while scenes *could* theoretically be arranged to track the diegetic content of each panel of a comic or shot of a film exactly, this would be an avant-garde strategy of performance at best (and a technical and narrative disaster at worst). The fact is that theater, in virtue of its media, is not well suited to the same types of narrative breakdowns that are so naturally present in comics and film.

Theater, then, lacks a vital affinity to film that comics share. And that has implications for adaptation: adapting from one gappy art form into another is much more natural and straightforward than adapting from a nongappy art form into a gappy art form. So comics are better sources for film adaptation than theatrical works are.

At the end of the previous chapter, I hinted at ways in which comics and film use closely related means of pictorial storytelling. Any art form with visual components employs a range of techniques to direct the attention of its audience to (or, in some cases, away from) narratively salient elements. In theater, these techniques notably include blocking—the ways actors are to move about onstage—and lighting (the spotlight, for example). In film, they notably include (as Carroll identifies them in 1985a) *indexing*, guiding the viewer's attention via camera movement like pans, zooms, and tracking shots; *bracketing*, framing each shot so as to include or exclude certain features of the diegetic world; and *scaling*, positioning the camera in such a way as to foreground prominent and (often) narratively significant objects and events while minimizing others.

When it comes to its attention-directing techniques, comics is a lot like film. Indexing is achieved through a succession of panels that alter the reader's viewpoint with respect to the distance or orientation of an object, or by showing us where a character is looking (called a "point-glance" shot in film theory). Bracketing is done in comics of necessity: since panels cannot be infinitely wide or tall—even those that bleed to the edge of the printed page—they must exclude some of the diegetic space. Scaling is a similarly straightforward effect, accomplished by drawing represented objects as if seen from various distances.

The outcome achieved by these techniques is similar in all three media: if the narrative is presented adequately, the audience will know where to look.

But the degree of control allowed by comics and film far surpasses that allowed by conventional theater. For instance, in theater, it's extremely difficult and awkward to alter significantly and quickly the audience's perspective of the characters and the props. Consider the challenges that would be involved with transitioning from a panoramic view to a tight view of an actor's face, or of foregrounding a small object such as a potato or a bloody knife. In comics and film, manipulating such spatial relations is easy and natural. Creators of comics and film can exert fluid control over the reader or viewer's access to any object, from any perspective.

Because the degree to which they admit of visual control over presentation of the narrative is equivalent to that found in film, comics can serve as a basis for film adaptation to an extent unknown in other art forms. A comic, in ways a theatrical performance (to say nothing of a theatrical script) doesn't, has already broken down the visual presentation into the equivalent of shot transitions. And comics offer ideas about how to use the camera within a shot. It's no accident that storyboards for films look almost exactly like comics. Even when a filmmaker isn't adapting a comic, the filmmaking process is strengthened by acting—through the creation of the storyboard—*as if* the film was based on a comic all along.

Some examples in which directors of comic-to-film adaptations used the comics as storyboards might prove helpful at this point. I'm in the company of those who think that the film adaptation of *Watchmen* is a failure in many ways. However, a few scenes in it demonstrate how smoothly the transition from comics to film can occur. The famous opening page of the comic is imitated directly in the film adaptation in the shot immediately following the opening credits (from 11:12 to 11:39). Both comic and film begin the sequence with a tight close-up depicting the bloody happy face button and then transition through a succession of images that bring us up from the street level to the skyscraper window from which the Comedian was pushed. This zoom in the film even includes Rorschach, whom we see quickly in panel 3 of the comic.

A better and consistently rendered exemplar of comic-to-film adaptation is *Sin City* (2005). (Don't see the sequel: the less said about that, the better.) The use of Frank Miller's comics as a storyboard is evident from beginning to end. Miller even gets credit as a codirector. There is no point (or space here) in describing all of the ways in which the shots of the film are synchronized with the panels of the comic. To get a taste of the correspondence, watch the film from 13:02 to 16:21 and follow along in *Frank Miller's Sin City Volume 1: The Hard Goodbye* from pages 10 to 28. Save for a few extraneous images and a few snippets of narration in the comic that do not appear in the voice-over, the film uses the framing, focus, and narrative of the comic as much as can possibly be achieved in a cross-media context.

5.4. Conclusions

My argument in the previous section is that close attention to the media of comics and film reveals striking commonalities. Both tend strongly toward the narrative; both employ largely mimetic, visual narration; both are gappy; and both control the percipient's attention to a similar degree and with similar techniques. No other art form—neither literature, nor theater—shares these affinities with film to the same degree that comics does. And that's why comics is the best source for film adaptation.

Even so, we need to remain mindful of the difficulties with adaptation, canvassed earlier in the chapter. To say that comics provide the best sources for films isn't to say that adaptation from one to the other preserves perfect viability. There are still plenty of legitimate barriers to that. Rather, the standpoint we've arrived at is much more modest. All else being equal, when a comic is adapted for film, the likelihood that the story the comic tells and the way the comic tells it can be preserved is higher than it is for any other art form adapted into film. That's compatible with the extent of viability in adaptations from comics to film—or from any art form into any other art form—being quite low.

So maybe theorists like Wolk, Miller, and Moore are right to be worried about the failure to recognize that comics and film have different medium-specific capacities. Moore writes that "any emulation of film technique by the comics medium must inevitably suffer by the comparison," since "you will be left with a film that has neither movement nor a soundtrack" (2008b, 3). When comics authors create their work with film in mind, there's a real risk of not using comics media well. Moreover, because comics and film have different medium-specific capacities, it's a mistake to think critically about comics exclusively in terms drawn from film criticism. That's the payoff of Cook's argument in "Why Comics Are Not Films" (2012): understanding comics requires a philosophy and theory of comics independent from philosophy and theory of film.

Let me close this chapter with a point that pushes us forward into our next issue. What effect does adaptation have on value? We can't handle this question fully here, but intuitively, the more viable an adaptation is, the more closely the value of the source will transfer to the adaptation. That is, a good source, adapted with a significant amount of viability, should eventuate in a good adaptation; a bad source, adapted similarly, should eventuate in a bad adaptation. However, if viability is lower, all bets are off. A bad source comic could become adapted into a good film (it's hard to find examples of this); a good source comic could become adapted into a bad film (sadly, it's all too easy to find examples of this). A good comic could even be adapted with low viability into a good film, or a bad comic with low viability into a bad film.

But what makes a comic good in the first place? I used *Sin City* as a case of very close adaptation from comic to film. If highly viable adaptations preserve value, is this an example of a good source comic with a good film adaptation? Or is it an example of a bad source comic with a bad film adaptation? Or something in between? This isn't a book about film, per se, but it is about comics, and while I'm probably not going to definitively settle the status of *Sin City* for you, I hope to provide a framework in the next chapter for what an evaluative theory of comics should look like.

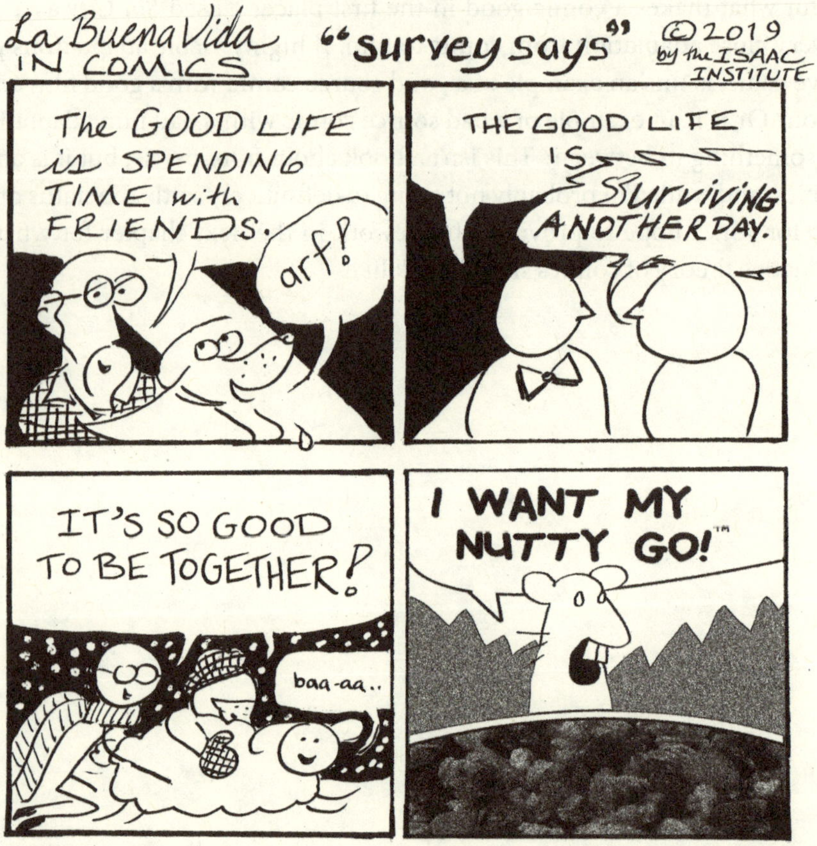

La Buena Vida IN COMICS
"Survey says"
©2019 by the ISAAC INSTITUTE
The GOOD LIFE is SPENDING TIME with FRIENDS.
arf!
THE GOOD LIFE IS SURVIVING ANOTHER DAY.
IT'S SO GOOD TO BE TOGETHER!
baa-aa..
I WANT MY NUTTY GO!™

fig. 6.1

6
Evaluating Comics

6.1. Criticism and Relativism

According to Noël Carroll, "Criticism comprises many activities, including: the description, classification, contextualization, elucidation, interpretation, and analysis of the artworks on the docket . . . precisely for the purpose of providing the grounds for the critic's evaluation of the artwork in question" (2009, 13–14). On this account, you are most probably a comics critic. I don't mean that you do it professionally, or that you post about comics on a blog or some form of social media, or even that you share your take on comics with others. There are, of course, plenty of people who do those things, and you might be among them. But as long as you read comics and arrive at judgments about their value based on your interpretive activities, you're a critic.

This chapter is about those evaluative judgments. We've occasionally touched on issues of value before, most recently in the previous chapter. Some comics theorists, remember, claim that the value of particular comics is lost through adaptation: we traced the source of those claims to specific capacities for representation and expression enabled by the media of comics. I've also smattered this book with some of my own value judgments about particular comics, with which you might or might not agree.

And that leads us to an issue about evaluation it's worth considering right at the outset: relativism. When we attribute a property to an object, the truth value (i.e., truth or falsity) of that attribution is relative when it shifts depending on the context of the attribution. Suppose I tell you that one of my old cats, Perry, was big. The natural way to interpret this claim is that I'm making a comparison of Perry to other cats. If that's the background context for my utterance, it's true. Perry was truly huge for a cat (I'm pretty sure of Norwegian forest cat lineage—look it up if you're curious). However, if the comparison is not between Perry and other cats, but between Perry and people, or tapirs, or canyons, Perry was small. There's no context-independent fact of the matter about whether Perry was big or small—it's all relative.

Some think that all evaluative judgments—those involving right and wrong, good and bad—are relative. Most prominently, relativism has been a

The Philosophy of Comics. Henry John Pratt, Oxford University Press. © Oxford University Press 2023.
DOI: 10.1093/oso/9780190845445.003.0006

salient issue in ethics, where it needs to be handled with some care, at the risk of unpalatable results. It's hard to envision, for example, how killing innocent children for fun could be morally obligatory within a certain culture just because it's accepted within the context of that culture.[1] But relativism in the evaluation of artworks, comics included, seems less worrisome. Does it really matter if I judge Eric Powell's *The Goon* series to be great and you judge it to be terrible? It seems not. Nothing of import hinges on our divergent critical judgments, any more than if I like marmalade sandwiches and you don't. *De gustibus non est disputandum*, as the Latin proverb has it: there's no disputing taste.

Or is there? I can put it no better than David Hume in his essay "Of the Standard of Taste":

> Whoever would assert an equality of genius and elegance between Ogilby and Milton, or Bunyan and Addison, would be thought to defend no less an extravagance than if he had maintained a molehill to be as high as Tenerife, or a pond as extensive as the ocean. Though there may be found persons who give the preference to the former authors, no one pays attention to such a taste; and we pronounce without scruple the sentiment of these pretended critics to be absurd and ridiculous. The principle of the natural equality of tastes is then totally forgot, and while we admit it on some occasions where the objects seem near an equality, it appears an extravagant paradox, or rather a palpable absurdity, where objects so disproportioned are compared together. (1996, 137)

Hume's literary comparisons might be antiquated—his essay was originally published in 1757—but his grasp of our critical practices is not. Substitute "Chris Browne–era *Hagar the Horrible*" in for "Ogilby" and "1950s *Peanuts*" in for "Milton" to see what I mean. (OK, maybe that comparison is also antiquated. Feel free to substitute your own.) There are some evaluative judgments, even of comics, that we treat as just plain incorrect. We think of those who make such judgments as misinformed, willfully contrarian, or not in their right minds. Those are the same kind of verdicts we reach about people who get matters of fact incorrectly.

Our treatment of some evaluative judgments of artworks as more correct than others is evidence, for Hume, that they really *are* more correct. According to the strongest form of relativism, no evaluative judgment of artworks is more correct than any other, since such judgments are relative to the particular taste of the critic. Hence, if Hume is right that some evaluative judgments of artworks are more correct than others, that strong form of relativism is false.

Applied to comics, that's the fundamental position I'll be endorsing going forward in this chapter. Some comics critics are better at it than others, and the evaluative judgments that they render can be better as well. If a good critic judges that Grant Morrison's *The Invisibles* is a great comic and a bad critic disagrees, the good critic's verdict is the correct one. On Hume's view, the consensus judgment of good critics supplies what he calls the "standard of taste": "a rule by which the various sentiments of men may be reconciled; at least a decision afforded confirming one sentiment and condemning another" (1996, 136). In more contemporary terminology, the standard of taste allows us to resolve conflicting evaluations of comics and provides grounds for determining who got it right and who got it wrong.

If the standard of taste for comics is going to be fixed by what the good comics critics think, it had better be the case that we can make sense of what it is to be a good comics critic. Hume defines these (though he's not concentrating on comics, of course) in terms of "true judges": their characteristics include "strong sense, united to delicate sentiment, improved by practice, perfected by comparison, and cleared of all prejudice" (1996, 147). Fleshing that out a bit more, the true judges (or good critics) of comics are persons who are good at using reasons and logic to support their judgments. They're sane and healthy. Their perceptual capacities are finely attuned—they can pick up on not only the obvious but also the subtle properties of a comic. They've got extensive experience reading great and terrible comics and comics in between. They don't come to their critical tasks with any biases one way or another, and their good sense allows then to confirm and (if possible) eliminate any lingering traces of bias that they might detect.

Hume believes that true judges are rare. Maybe some of the characteristics he lists (particularly the absence of prejudice) are impossible to attain. But we can still use his view to establish a standard that's based on a continuum: the better a comics critic conforms to Hume's description of true judges, the more correct their evaluative verdict will be.

There's a wrinkle that brings us right back to relativism, at least at a limited scope. Can true judges disagree? Some commentators on Hume think that the true judge is an ideal and as such always reaches a single best verdict.[2] But on the opposing view that actual critics can be true judges, it would be unsurprising if they produced incompatible verdicts. After all, Hume's critical standard is grounded in taste, and taste varies from person to person. For Hume, when such variations are produced by differences in respects like personality, age, and historical-cultural background, they're blameless, and the critics' verdicts are still to be trusted.

What this part of the Humean view implies for comics is that their value is going to be relative to those aspects of readers. A contemplative old man reading comics in 1920s France will have a different set of comics that are "good for him" than an adventurous young woman in 1990s Ohio. But for both, the value of the comics they read will be specified by the true judges appropriately like them in character and circumstances. Perhaps this result mirrors some of your own experiences: if you're trying to get recommendations about which comics to read (or avoid), you might seek out critics as much like you as possible (with the addition, if applicable, of a greater degree of the qualities of the true judge).

Is this too much relativism? Suppose I think *The Goon* is great and the true judges most like me agree. Suppose you think it's awful and the true judges most like you agree. Is *The Goon* great or not? It appears that Hume's theory won't let us settle the issue of who's right, and that effectively negates its stated purpose. If you believe that some comics are just plain good, full stop, irrespective of anybody's critical opinion, then the Humean standard of taste might not be the strategy for you.

To alleviate this problem, we could revisit the idea that true judges are ideals who can't disagree, and that there's one evaluative verdict that's equally applicable for all comics readers. The cost of this option is that it's going to be harder to find out which comics are good, since it's challenging, to say the least, to consult an ideal. We'd just have to do our best to approximate the true judge's characteristics (or find somebody else who can get as near as possible), and be hopeful that we're getting close enough to a critical standard.

Alternatively, we could refine Hume's notion of blameless disagreement. The more blameless disagreement we allow among true judges, the more relativism results. In ethics, nuanced relativists have exploited this relation by connecting ethical values to very broad cultural circumstances. David Wong, for instance, argues that whether an action is right or wrong depends on whether it occurs in the context of "the modern West" or "traditional cultures found in Africa, China, Japan, and India" (1991, 445). Whether the particular cultural division he's picked is plausible or not, it's about the broadest level possible, and something similar could be done with respect to the evaluation of comics (and artworks in general). We wouldn't get the result that for everybody, everywhere, at all times, *The Goon* is great, but we could get the result that it's great for me, you, and all your friends (provided that we all hail from the same culture, broadly construed).

Sophisticated relativists have another refinement to offer as well. In traditional poker, there are better and worse hands, but there's no single best hand. In the unlikely event that two or more players have a royal flush, there's a tie and the pot is split. For Wong, the broad cultural divisions he cites are like the royal flush. They sit at the top of moral systems (much higher than, say, Nazi morality), but since they fulfill the functions of morality equally well, there's no way to adjudicate between them. Analogously, the relativist can say, along with Hume, that there are better and worse standards for evaluating comics, but there's no one single best standard.

This refinement would support the result that any standard of comics criticism on which *Hagar* is better than *Peanuts* is inferior (all else being equal) than any standard on which *Peanuts* is better than *Hagar*. These are what Ruth Chang calls "nominal-notable" comparisons, between works that clearly are at different ends of the evaluative spectrum (1997, 14–17). Just as any acceptable moral system should agree that the obviously obligatory actions (e.g., don't murder) are better than the obviously impermissible actions (e.g., get out there and murder for fun), any acceptable standards for evaluating comics should agree that the notable masterpieces of comics (e.g., *Peanuts*) are better than the comics with nominal value (e.g., *Hagar*).

When it comes to closer comparisons, however, there seems to be more room for relativism in comics evaluation. Perhaps we should be comfortable with relativistic judgments about, say, the comparative value of *Peanuts* and *Pogo*, or *Little Nemo in Slumberland* and *Krazy Kat*, or Allan Moore's run on *Swamp Thing* and Grant Morrison's run on *Animal Man*, or Charles Burns's *Black Hole* and Daniel Clowes's *Eightball*. If a true judge from one comics culture were to determine that all of the former are better than all of the latter, and a true judge from another comics culture were to determine that all of the latter are better than all of the former, their disagreement might really be blameless. There'd be nothing further we could use to decide between their verdicts, and we'd just have to accept that the relative value of these comics can be flipped depending on cultural context.

Hume's standard of taste has some notorious problems with it. In addition to those gestured at above, these include a potential circularity or regress involved in identifying true judges, a conflation of liking with evaluating as good, and the priority Hume appears to afford to elite over vulgar taste. Maybe these problems have solutions; more likely, as is the case for most any philosophical position, there are bullets to bite. Nonetheless, the Humean view provides us with a way to fix the value of comics as best we can. And that's a good thing. There are far too many comics out there to read, and we need a way of ensuring to whatever degree possible that we're finding the good ones and not wasting our time on the bad. Good criticism gives us our best shot at finding good comics and understanding what has been achieved in them.

6.2. Value-Making Properties

Hume isn't writing directly about comics, of course, and so doesn't supply general principles for what makes particular comics good or bad. Maybe a true judge of comics could give us a grasp of those principles or the properties of comics to which they advert. Since it's not clear whether we actually have true judges among us, let's look for some representative examples of value-making properties offered by a comics critic, a philosopher, and a comics theorist. If these properties are correctly identified, they're what true judges will be basing their judgments on—and what the rest of us should try to detect in comics as well.[3]

Most comics critics aren't particularly explicit about the grounds of their evaluative verdicts. Wolk is something of an exception. In *Reading Comics* (2007), he mentions, at least in passing, the following as potentially valuable properties for comics to have:

- Entertainment value (22–23)
- Pacing, storytelling quality, and coherence (24, 80)
- Affording pleasure (31)
- Being memorable (Wolk's term is "resonant") (31)
- Stylistic adventurousness (32)
- Technical competence (33)
- Stylistic distinctiveness (34)
- Beauty (including the beauty that can be found in ugliness) (58)
- Multidimensional characterization (80).

Wolk doesn't think that all of these are equally important. Rather, he appears to prioritize whether comics are entertaining, pleasurable, and memorable.

Meskin is one of the few philosophers who have touched on evaluative criteria for comics, albeit in passing. In one of his arguments against the possibility of defining comics, according to which definitions are necessary for evaluating them, Meskin writes:

> To focus on evaluation, I would suggest that what we need is some grasp of the various styles, techniques, and purposes found in the art form, as well as a broad grasp of how to evaluate the variety of elements that are typically (but not necessarily) used in it, such as narrative, drawing, dialogue, and coloring. The virtues of Humean true judges may be of assistance. (2007, 376)

The reference to Humean true judges obviously fits well with the view I stake out in the previous section. And the "elements" he selects here as relevant will loom large shortly.

In the context of his discussion of comics as literature (2009), Meskin concludes ultimately that comics is a hybrid art form descended in part from literature. The verbal dimension, as I called it in Chapter 4, is part of most comics and, of course, paradigmatic literature. So too, Meskin points out, comics has appropriated literary genres like novels and memoirs (2009, 19). Because of these hybridizations, using literary tools to assess comics—applying evaluative principles and techniques imported from literary studies—is at least sometimes appropriate.

In the process of investigating whether comics can be equal in value to great works of literature, Meskin argues that certain good-making properties are shared across the art forms. Because these properties can, for Meskin, make both literary works and comics good, we can reasonably take it that he's committed to them as critically relevant to comics.[4] Meskin's examples of value-making properties in comics (and literature) include being "creative, original, well-structured, and unified" (2009, 2), and being "well-written, having depth of characterization, exhibiting . . . 'moral seriousness' in tackling 'humanly interesting themes,' and being well-plotted (if they are narrative in form)" (2009, 2).

Harvey is the theorist who might have most explicitly endorsed and defended specific criteria for comics evaluation. For years, Harvey has been advocating consistently for the view that the most important evaluative property of comics is what he calls the visual-verbal blend: "A measure of a comic strip's excellence," he writes, "is the extent to which the sense of the words is dependent on the pictures and vice versa" (1979, 642). We discussed in Chapter 2 (see Section 2.4) why this isn't a plausible element to bring in to a definition of comics. Nor should we endorse Harvey's claim that the visual-verbal blend "exploits the unique character of the artform" (1979, 642), since other art forms blend the same sorts of features. But maybe the visual-verbal blend lies behind a plausible evaluative criterion, at least for the comics with both verbal and pictorial dimensions. After all, if what those comics do is to use verbal and pictorial media in ways that are mutually reinforcing, then to be a good comic is, in part, to do that well. The blend of the visual and verbal in Figure 2.9, previously used to illustrate Harvey's notion, is part of what gives it its value.

At the same time, Harvey recognizes that effectively blending the visual and verbal isn't the sole contributor to the value of a comic (1998, 68). Aside from the sort of literary values mentioned by Meskin, Harvey raises preservation of comics traditions (a form of what I'll classify as intertextuality) or originality (1979, 645); graphic variety (1979, 646); and compositional clarity that maintains a "graphic center of narrative focus," concentrating reader attention on the visual elements that contribute most centrally to the story being told (1979, 650). For Harvey, these properties don't weigh as heavily as the visual-verbal blend, which serves as a framework for all other comics evaluation, but they matter.

The properties cited by Wolk, Meskin, and Harvey certainly aren't an exhaustive list, but they provide a basis for a rough framework of comics evaluation. While there are multiple ways to group them, I'm going to sort these properties into four categories (except for the visual-verbal blend, and some of the properties Wolk cites, about which more later).

1. *Narrative properties*: connected to the stories that comics tell. These include properties contributing to pacing, storytelling, coherence, writing mechanics, plotting, structure, and characterization.
2. *Pictorial properties*: connected to visual and graphical elements. These include depictive style, graphical composition, coloring or lack thereof, unity, technical competence, and beauty.
3. *Historical properties*: connected to circumstances in which the comic originates. These include creativity, originality, and intertextuality.
4. *Referential properties*: connected to the correspondence between what comics represent and facts about the actual world. These include accuracy, realism, and ethical content.

I'll make a few remarks about each of these and then add an umbrella category.

In your role as a comics critic, when you think about the writing of a comic, you're adverting to properties in the first category of value-making properties—narrative properties. The properties listed in that category are fairly standard for evaluating narrative works in general. It's these aspects of narrative comics that are imported from literary criticism, and connect them most closely to literature. On the face of it, there's nothing particularly unique to comics in the list of narrative properties. But that's not to say that we can simply evaluate comics narratives using the same methods we employ for nongraphic literature.

Over the last two chapters, I've offered arguments for the position that comics tell stories using medium-specific techniques that can't easily be replicated in works of other art forms. When comics tell stories, they do so in part by spatially juxtaposing pictures, and that entails that narrative properties like being well-paced are going to take a different form and have different grounds than they would in works that are nonpictorial. Accordingly, evaluating the writing of a comic's narrative (and, indeed, writing the narrative in the first place) requires paying attention to more than just the ways that the words are put together. It requires paying attention to the arrangements of elements within panels, the size and shape of the panels, the tabular organization of the page, and the relation of the pages to each other. All of those are obviously irrelevant when there's no sequence of pictures.

While it's crucial, when evaluating comics, to consider the medium-specific aspects of the construction of narrative, that can't be all there is to comics criticism. As we saw in Chapter 2, Section 2.4, the status of nonnarrative comics is unsettled. But if works like Figure 6.2 are indeed properly categorized as comics, then they can't be evaluated by paying attention to features like the quality of their storytelling or characterization.

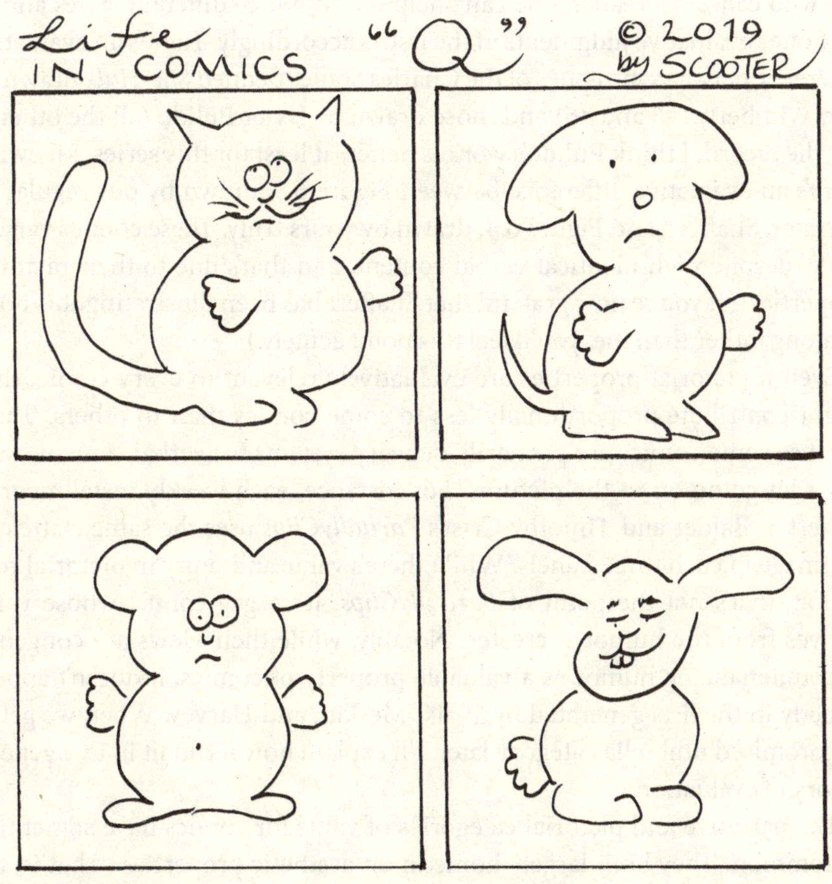

fig. 6.2

Similarly, a few of the properties I've grouped under the narrative heading won't be useful ways for evaluating pantomime comics (i.e., those without word balloons—such as Figure 2.9). If there are no words that have been put together in a comic, then the quality of writing mechanics—understood as referring exclusively to the words—is irrelevant. Understood as referring to the overall ways in which a comic's media combine to tell a story, writing mechanics will be relevant to any narrative comic.

If I'm right that all comics are pictorial, then attending to pictorial properties (the second category) will be a part of the evaluation of any comic whatsoever. A primary concern of most (and maybe even all) readers is how comics look. Case in point: major comics publishers frequently assign to different pencilers different issues of a comic series written by a single writer. This is a common practice because it takes a long time to draw a comic, and when busy artists can't meet their publication deadlines, work gets passed to somebody else who can. As a reader, one can't help but to notice different styles and to alter one's evaluative judgments of the issues accordingly. There's an evaluative difference between the issues of the Charles Soule–penned *She-Hulk* drawn by Ron Wimberly (#5 and #6) and those drawn by Javier Pulido (all the others). For the record, I think Pulido's work is better, at least for this series. Likewise, there's an evaluative difference between Figure 6.3, drawn by our regular illustrator, Shaffert, and Figure 6.4, drawn by yours truly. These comics vary in value, despite nigh identical verbal content, and that's due to their pictorial properties. (If you're now grateful that Shaffert has been illustrating this book all along rather than me, you'll feel this point acutely.)

Even if pictorial properties are evaluatively relevant to every comic, they might contribute proportionally less to some comics than to others. That's because some comics are primarily delivery systems for verbal content, with not a lot going on in the pictures. For instance, each weekly installment of Robert T. Balder and Timothy Crist's *PartiallyClips* uses the same static clip art image in each three panels. While there's value and unity in pictorial repetition, that's not the point of *PartiallyClips*. It's a gag comic, whose value derives from the humor it creates. Notably, while their views are congenial to countenancing humor as a valuable property of comics, it doesn't appear directly in the lists generated by Wolk, Meskin, and Harvey. When we get to the promised umbrella category later, I'll explain how it can fit in to a general theory of evaluation.

The narrative and pictorial categories of value for comics have something in common. They both largely home in on aesthetic properties—that is, the manifest properties that can be discerned merely by attending closely to a comic, apart from its relations to anything else.[5] If the pictures in a comic are,

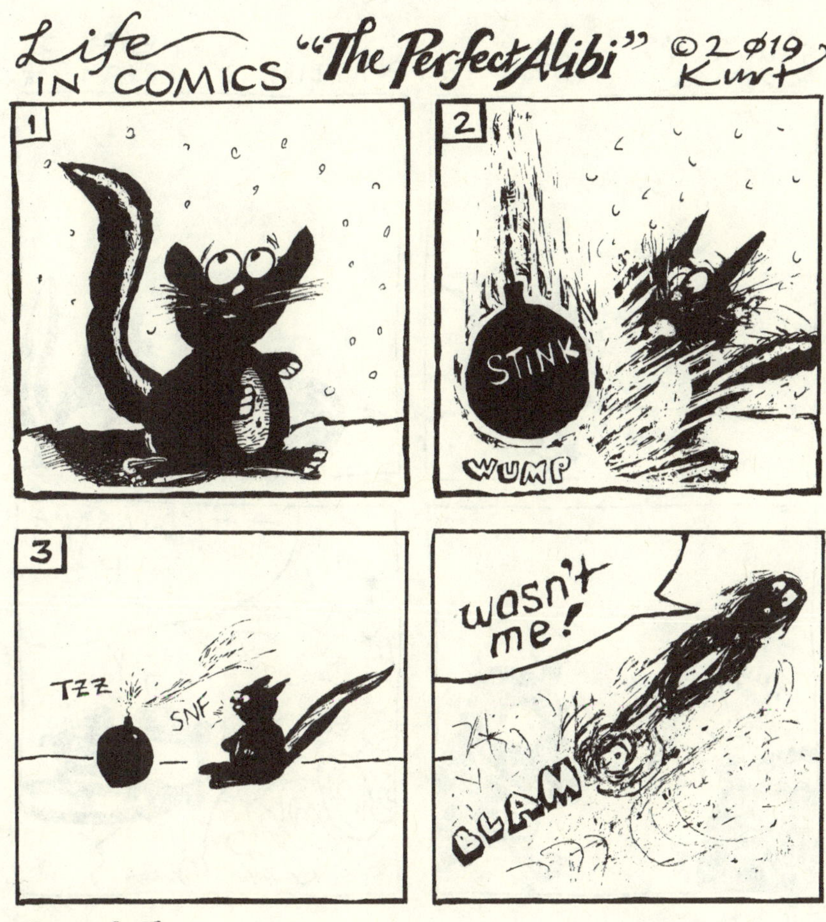

fig. 6.3

e.g., beautiful, that's value-adding, and you don't need to know anything about what a comic represents in order to pick up on beauty. Similarly, if a comic is well and intricately plotted, the elements that make it so are revealed exclusively through careful attention to the comic's manifest structure.

Before moving on to the third and fourth categories, thoroughness requires further attention to Harvey's notion of the visual-verbal blend. I didn't list the visual-verbal blend in the four types of evaluatively relevant properties of comics not because it doesn't belong there, but because it doesn't fit neatly into any of the categories. Rather, it's an aesthetic property that can contribute to the realization of valuable narrative properties (all of Harvey's examples

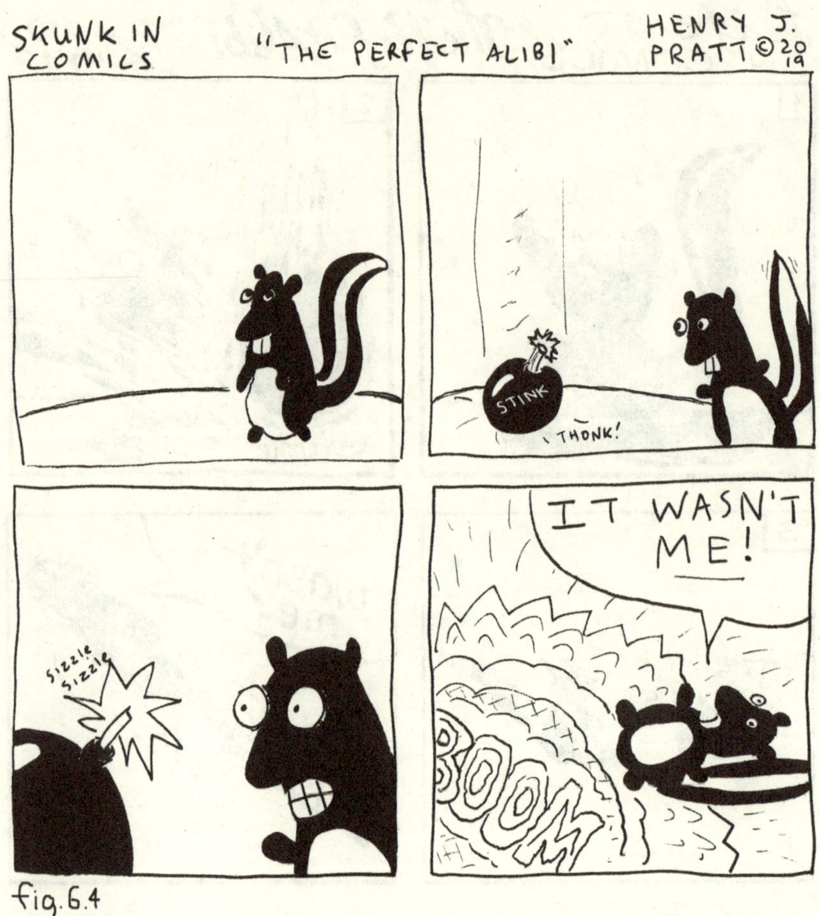

fig. 6.4

are of narrative comics). When different modalities of information transfer come together in a way that's in mutually reinforcing dialogue, that adds value by enhancing the unity of and reader engagement with the story that's being told. *Watchmen*, which we've encountered before, is a good example of that effect. If visual and verbal elements are working at cross-purposes—say, if the pictures are inappropriate to the overall style of the comic's writing—the likely effect will be to distance readers and interfere with their enjoyment.

Like other aesthetic properties, the visual-verbal blend is manifested directly in the comic and doesn't depend on its relations to anything outside it. The third and fourth categories—historical and referential properties—are rather different, and more controversial. There's a long-standing debate in philosophy and literary studies about whether critics ought to attend to anything other than aesthetic properties. On one side, we find formalists like Monroe Beardsley, who argue that when approaching a work critically, the *only* thing we should be paying attention to are the aesthetic features we can directly perceive in the work.[6] This view rules out as critically relevant any nonmanifest properties having to do with the author's circumstances, the conditions of the origin of the work, and how the work interfaces with the actual world (though formalists typically acknowledge that these might be relevant to the historical value of the work or a biographical account of the author).

You can perceive a visual-verbal blend directly *in* a comic, but you can't do so with creativity, originality, or intertextuality. These aren't manifest properties: they're only available to those who have specific background information about the relation of the comic to other comics that preceded it. If Beardsley and his ilk are right, then the historical properties cited above are critically irrelevant.

But are they right? We've got examples of comics critics who use those properties. My guess is that if you read a comic that's strikingly original, you'd judge that to be a value-making property. To divorce critical evaluation entirely from historical properties runs roughshod over standard critical practices. Maybe that's the point—maybe Beardsley and other formalists are comfortable with the implication that we're doing it all wrong—but the burden of proof here is pretty heavy. And there are strong reasons for thinking that evaluation should encompass properties beyond the merely formal. If Danto is right that artworks can't be understood or even exist independent of artworld context (a theory we encountered in Chapter 1, Section 1.4), then formalism is a nonstarter. So too, according to Walton's theory of categories (1970), which properties of an artwork are standard, variable, or contrastandard is determined by category membership, and category membership is determined by nonformal (including historical) considerations. (We discussed these terms briefly in Chapter 2, Section 2.1.) Walton's theory is about as close to widely accepted as one gets in the philosophy of art: since it entails that critical relevance is determined by how properties are classified, and since classification isn't done on formalistic grounds, then Walton gives strong reasons to reject formalism in evaluation.

Until it can be shown that the arguments for the irrelevance of historical properties to comics criticism can overcome the challenges from the likes of Danto and Walton, it's worth keeping them under consideration when making evaluative judgments of comics. If Jim Starlin's *Warlock* comics are particularly original, that's an important part of their value. If *Crisis on Infinite*

Earths resonates with an incredibly comprehensive set of connections to past DC comics continuity, that matters evaluatively.

Formalists dismiss referential properties just as they do historical properties. I think this stance is just as mistaken. Referential properties are indeed irrelevant to the extent that a comic's content sets it apart from the actual world: if there's a comic that's supposed to be appreciated merely in light of how it looks or is structured, and there's nothing to take away from it other than that, then referential properties don't contribute to its value. Abstract comics (if they exist) seem to be like that. A work like Figure 2.11 doesn't have any connections whatsoever to the actual world—it's just a series of patterns that represent nothing—and so doesn't have referential properties that can be used to evaluate it.

But ignoring referential properties brackets off a significant source of value that some comics have. If readers are supposed to gain knowledge or insight from a comic, then referential properties loom large. The use of referential properties for evaluating comics is especially key when assessing comics on two grounds: moral value and realism.

Moral value is the topic of Chapter 7. The only way that comics can even be assessed morally in the first place is to attend to their referential properties—to inquire into the sorts of actions, events, and attitudes a comic represents, and how it portrays them. That's not something that can be determined merely by attending to aesthetic properties. The critic concerned with ethics must relate the comic to the actual world.

Realism is tricky. Let's avail ourselves of Allan Hazlett and Christy Mag Uidhir's theory of what makes a work in any art form, comics included, realistic. As they argue in "Unrealistic Fictions" (2011), we can't just straightforwardly understand realism in terms of the match between the diegetic world and the actual world, since all fictions would thereby automatically be unrealistic. Rather, as part of their complex analysis, Hazlett and Mag Uidhir claim that works are unrealistic to the extent that there's an inconsistency between (a) the beliefs that works invite audiences to import from the actual to the diegetic world and (b) the beliefs that works invite audiences to export from the diegetic to the actual world. To cite one of their examples, the television show *ER* presents CPR as an incredibly effective life-saving technique. As a medical drama, the show invites viewers to understand it through our real-world expectations about how medical practices work. Since in the actual world, CPR isn't nearly as effective as it is on *ER*, and since viewers are expected to take the show's portrayals of medicine as accurate, *ER* unrealistically depicts CPR.

It's not a mark of unrealism that penguins can talk in Berkeley Breathed's *Bloom County*, or that human cloning is a viable technology in Sean Murphy's *Punk Rock Jesus*. According to Hazlett and Mag Uidhir, that's due to the norms of the genres in which those comics are embedded. The genre norms of hospital dramas have it that we're supposed to understand the diegetic world of *ER* as conforming to our own, at least with respect to medical facts. But given the genre norms of funny animal comics and dystopian science fiction comics, readers of *Bloom County* or *Punk Rock Jesus* (respectively) are not invited to import our beliefs about talking penguins or cloning (respectively) into the comics, nor invited to believe in those things in response to the comics.

Realism, so construed, is evaluatively relevant for journalistic and autobiographical comics, and other types of nonfiction. Here, due to the genre norms of nonfiction, the diegetic and actual worlds are presupposed to be the same place. Any inconsistency between the two is a misrepresentation of reality; any consistency is truth-telling. All else being equal, if being deceptive is an ethical defect, and being truthful is an ethical virtue, then, effectively, standards of realism in nonfictions become ethical standards. If the moral value of a comic affects its overall value *as* a comic, then the realism of a nonfiction comic affects its overall value.

Of course, the only way in which the realism of a work of nonfiction can be determined is by comparing it to the actual world, via attention to its referential properties. Joe Sacco's *Footnotes in Gaza* wouldn't be as good if it didn't accurately represent his experiences of Israeli-Palestinian relations. Allison Bechdel's *Fun Home* wouldn't be as good if it didn't afford the reader knowledge of what it's like to come to grips with one's own sexuality and family history. These comics are aesthetically stellar, in light of their strong narratives and pictorial mastery. But unless referential properties are taken into consideration, significant contributions to their value will be lost. It's not accidental that when critics evaluate these works, they (including you, if you've read them) don't just focus on the pictures and the storytelling. If formalists were right, that would be an error. It isn't. They're wrong.

What about fictions? There are all manner of ways in which fictions diverge from the actual world without being unrealistic. Superpowers typically violate the physical laws of our universe, but that doesn't make superhero comics unrealistic. Readers (hopefully) understand genre norms and know both that (a) they aren't supposed to believe that, e.g., super speed is impossible in the DC universe and (b) they aren't supposed to believe that super speed is possible in the actual universe. Nor is realism, where found, necessarily a good-making feature of comics that are works of fiction. Even superhero comics invite readers to import into and export from the diegetic world the fact that ordinary humans need to breathe air in order to live—and that doesn't make those comics better.

As Hazlett and Mag Uidhir point out, though, being unrealistic can be a flaw in a fiction, when unrealism interferes with readers' abilities to understand and enjoy it given the genre in which it's situated. Think about Batman. While he's claimed to be at the peak of human physical form, he's not supposed to have any superpowers. That means we're supposed to import from the actual world our knowledge about what's humanly possible. Nonetheless, it's not unusual for Batman to perform actions that aren't within human capacities, like kicking cleanly through an entire tree trunk (appearing to be at least three feet in diameter) in *Batman* #404, or holding up a thousand-pound ceiling while having a conversation (*Detective Comics* #484). If Batman comics are purely fantasy, and readers aren't expected to believe that these actions could happen in the actual world, then Batman's actions aren't bad-making features of the comics. They might even be good-making features. But if we *are* supposed to export the possibility of his feats into the actual world, the comics are unrealistic, and hence evaluatively flawed. Personally, I think the latter alternative is the more plausible interpretation of *Batman* comics, at least in the post–Frank Miller era, in which the supposed realism of the comics and Batman's actions therein is emphasized.

6.3. The Umbrella Category

I've argued that both aesthetic and nonaesthetic properties need to be kept in mind when evaluating comics. I've also pointed out that not all of the critically relevant properties of comics are applicable in each and every case of evaluating particular comics. The properties might, then, seem like a miscellaneous grab-bag. However, there are two fundamental commonalities among them, having to do first with what makes them valuable for comics that bear them, and second with the social practices particular to the community that constitutes the comics world.[7]

Fundamentally, it's my view that all of the properties cited in the four categories listed—narrative, pictorial, historical, and referential—are relevant to the value of comics because they have the capacity to afford valuable experiences. That's what Wolk is getting at when he mentions valuing comics when they're entertaining or give pleasure or are memorable. He finds value in these kinds of experience, and when comics can produce them, they're valuable because of it. Incidentally, if we like being amused, the funniness of a comic (based in the visual-verbal blend or other factors), is another property that can contribute to valuable experiences.

When it comes to artistic value in general, theorists are divided between those who endorse *objective* accounts, on which artistic value has nothing to do with our experiences of artworks, and those who endorse *subjective* accounts, on which it does. Continuing along the Humean lines introduced in Section 6.1 above, I side with the subjectivists. What the true judges are using to determine their critical verdicts is nothing beyond their experiences of art—how artworks make them feel.

What else *could* they go on? If the value of comics is supposed to be objective, then it's hard to see how we could ever access it, except through our experiences of comics. And at that point, we might as well be subjectivists. Then too, the very notion of objective value is exceedingly weird. As J. L. Mackie famously points out (1977, 95–97), it's hard to see what it would be like for any object—comics included—to be valuable if it was severed entirely from anything or anybody.

Wolk mentions pleasure, and that's an obvious candidate for a valuable experience. When comics are pleasurable to read, all else being equal, that's a good thing. However, we should resist hedonism, the view that the *only* kind of valuable experience is pleasure. Sometimes comics are good because they teach us something about the world (via referential properties): knowledge gained is not smoothly reducible to mere pleasure. Sometimes they're good because they're difficult or disturbing to read. I trust that I'm not alone in finding the experiences of reading David B.'s *Epileptic* and Derf Backderf's *My Friend Dahmer* tremendously uncomfortable. I wouldn't describe those experiences as pleasurable. But they're valuable experiences to have nonetheless, experiences that I appreciate having had.

Accordingly, what it is to have a valuable experience of a comic should be understood broadly, to encompass a variety of valuable mental states, not all of which are pleasurable. A standard way of classifying this position is as a "mental state view."[8] It isn't just coincidental that mental state views accord nicely with the standard of taste discussed in the first section of this chapter. Each of us derives experiences of some degree of value from reading comics. When the value of those experiences lines up with the value of the experiences that the true judges have, then our evaluative judgments based on those experiences are correct. To the degree that our judgments diverge, they're incorrect.

A standard objection to mental state views comes in the form of a thought experiment of the kind originally proposed by Robert Nozick (1974, 43–44): imagine a virtual reality "experience machine" that, when used, provides you with exactly the same mental states that you'd get reading Kate Leth and Brittany Williams's *Patsy Walker, A.K.A. Hellcat!* #1 (2015), without you reading it. Would you rather use the experience machine than read the actual comic? For that matter, would you rather use the experience machine to acquire the mental states you'd get from every comic you've ever read? Would the experience machine allow us to dispense with comics entirely, replacing them with virtually produced mental states? If you think something would be missing, and that the actual *Patsy Walker, A.K.A. Hellcat!* #1 (or any other actual comic) is more valuable than the mental states you'd get via the experience machine, then you should reject the mental state view. And you should reject it if you think that comics can have value even if you can get the same mental states from something else.

Despite the threat of the experience machine scenario, I think we shouldn't be so quick to abandon the position that comics are valuable when they have the capacity to provide valuable experiences. We need to remind ourselves that it's a hypothetical thought experiment. Until there is an actual experience machine that can provide us with mental states *identical* to those that we would experience while reading comics, there's no telling exactly how we'd react to it.

And let's think about what the experience machine would actually give us. Suppose that it produces *all* of the experiences of reading comics, e.g., having a comic in one's hands, letting one's eyes play over the panels, piecing together the narrative, anticipating what's going to happen during a page turn, as well as the knowledge gained from reading and an awareness that the experience is distinctive (if the comic is particularly original). What's left out? It seems entirely possible that trepidations about the experience machine are due to the suspicion that it wouldn't work well enough, whereas a truly comprehensive experience machine would leave us completely satisfied with the result and all too happy to get dispense with genuine comics entirely.[9]

Now, one thing that the experience machine wouldn't be able to provide is ownership of comics. To collectors, comics are good in part because they're real things to put on one's shelf and (as the case may be) to be bought and sold. Accordingly, some types of value that a comic has, such as monetary value, go beyond the experience of reading it. Such considerations motivate a refinement of my explanation of the umbrella category. For example, I expect that buying or selling an issue of *Action Comics* #1 for $3.2 million is a satisfying experience for some. So too, one could avoid an uncomfortable feeling by using the comics section of a Sunday paper to shield one's immaculately coiffed hair from the rain. But does either of those uses of comics make them better *as* comics? It seems not. If *Action Comics* #1 is a good comic, that's not because it's expensive or rare, but because it's original (containing, as it does, the first appearance of Superman). If those Sunday newspaper comics are good, it's not because they're printed on something that takes a while to soak through. While all value might ultimately trace back to experiences, there are all kinds of ways in which comics can produce valuable experiences that have nothing to do with their value qua comic.

Talk of valuable experiences is useful for explaining why the properties listed in the four categories of the previous section are valuable. But it's not useful for explaining why they contribute to comics' value qua comic, rather than qua financial investment or rain hat. What's needed is the second commonality among them, briefly alluded to at the outset of this section.

Let's return one last time to Beaty's description of the comics world: "the collection of individuals necessary for the production of works that the world defines as comics, [including] writers, pencillers, inkers, colourists, letterers, editors, assistant editors, publishers, marketing and circulation personnel, printers, distributors, retailers, and retail employees" (2012, 37). As in Chapter 1, where we first encountered the comics world, I append comics readers to Beaty's list.

In Section 3.2 of Chapter 3, I argued that the comics world provides a framework for identifying the media of comics: the practices constitutive of the comics world include (strong, if not inviolable) norms that govern the ingredients used to make comics and how those ingredients are to be combined. More importantly for our current purposes, the norms of the comics world also select which properties are relevant to a comic's value. That is, it's the people working on, selling, and reading comics who pick out as valuable some properties rather than others as valuable to comics qua comics.

We can see what they've selected by considering the categories that are part of the Eisner, Harvey, and Ignatz awards.[10] The most significant portion of the categories breaks down into the four types of properties listed in Section 6.2. Narrative properties are recognized by means of awards for writers and stories. Pictorial properties are recognized by means of awards for artists, pencilers, colorists, letterers, cover artists, and combinations thereof. Historical properties are recognized by means of awards for archival collections and reprints, and in other awards that recognize originality and distinctive new or lifetime achievement. Referential properties are recognized by means of awards for reality-based, educational, and journalistic comics (and presumably also factor into awards for artistry and writing whenever pictorial and narrative realism is considered). Remaining award types include those for best comic overall, continuing series, single issue, short story, minicomic, graphic novel, webcomic, children's comic, and humor comic. I submit that which comics are selected for these are, at least aspirationally,[11] based in combinations of the above properties, appropriately restricted to the relevant category or subcategory of comics, in consideration of the overall value that the experience of reading the candidate comics yields.

Why did the comics world select these properties as valuable rather than others? I suppose it's possible to conceive of an alternative scenario in which the value-making properties of comics are very different—say, being able to be thrown the farthest, or being legible when read underwater, or having been blurbed by Stan Lee. But I think the extant value-making properties of comics in the actual world aren't just a historical accident. That's because they're generally closely tied to the media that comprise comics. (And, returning briefly to our topic in Section 6.1, that's why any relativism in comics evaluation is unlikely to emerge from disagreement about which properties of comics are value-making.)

I've previously identified the media of comics as pictures spatially juxtaposed (perhaps essentially so), with narrative as the predominant means of unifying those pictures, and with words typically (if not essentially) integrated with the panels by means of speech and thought balloons, narrative boxes, and captions. If that's right, then it should be completely unsurprising that the three comics theorists we surveyed in Section 6.2 above describe as valuable the particular pictorial, narrative, and referential properties that they do. Since comics use an arrangement of pictures, of course the visual and graphic elements of these pictures and how they're arranged are going to be evaluatively relevant. When comics are narrative, properties related to storytelling become evaluatively relevant, including those having to do with the use of words insofar as they contribute to the narrative a comic presents. To the degree that a comic's pictures and narrative stand in the appropriate import/export relations to the actual world, referential properties will be evaluatively relevant. Harvey's visual-verbal blend criterion (which I've argued is a way in which words and pictures can combine to affect the reader's uptake of a comic's narrative) results naturally from considering both pictures and words as comics media.

Historical properties are a bit different. Their relevance to the value of a comic isn't produced by medium-specific tendencies. That is, given the media that typically comprise comics, the comics world could have selected against historical properties as value-making features of comics qua comics. At the same time, this seems pretty unlikely. For whatever reason, we humans typically value the experiences of encountering something that's never been done before, and of drawing connections among the artistic products that we make. That appears to be true across art forms: originality, creativity, and a work's self-conscious situatedness within its genre and broader cultural context are generally esteemed. Why? Here's where McCloud would engage in unsupported psychological speculation, and where I defer to empirical science.

6.4. Conclusions

Let's take stock. When evaluating comics, not every critical judgment is equally correct. I've endorsed Hume's view that the standard of taste is fixed by the verdicts of the true judges. Given the possibility that such verdicts admit of blameless disagreement, I argued that at least some relativism is probably inevitable, but that sophisticated versions thereof can mitigate relativism's less palatable consequences. Attention to the comics world reveals four kinds of value-making properties for comics, which acquire their value from their capacities to produce valuable experience and are selected largely as a result of the media from which comics are constructed.

Evaluation of comics is a challenging topic, and there's a lot more to be addressed—too much to fit comfortably in this book. I'd like to conclude this chapter by tying up a loose end that gets generated by some considerations initially broached in Chapter 3. Comics critics, on my account, are supposed to be focusing to a significant degree on medium-specific properties of comics. So should comics authors aspire to exploit maximally the capacities that comics media afford?

The looming worry here goes back to some of Carroll's long-standing criticisms of medium specificity. Carroll argues (2008, chap. 2) that just because a film uses its media especially well (whatever that amounts to), that doesn't make it good. For instance, film media seem to abet editing effects such as montage better than the media used in other art forms. If filmmakers succeed when they employ that capacity to its fullest extent, then Michael Bay turns out to be a great director: he's well practiced at splicing shots together in ways that are impossible in other art forms (e.g., theater). *Transformers* (2007) is much better than any film that doesn't use any fancy editing at all, like *Vanya on 42nd Street* (1994). But that's the wrong verdict. Michael Bay has style, and it's a style only possible given the media used by film, but his films are terrible. Analogously, one might worry about comics that successfully follow medium-specific tendencies—use pictures and words to tell a referential narrative—but are still bad.

The best way to respond here is to revisit a point made in Chapter 3: Carroll's challenges target strong medium specificity, but don't really impact moderate medium specificity. According to moderate medium specificity, as I've laid it out, the media that comprise comics make them well suited to have narrative, pictorial, and referential properties. That is, it's easier to make a comic that has those sorts of properties than it is to make works in at least some other art forms that have those sorts of properties (e.g., it's hard to make effective narrative paintings, or films that just use words and no pictures, or referential instrumental music). Responsible comics authors should be conscious of the tendencies produced by means of comics media—either by intentionally using the media of comics according to the pressures that they exert, or by deliberately defying those pressures.

When evaluating comics, critics should be mindful of those media and their tendencies as well. That's what Gaut has in mind when he approves of what he calls *evaluative* medium specificity: "Some correct artistic evaluations of artworks refer to distinctive properties of the medium in which these artworks occur" (2010, 286). This is eminently plausible. If comics are made of pictures, then critical assessment of a comic will naturally refer to those pictures and what the pictures allow the comic's author(s) to do. If comics media produce tendencies toward storytelling, then criticism will advert to narrative properties of comics—or, if those properties are absent, their absence. If comics media are referential, that's critically relevant as well.

It does *not* follow from any of this that merely going with the flow—making comics according to medium-specific features they abet—is either necessary or sufficient for making a comic good. Authors who create a comic that's a pictorial narrative with referential features have succeeded in only a very minimal way. They've produced an object with what I've called elsewhere *recognition value*: a work that needs to be taken into consideration when engaging in the practices of comics criticism. They haven't created an object with *appraisal value*, which stems from properties the presence of which merits a positive critical judgment.[12] To attain appraisal value, a comic must manifest medium-specific (and, presumably, other) properties in a way that's good—that produces valuable experiences.

What I've done in this chapter, in part, is to connect the value of comics to the media out of which they are made—a medium-specific position. Carroll writes that "no one has ever succeeded fielding a medium-specificity hypothesis of any great degree of detail that has not been immediately accosted by counterexamples" (2008, 48). His focus, as we saw back in Chapter 3, is on strong medium specificity, which is indeed prone to counterexamples. I don't think that the medium-specific claims I've made in this chapter are similarly vulnerable, since they're based in a more moderate approach. But, as always, I encourage the reader to prove me wrong. If you can find some comics whose value derives to a significant degree from properties that don't fall into any of the categories discussed above, then I'd love to hear about them.

In the next, final chapter, I'll take up one more aspect of the value of comics to which I've briefly alluded: the social and ethical value of particular comics and the category of comics itself. Medium specificity looms large there as well. Do the medium-specific pressures comics exert make them immoral?

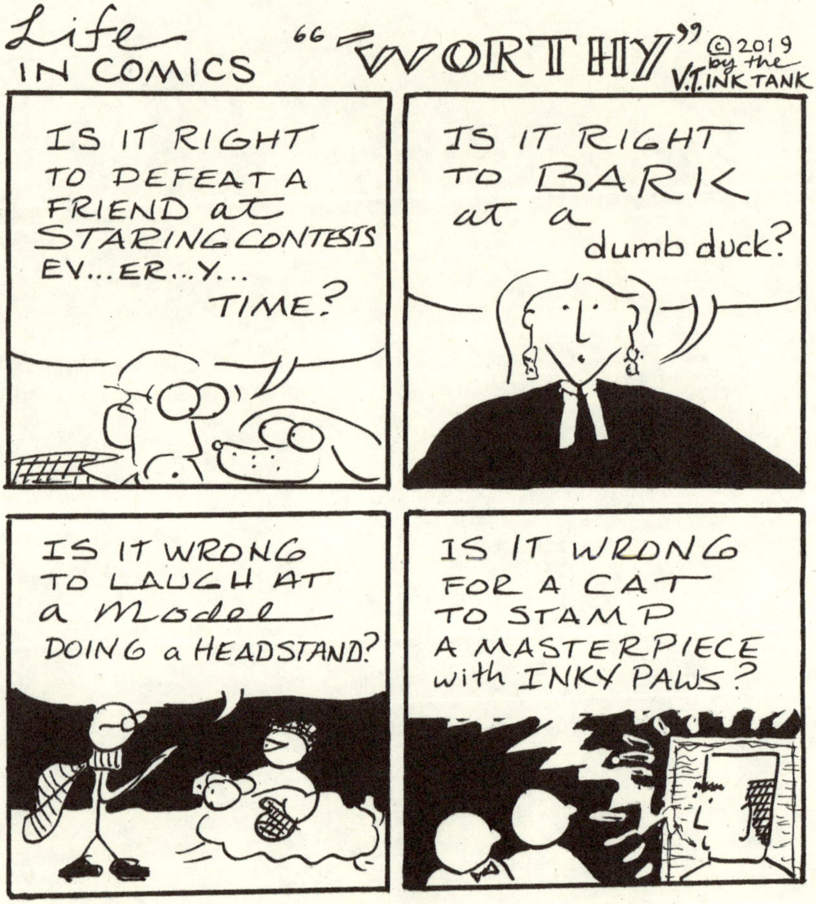

Life IN COMICS
"WORTHY"
© 2019 by the V.T. INK TANK
IS IT RIGHT TO DEFEAT A FRIEND at STARING CONTESTS EV...ER...Y... TIME?
IS IT RIGHT TO BARK at a dumb duck?
IS IT WRONG TO LAUGH AT a Model DOING a HEADSTAND?
IS IT WRONG FOR A CAT TO STAMP A MASTERPIECE with INKY PAWS?

fig. 7.1

7
Social and Moral Problems

7.1. The Platonic Strategy

Concerns about the social and moral value of comics go back at least to Plato (some twenty-four hundred years). Of course, putting ahistorical definitions aside for the moment, Plato wasn't aware of comics. But he was deeply worried about what the plays and poetry of his time were and weren't teaching people, and how they were encouraging people to act. For Plato, these works, like all the arts, are mere imitations of reality—a flawed mirror held up to nature, as it were. And this imitation, together with our tendencies to take that which imitations represent as real, has pernicious effects on the development of the just person and the just state.

To the contemporary mind, Plato may appear to be a crank or even an embarrassment. After all, the poetry and theater he targets in dialogues like the *Republic* (especially Book X) and the *Ion* are now considered to be among the classics of Western art. However, as Alexander Nehamas relates (1988), it's a mistake to think that Plato disapproves of high literature or fine arts at all. Those concepts didn't exist at his time. Rather, Plato is targeting the ancient Greek equivalent of contemporary mass-media narrative forms. At root, Plato's attacks on poetry and theater are identical to attacks that have recurred periodically to this day, on television, film, video games, popular music, and our topic, comics. Arguments that these are immoral or unethical tend to relate closely to the same motivations that Plato originally articulated.

Before investigating variants of what I'll call the *Platonic strategy*, and whether they have merit, let me offer a very brief defense of the position that individual comics can be evaluated morally.[1] They're not like trees or spoons. These can, of course, can have immoral origins (e.g., a spoon carved tortuously from the fingerbone of a living person), or be placed immorally (e.g., a tree I plant out of spite, in order to ruin my neighbor's view) but don't themselves appear to have any moral status. There aren't any righteous or evil trees or spoons. Contrastingly, comics can be morally better or worse—at least, that's how we treat them. That's because comics can represent states of affairs and mandate responses to those states of affairs. If a comic, properly interpreted,

The Philosophy of Comics. Henry John Pratt, Oxford University Press. © Oxford University Press 2023.
DOI: 10.1093/oso/9780190845445.003.0007

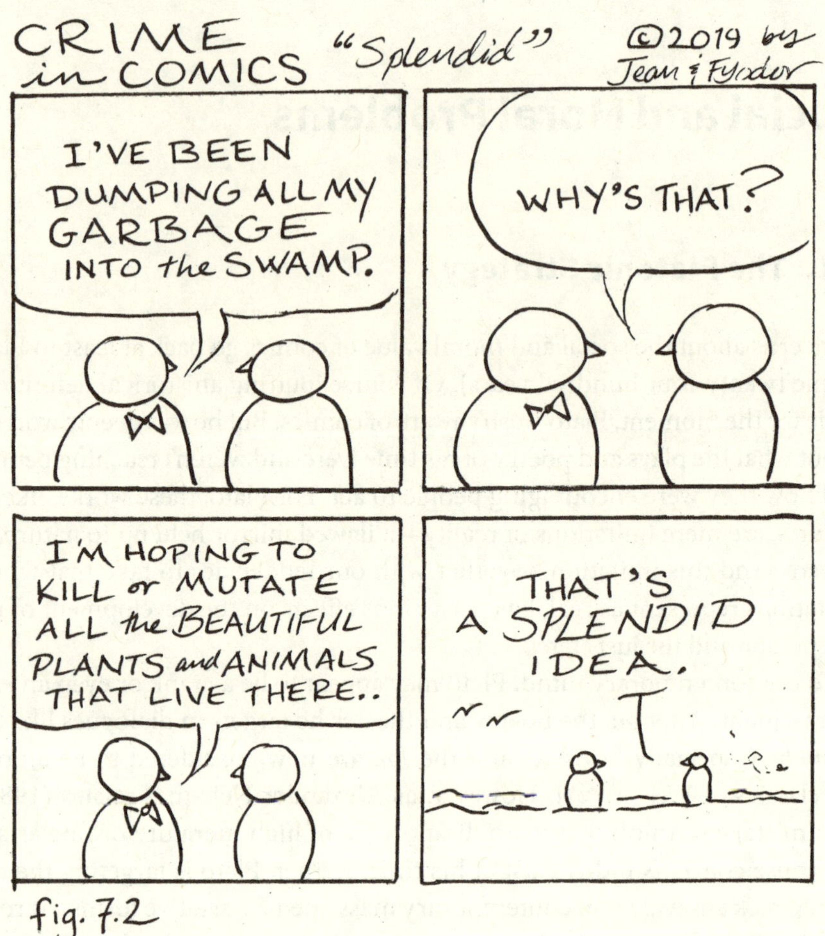

fig. 7.2

prompts the reader to adopt the wrong moral attitudes (approving of that which is morally bad, disapproving of that which is morally good), then it's morally flawed, as in Figure 7.2. If a comic, properly interpreted, prompts the reader to adopt the right moral attitudes (approving of that which is morally good, disapproving of that which is morally bad), then it's morally laudable, as in Figure 7.3.

In the same way that if I tell you that you should adopt an attitude of kindness and respect toward dogs, I'm doing something with positive moral value, *Captain America* #1 (1941) is morally good because it mandates disapproval of Nazism. Correspondingly, if I tell you that you should wantonly steal the ideas of others without crediting them, I'm doing something with negative moral

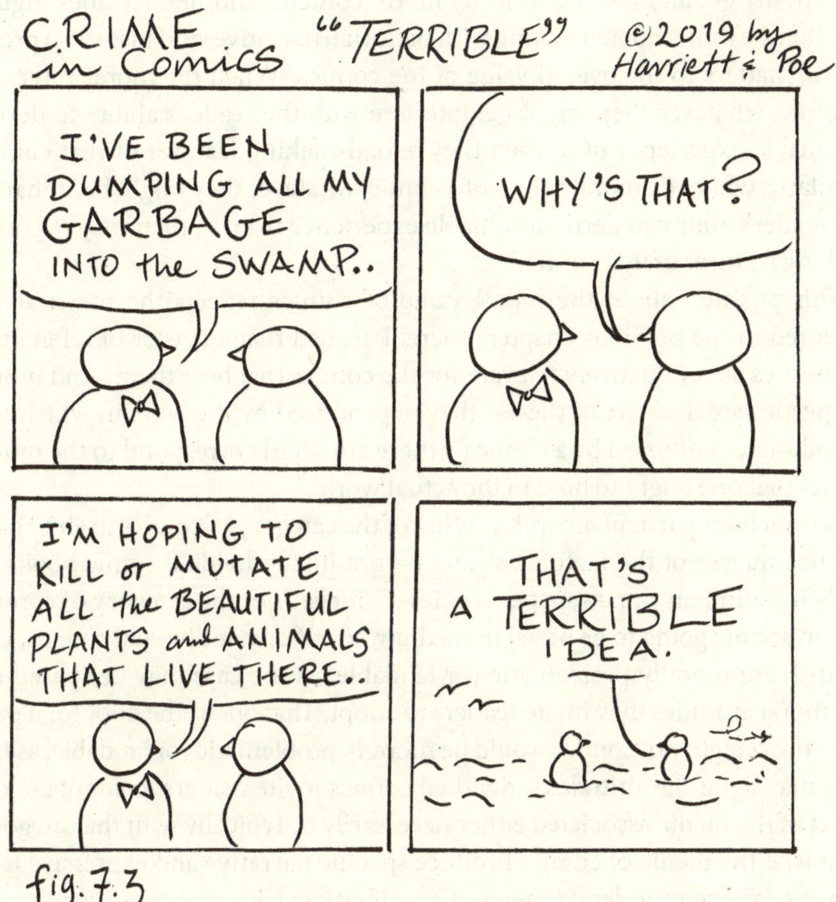

fig. 7.3

value, just as *Green Lantern* #54 (1994) is morally bad because it mandates viewing female suffering chiefly as a motivation for male action (Gail Simone deserves credit for exposing this "Women in Refrigerators" trope).

How exactly moral value affects value as work of art, if at all, is a fraught issue, about which I don't want to generalize here.[2] However, for comics, I think it's pretty clear that critics consider moral properties in their overall evaluative verdicts. That's not to say that being morally problematic necessarily entails that a comic is overall bad, or that being morally laudable necessarily entails that a comic is overall good. To offer some more concrete examples: Dave Sim's sexism doesn't by itself mean that *Cerebus* is a bad comic series, and the stance taken against teen drug addiction in the "Plague" issue of the *New Teen Titans* (1983) doesn't in itself mean that it's a good comic. Figure

7.2 doesn't get all its value from its moral content, and neither does Figure 7.3. But the moral content, along with pictorial, narrative, and historical properties, matters to the overall value of the comics. When the moral values of a comic, whatever they might be, interfere with the reader's ability to derive a valuable experience of it, then they're bad-making features of that comic. Similarly, when the moral values of a comic, whatever they might be, enhance the reader's ability to derive a valuable experience from it, then they're good-making features of that comic.

This position about the moral value of comics reflects the material we explored in the previous chapter. There, I argued that a cluster of referential properties are evaluatively relevant for the comics that bear them. And moral properties are a subset of these—they're produced by the ways in which the moral values endorsed by a comic (if there are such) correspond to the moral values that one ought to hold in the actual world.[3]

So much for particular comics. What of the category of comics itself? That's the real quarry of the Platonic strategy—not just individual comic books or daily installments of newspaper comics. Criticisms of the category of comics are invariably going to be based in medium specificity. Individual comics, I've argued, are morally problematic (or laudable, as the case may be) based on the moral attitudes they invite readers to adopt. That opens the door for a parallel: the category of comics would be morally problematic (or laudable, as the case may be) if the attitudes individual comics invite readers to adopt are the effect of the media associated either necessarily or typically with the category. That is, if the media of comics produce specific narrative and expressive tendencies (as even moderate medium specificity has it), and those tendencies are morally suspect, then the category of comics itself is morally suspect.

Overall, defenders of the category of comics against various permutations of the Platonic strategy have two possible avenues of response to it. One is to reject medium specificity. If the media of comics don't produce tendencies of any interesting kind, then it can't plausibly be argued that the category itself has negative moral value. For reasons that should be obvious at this point of the book, that's not the response I'll use. Rather, in the remainder of this chapter, I'll pursue the second available strategy: to argue that even though moderate medium specificity is correct, the media of comics are morally neutral. Comics media can be used for good or ill as one chooses (with one possible exception, to be considered later).

One quick comment before investigating the charges against comics. There's a risk that what we're confronting here is a straw man. If it were the case that, historically speaking, nobody has applied the Platonic strategy to comics, or if it were the case that it was just plain inapplicable, then responding to its attacks would be all too easy.

It's no straw man. There is a long, well-documented history of condemning the comics category itself (and not merely individual comics or comic subgenres) on moral grounds. Most prominently, as related briefly in Chapter 1, there was a surge of arguments against comics culminating in Fredric Wertham's *Seduction of the Innocent* (1954), a book that, together with associated social pressures, led to hearings on comic books in the US Senate and the establishment of the Comics Code Authority, a powerful self-censorship mechanism in the comics industry.[4] Furthermore, despite the growth of more reputable comics marketed as graphic novels, attacks on comics continue into the present. For example, a teacher in Guilford, Connecticut, was suspended not that long ago (see Arnott 2007) for assigning an issue of Dan Clowes's acclaimed *Eightball* series to a student as summer reading, and the problem seems not to have been the content (much more controversial content was deemed acceptable when conveyed in the form of literature), but the delivery of that content in a comic. Consider also a phenomenon I mentioned in the preface to this book: much academic work on comics is still introduced by disclaimers about the value of studying such a disreputable subject. And ask yourself which alternative typical parents in contemporary society would be more likely to be proud of: their child reading a comic, or their child reading a (nongraphic) novel. In general, people are worried about comics in a way that they are not worried about, e.g., novels. Addressing those worries, accordingly, is worthwhile.

7.2. Creators and Audiences

The means of producing comics are somewhat complex, at least when compared to paradigmatic works of literature. Comic production generally requires some combination of writing, layout, penciling, inking, lettering, and coloring (if applicable). Sometimes a single person does all of these tasks—most often in alternative or underground comics—but the vast majority of mainstream, mass-marketed comics are collaboratively created. Will Eisner likens the process to an assembly line: "We made comic book features pretty much the same way Ford made cars" (quoted in Wright 2001, 6).

Moreover, historically speaking, comics authors have tended to come from backgrounds of low social and economic status. Many of the pioneers in comics were immigrants to the United States or children of immigrants, and often Jewish (at a time when this put one at a significant disadvantage). As emphasized by David Hajdu (2008, chaps. 1 and 2), others were women, homosexuals, or African Americans, many driven to comics because they could not find work in more esteemed fields of art. Comics has been understood primarily as a lowbrow art form; correspondingly, the lack of respect typically afforded to comics authors has provided job opportunities for talented but marginalized individuals.

It seems unlikely that support for the Platonic strategy could be found by attending merely to the social or economic status of comics creators. While factors having to do with class, race, and gender no doubt contribute causally to hysteria about comics, to suggest that there's a significant correlation between these factors and either artistic talent or moral virtue is sheer bigotry. Moreover, the low status of comics authors can lead to experiments in both narrative and ethics that are rather difficult to achieve in more highbrow art forms, a point to which I'll return at the end of this chapter.

The fact that most comics have multiple authors does raise several interesting possibilities for critical attention. One is that group-think can overwhelm individual ethical qualms. Participants in the creation of a comic may feel pressure to go along with the others in crafting a narrative whose moral values they don't personally endorse. Alternatively, it might be argued that when multiple points of view are involved, it's less likely that a single, morally problematic vision will predominate. It's notable that underground and alternative comics, which typically express individual (or even idiosyncratic) values and sensibilities, tend to be much more morally controversial.

With this in mind, more forceful objections to comics as a narrative art form (again, I've argued that comics media lend themselves to narrativity) might target comics that are individual rather than collaborative productions. But is being the product of a distinctive moral vision enough to condemn an entire category of art? Probably not: the moral views of artists are just too widely divergent. For every Mike Diana (sole creator of the controversial *Boiled Angel*, convicted in Florida in 1994 on obscenity charges) there is an Art Spiegelman (sole creator of the powerful and acclaimed *Maus*). It would be hard to show that comics narratives by individual artists have such a high probability of inviting immoral responses or promoting immoral values that condemnation of comics as a category is justified.

However, what if we turn our attention from creators to audiences? If comics are created for audiences inappropriate to them, then even if their creators aren't at fault, there's something troubling about the art form that deserves attention. Stereotypically, the actual audience for comics, at least in the United States, is children and teenagers. But is this the audience that comics are created for? What is the relationship between the actual audience of comics and what Peter Rabinowitz (1977, 126) terms the *authorial audience*, the specific hypothetical readership for which an author designs their work?

A dilemma arises. If the authorial audience dovetails with the actual audience of children and teens, a significant portion of comics narratives is (intentionally) morally inappropriate for their actual audiences, because the narratives invite those audiences to respond in ways inappropriate for children. However, if the authorial audience for comics is adults—a common defense made by comics publishers against censorship—there might be a different problem. Rabinowitz claims that most authors "will only call upon those moral qualities which they believe the actual audience has in reserve, just as they try not to rely on information which we will not in fact possess" (1977, 126). Authors generally do this in order to minimize the gap between authorial and actual audiences. But if the authorial audience of comics is adults, and the actual audience isn't, then comics seem to function differently. Comics creators are calling on a set of moral qualities, particularly the capacity to exercise moral judgment, that they know their actual audience doesn't possess.

Though the first horn is pressing, I'll put off discussing it until we can take a closer look a bit later at the content of comics. The second horn can be confronted here. A disparity between actual and authorial audiences might interfere with reader uptake: when the actual audience isn't the intended audience, they might have difficulty reading the comic in the mandated way. However, this doesn't produce a moral failing in the comics themselves. At most, it's a moral (or perhaps just epistemic) failing of those who create and publish comics. If we accept the supposition of the second horn, we can, at most, criticize comics creators for going over the heads of their audience and comics publishers for dishonestly marketing to children narratives best suited for mature readers.

Attention to marketing reveals another potential avenue for criticizing comics. The real authorial audience, it may be argued, is just whoever will buy comics. Comics are produced with an eye to making the most profit possible from whatever readership for them can be found. Comics are not made for artistic fulfillment, but rather to move units—explaining why, among narrative art forms, they can be the cheapest, most disposable (what happens to newspaper comics once they're read?), and most instantly gratifying. The emphasis is on quantity over quality, and production via easily duplicated narrative formulas that are instantly familiar to the readers, but that give the impression of newness nonetheless. As Wertham puts it, "The writers of comic books rarely want to be professional crime-comic-writers. . . . They want to get their ten dollars a page and pay the rent. They do not write comic book stories for artistic or emotional self-expression" (1954, 263). Even celebrated comics authors like Spiegelman, Wertham would no doubt claim, are working with mass media, and even they want to get paid.

Concentrating on mass media and the profit motive, Theodor Adorno famously crafted an argument against popular music along Platonic lines.[5] Transposed to the category of comics, it might look something like this:

1. Comics use mass media, in that its components are cheap, easy to use and understand, and easily disseminated to great numbers of people.
2. So comics are commodities created for their exchange value.
3. The goal of creating something for exchange value is incompatible with the goal of creating something with aesthetic value (which is supposed to stand apart from everyday concerns and interests).
4. Therefore, the media of comics interfere with the production of aesthetic value.

This argument clearly bears on the *aesthetic* value of comics, but does it tell us anything about their *moral* value? Perhaps: Adorno thinks that works of mass media prevent "the development of autonomous, independent individuals who judge and decide consciously for themselves. These, however, would be the precondition for a democratic society which needs adults who have come of age in order to sustain itself and develop" (1975, 19). In effect, when the media used in the production of art forms render those art forms largely incapable of providing access to expressive, autonomous art, they fail to nurture us as moral beings—at root, a very Platonic concern.

While the Adorno-style argument could well be used to target individual comics, does it ground a conclusion about the art form itself? It's hard to imagine that Gary Panter had exchange value in mind when he wrote *Jimbo in Purgatory*. Examples of this kind show that premise 2 seems to be a flawed account of the exclusive motivation of comics authors. Furthermore, even if they retain economic motivations, artists like Lynda Barry, Will Eisner, Mike Mignola, Marjane Satrapi, Chris Ware, and countless others produce works that are highly expressive aesthetically. Premise 3, then, is false. At most, the argument shows that comics are *generally* commodities and not artworks. Then too, one might respond that even generic, mass-marketed superhero comics can provide rich aesthetic and moral experiences. The narratives presented in these comics allow readers to exercise their imaginative capacities, to contemplate contrasts between good and evil, to think about prejudice and the sociocultural nature of the self (issues nearly all superheroes face), and, perhaps, to an even greater extent than the novel, to engage in empathetic exploration of the minds of others.

7.3. Reading Process and Format

Several other potential medium-specific criticisms arise from attention to the format of comics and the process of reading the narratives that they present. Regardless of whether they appear in a printed or electronic format, comics have a strong tendency to be issued in easily digested installments. Comic books are small, short, and eminently portable. Webcomics are designed to fit easily on the screen of a personal computer or smartphone. Newspaper comics (where these still exist in print) fit to the page and arrive and depart daily. By and large, comics technology is much less sophisticated than, e.g., film technology: comics are easily produced, affordable, and disposable.[6]

In addition, the processes of reading comics and paradigmatic works of literature like novels have some strong similarities. As we saw in Chapter 4, readers of comics, like readers of literary works, control the pace of their engagement with the text. To summarize: in film, narratives are presented at a rate predetermined for the viewer by the filmmakers, whereas comics creators exert far less temporal control over the reading experience. It's the readers themselves who, via closure, have to make sense of spatiotemporal relations within the diegesis. As a result, the process of reading comics is particular to each individual. It's private and personal rather than public and shared.

The private, individual nature of reading comics, combined with their financial accessibility and ease of concealment, motivate one of Wertham's chief concerns (1954, 300). Reading comics, in contrast to viewing film, is almost impossible to supervise. Mature adults are unable to exert moral authority over the reception of narratives the experience of which is highly privatized. "We who care about things," Wertham writes on behalf of parents concerned with the comics their children are reading, "feel so helpless" (1954, 300). Accordingly, because of the nature of the media in which comics are published, they have a high potential both to contravene public, social standards of appropriate conduct, and to do so in a way that cannot easily be corrected.

Is it possible to use this variant of the Platonic strategy on comics without also condemning nongraphic literature? Not likely. Literature, particularly in the form of novels, is often held to contribute positively to the moral development of readers.[7] But literature shares all of the same aspects of comics that are being targeted by this line of argumentation—books are relatively inexpensive, just as portable as comics, and read privately through a process that involves unsupervised, individual construction of narratives.[8] Condemnation of comics risks inconsistency: unless something else can be found that differentiates them, comics and literature rise or fall together as narrative art forms. And because literature seems not to be susceptible to medium-specific objections on this score, comics should not be either.

While there is, as we'll see shortly, a significant difference between comics and literature that could be used to drive a wedge between them, I want first to draw attention to another potential difficulty stemming from publication format. Because comics, at least in comic book form, are short, they are susceptible to a medium-specific concern similar to that about broadcast television articulated by George Gerbner and Larry Gross, as described by Nehamas (1988, 220). On their analysis, narratives on television are typically short in viewing duration—either twenty-two or forty-two minutes of programmed content, give or take. Gerbner and Gross point out that a viewing audience expects narratives to be largely resolved within that time frame, and claim that the simplest and most effective resolution comes through action, often in the form of violence. The violent nature of much television programming is not an accident, but a by-product of the temporal constraints that have been imposed conventionally by the media.

It would be more difficult to take the attack of Gerbner and Gross on television seriously after the streaming revolution, which encourages long-form serialized shows with narrative arcs stretched over multiple episodes. Most comic books are like that—with an overarching plot line that is parceled out in small installments. The key to serialized television and comics is not a quick, violent resolution (though many comics are indeed violent), but just enough resolution to satisfy readers while simultaneously priming them for the next installment. Plot lines in comics can last for many issues, graphic novels tend to be increasingly lengthy (*Bone* runs for 1,332 pages), and manga can be thousands of pages long. Comics narratives have the potential to be quite sophisticated.

Perhaps the equivalent of Gerbner and Gross's argument could be better applied to newspaper comics. After all, these rarely feature any serialization nowadays, so any narrative resolution must occur within the space of just a few panels. Attention to newspaper comics, however, reveals that there's another way to tidy up narrative strands quickly: with a punch line. Unless humor is morally problematic in itself, it's hard to see how gag comics are rendered objectionable because of their format.

The real nail in the coffin for Gerbner and Gross is that no one tends to equate brevity in literature with moral deficiency. Short stories aren't any more immoral as an art form than epic fantasy. Hemingway isn't any more immoral than Proust. So why should brevity, where present, be a problem for comics?

Nonetheless, comics and (paradigmatic) literary texts do have one obvious, glaring difference. Comics use pictures. They can narrate mimetically, showing rather than merely telling. In Chapter 3, Section 3.4, I argued that the narrative capacities of comics media make them well suited for instructional and educational purposes. In part, that's because picture recognition is a basic skill and easily acquired. Consequently, comics are readily accessible to children, even when semiliterate.

Most comics are drawn (rather than created photographically). What's depicted is limited only by the visual skill and, importantly, the taste of the artist. In consequence, comics is a predominantly narrative art form that's inexpensive to create and purchase, but whose content is restricted only by the moral scruples (if any) of its creators. If we combine these medium-specific traits with the accessibility of comics and the corresponding presumption that they're mainly read by children, we find grounds for moral concern. Consider a pivotal moment of the 1954 US Senate hearings: the testimony of Bill Gaines, publisher of EC Comics. As related by Hajdu (2008, 270), referring to the cover of a recent issue of one of EC's publications, *Crime SuspenStories*, Tennessee senator Estes Kefauver said, "This seems to be a man with a bloody axe holding a woman's head up, which has been severed from her body. Do you think that is in good taste?" Gaines replied, "Yes sir, I do, for the cover of a horror comic. A cover in bad taste, for example, might be defined as holding the head a little higher so that the neck could be seen dripping blood from it and moving the body over a little further so that the neck of the body could be seen to be bloody."

Effectively, Gaines's argument was that the cover was tasteful *because it could have been worse*. This was not a reason that the American public was prepared to endorse. The artists and publishers of comics appeared to have no good moral standards. But do comics really lend themselves to such unfiltered, tasteless content? Do they invite their readership, including children, to respond approvingly to depictions of decapitation and worse? The next section explores in more depth the issues at stake in Gaines's reply—issues that bring us into the domain of the narrative content of comics.

7.4. Content

The medium-specific qualms about comics that ground the Platonic strategy would seem to have to focus on the *ways* in which comics represent, the "how" of storytelling instead of the "what." Media, as I defined them in Chapter 3, are just the resources used in the production of a work, surrounded by a set of norms for the use of those resources. That's neutral about content, including moral content. And the media of comics, largely pictorial and verbal, are no exception. In this, I've tried to follow McCloud's aspiration to "do a little aesthetic surgery to separate form from content . . . the trick is never to mistake the message for the messenger" (1993, 5–6). This is what Berel Lang calls the *neutralist* model of the relation between form and content (1990, 11), as distinguished from the *interaction* model (1990, 18).

Can form and content really be severed as neatly as the neutralist thinks? Interestingly enough, when considering the attempt to condemn the category of comics on moral grounds, the answer doesn't really matter. On the one hand, if interactionism is true, and form and content can't be separated, to critique the narrative content of comics is to critique the category itself. On the other hand, if neutralism is true, and form and content *can* be separated, there might still be something about the form of comics that produces strong, if not inevitable or irresistible, tendencies toward certain content. If it could be shown that comics naturally (even if not essentially) lends itself to narratives that mandate or invite morally problematic attitudes and responses, then medium specificity would commit us to a Platonic condemnation of it.

So where could we locate the immoral content of comics? Not in genre. Although some genres of comics might tend toward content that merits scrutiny (crime, horror, and romance are probably the easiest targets—not to mention pornographic subgenres like Tijuana bibles or hentai manga), others (talking animal, biography, newspaper gag) seem harmless. More propitious lines of argumentation, then, would focus on commonalities of narrative content across the category of comics instead of on particular genres.

One such commonality returns our focus to creation and marketing. The creators of comics, as noted earlier, tend to be outliers, historically afforded little respect within the artworld and society in general. Outsider status, combined with the marketing need to appeal to a youthful demographic and the sense of rebellion it involves, might suggest that comics creators have a strong tendency to produce narratives that reflect a deep subversiveness and cynicism about the mainstream values that have pushed both the creators and audiences of comics aside. Batman is a case in point: like many superheroes, he is at odds with figures of government who fail to provide for public safety. Because *Batman* narratives represent the titular hero approvingly, they invite the adoption of negative attitudes about authority and the law, and misrepresent appropriate and just social structures.

Whether one finds this type of objection to comics compelling will depend on one's stance regarding authority and the proper function of the state. On one end of the spectrum is the view that the state has no de jure (legitimate) authority, but only de facto authority (in virtue of its power). On this view, espoused by the likes of Robert Paul Wolff (1970), questioning the authority of the state may be imprudent, but it is also a praiseworthy exercise of moral autonomy—so comics would be morally commendable. While his view about authority is rather different, even Plato (at least the Plato of the early dialogues) leaves the door open for warranted criticism of an unjust state: his claim that "if you cannot persuade your country you must do whatever it orders" (1961, *Crito* 51b) at least allows the attempt to persuade.

Only under a very strong (or even autocratic) political theory according to which the state may never be questioned will comics turn out to be a problematic on the grounds of general subversiveness. Furthermore, comics seems to afford opportunities for questioning authority in very personal, particular ways. Because technology provides few obstacles to the creation of comics, and because of its position outside the more established artistic forms, comics is well suited for giving voice to the narratives of marginalized people. For instance, Satrapi's *Persepolis* (the story of an Iranian woman), Paul and Judy Karsik's *The Ride Together* (about growing up with autism), and even Jack Kirby and Stan Lee's *The Fantastic Four* (The Thing's experience of growing up in the Brooklyn ghetto closely follows Kirby's) have allowed their creators to present empowerment narratives that facilitate reader understanding of diverse perspectives. Arguably, this is a morally commendable aspect of comics, rather than fodder for a condemnation grounded in medium specificity.

It's possible, however, that another strong tendency in comics trumps this positive aspect: the pull toward caricature. By caricature, I mean roughly the depictive style marked by simplification, distortion, or exaggeration of features of the human face and body. Caricature can occur in depictions of actual, individual humans (Richard Nixon, Joseph McCarthy, Donald Trump, the Clintons) by means of a cartooned style (see Chapter 1, Section 1.3). Examples can be found in politically inclined newspaper comics like *Pogo*, *Doonesbury*, and *Mallard Fillmore*. But caricature can also occur when comics depict characters who are members of racial, ethnic, and cultural groups by using exaggerated traits stereotypically associated with those groups. Caricatures of Africans and Afro-descendants (e.g., Windsor McCay's Jungle Imp, Steamboat in 1940s Captain Marvel comics, too many *Tintin* comics to mention) are a case in point, as are the caricatures of the Japanese prevalent in American comics during World War II.

Caricature isn't unique to comics by any means. It's found in editorial cartoons and made by fairground sketch artists. But it's still connected closely to comics. Many comics histories locate the historical origins of comics in caricature. And the proclivity for caricature in comics has persisted, for medium-specific reasons that we've encountered before (in Chapter 1, Section 1.3). If an artist is trying to draw a particular person or general kind of person identifiably at the small scale at which comics are typically printed, caricature is an easy way to do it, especially given the time constraints under which most comics artists work.

Christy Mag Uidhir plausibly links the means by which caricatures increase our ability to identify persons to the psychological mechanism of peak shift (2013a, 140–42). The unrealistic exaggeration in caricature is a superstimulus: viewers respond more strongly to it than they do to the nonreinforced stimuli provided by more realistic depictions. According to Mag Uidhir, the effect thereof is the potential for non-ideally rational viewers (i.e., all of us) to acquire or take as supported what are unjustified beliefs about the subject of the caricature.

That's a little abstract, so an example might help. Caricatures of Richard Nixon consistently exaggerated the size of his nose and the jowliness of his chin. Because it's a superstimulus, a caricature of Nixon is instantly and easily recognizable as Nixon (at least to those familiar with how Nixon looked). To the degree that a large nose and jowly chin are viewed as unattractive, the degree to which we're disposed to think of Nixon as unattractive and even vicious in character is reinforced by the caricatures (through, perhaps, the long-standing association of physical attractiveness with moral virtue, which Nixon conspicuously lacked).

And that's troubling. As Mag Uidhir is at pains to point out, caricatures, qua distortions, simplifications, and exaggerations, don't accurately depict reality. They aren't reliable sources of knowledge about the world—they're epistemically defective. But our ways of processing them cognitively make it easy for us to *take* them as reliable sources of knowledge, which is a mistake. Moreover, when caricature is used (as in editorial cartoons—Mag Uidhir's main subject) to convey a morally relevant message (e.g., Nixon is untrustworthy), the grounds of that message are suspect, undermining the justification for the message itself. Regardless of the particular moral content of a caricature, viewers are being epistemically manipulated to endorse that content, even though they don't have any warrant to do so.

It's indisputable that the tendency of comics to use caricature has led to many morally problematic results. Any casual survey of the history of depiction in comics will turn up a shocking amount of overtly bigoted caricatures of racial, ethnic, and cultural groups. In fact, it's those caricatures that drive parts of Wertham's attack on comics. While Wertham makes many scientifically and psychologically dubious claims, his description of many of the comics of his time isn't far off, and here at least, his heart is in the right place. These comics, he writes, represent two kinds of people. On the one hand, there are the white, "regular-featured" superheroes and "the pretty blond girl with the super-breast"; on the other, there are "the inferior people: natives, primitives, savages, 'ape men,' Negroes, Jews, Indians, Italians, Slavs, Chinese, and Japanese, immigrants of every description, people with irregular features, swarthy skins, physical deformities, Oriental features" (1954, 101). When it comes to the latter kind, Wertham argues, the negative and prejudicial attitudes of children are sometimes directly "derived from crime comic books"; sometimes, "distorted stereotypes acquired at home, on the street, in school, are given new nourishment and perpetuation by comic-book reading" (1954, 101), presumably through the peak shift mechanism.

The shameful legacy of caricature in comics shouldn't be minimized, and requires persistent vigilance and attention if it's to be avoided in the future. Should we, however, take caricature to provide sufficient support for the claim that comics as a whole can be castigated on moral grounds?

One thing to keep in mind is that not all comics caricature. Comics that use photographs and photorealistic illustrations don't have to engage in the exaggeration or distortion central to caricature. And not all comics depict actual individuals or actual groups of individuals—there's nothing in those comics *to* caricature. Accordingly, the entire category of comics itself can't be morally problematic, just the subset of comics that uses caricature.

Furthermore, as Mag Uidhir himself indicates, not all caricature is worrisome. Using newspaper comics like *Garfield* as examples, Mag Uidhir writes: "Cartoons with purely suppositional uptake look radically ill-suited to satisfy the sorts of epistemic aims taken to be the editorial *sine qua non*" (2013a, 145). That is, there is a substantial class of comics that do not aim to persuade or inform readers based on their depictive content. Instead of inviting readers to believe that the world is as the comic depicts, readers are merely invited to imagine what the world would be like if the characters represented looked the way that they're depicted. Given that readers are not expected to form beliefs about the actual world based on such comics, caricature within them isn't epistemically problematic, and that avoids any moral shadiness associated with epistemic manipulation.

We should also attend to a positive aspect of caricature in comics. Consider that Walt Kelly's caricatures of Joseph McCarthy in *Pogo* (beginning in May 1953) grounded what were among the first and most socially visible critiques of McCarthy's odious and repressive brand of politics. Mag Uidhir might be right that Kelly's caricatures are epistemically defective, using peak shift effects to produce the unwarranted belief that McCarthy was evil. Still, McCarthy *was* evil. His downfall was to the benefit of the United States and its citizens. According to at least one prominent tradition of ethical theory—consequentialism, of which utilitarianism of various stripes is the predominant subset—lack of epistemic warrant doesn't undermine this verdict. As the term for the tradition reflects, consequentialists believe that outcomes are all that we should pay attention to when engaging in moral evaluation. Hence, if a given caricature in a comic has the right kinds of outcome (e.g., maximizing human well-being in comparison to available alternatives), it's moral to use. And that would be despite any epistemic misgivings one might have about it.

Last, the presence of caricature in comics, and the cartooning style in general, has an important result. It enables the articulation of alternative viewpoints, expression of which is largely forbidden in more "reputable" contexts. Caricature and cartooning's prima facie opposition to representational fidelity provides a partial explanation for the perception that comics, like the Punch and Judy puppet shows of old, is not to be taken all that seriously. Paradoxically, the fact that comics are not regarded as serious allows them to be used to convey serious and profound qualms about the political establishment and prevailing institutional mores. Political cartoons are obvious (and common) examples. It's *because Pogo* was a comic that Kelly could get away with trenchant excoriation of McCarthyism that might not have been possible in more esteemed art forms.

Of course some comics caricature. And caricature can be used for morally unacceptable purposes. Many individual comics deserve condemnation on these grounds. However, since not all comics caricature, and since caricature can also be used for praiseworthy purposes—e.g., to reveal otherwise unspeakable truths about matters of social injustice—comics as a category cannot be condemned simply because of its reliance on caricature.

7.5. Conclusions

Despite its ancient origins, the Platonic strategy is still very much with us, and shows no signs of going away any time soon. Surely its proponents are right that there are comics that have content that's morally objectionable. Whether the existence of immoral comics should be met with any form of censorship by the state or the industry is a different, if related issue. Without going into detail here, suffice it to say that there are arguably greater values in play, such as freedom of expression, that can come into conflict with the obligation to protect the vulnerable from immoral content, and it's not always clear which should triumph.

Regardless, censorship has a real risk of suppressing comics that it shouldn't. That's an entailment of the failure of the best versions of the Platonic strategy to reach the conclusion that the category of comics itself is immoral or socially problematic. To object to comics itself on medium-specific grounds, the most plausible options are to claim that artworks made by certain marginalized creators are generally unethical, that mass media such as those comics use cannot contribute to the development of ethical persons, or that subversion of dominant social paradigms through caricature or otherwise is generally unethical. While there could be other variants of the Platonic strategy I haven't encountered or tackled, I hope to have shown that these arguments, at least, are untenable.

More generally, perhaps comics can serve as a test case for the intersection of medium specificity and moral condemnation of entire art forms. If strong arguments against comics, long thought one of the most disreputable arts, can't be found, then it's probable that condemnations of television, video games, various internet interfaces like YouTube, and the like can't be found either. Defenders of moderate medium specificity of the type I've laid out in this book, let alone comics, have one less thing to worry about.

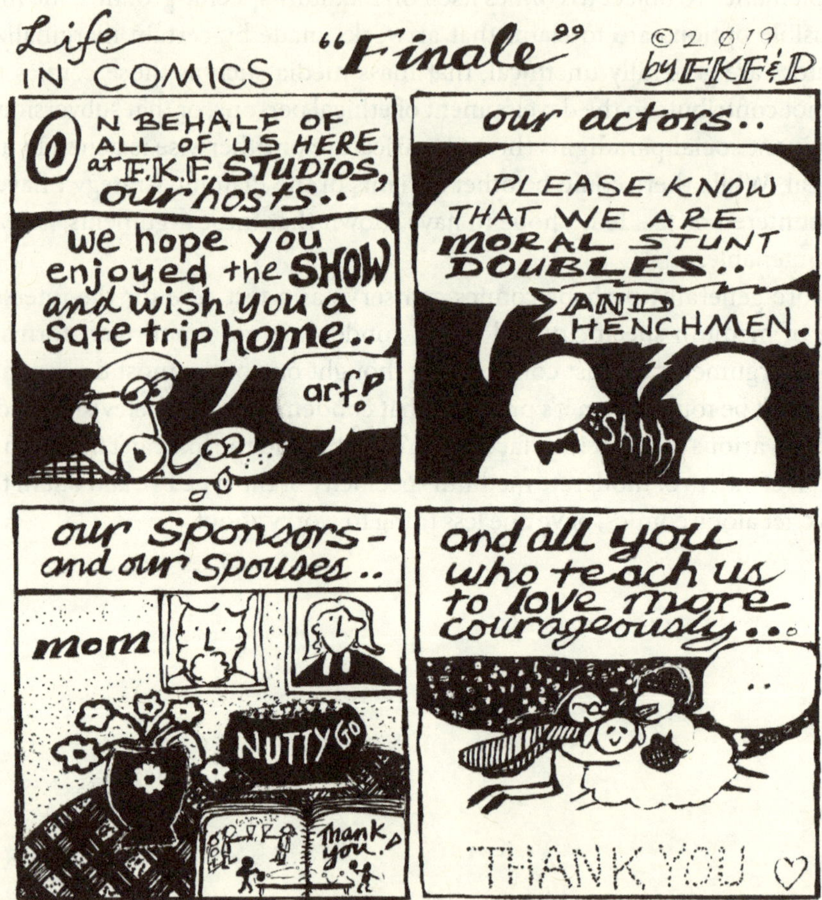
Life
IN COMICS
"Finale"
©2019
by FKF&P
ON BEHALF OF ALL OF US HERE at F.K.F. STUDIOS, our hosts..
we hope you enjoyed the SHOW and wish you a safe trip home..
arf!
our actors..
PLEASE KNOW THAT WE ARE MORAL STUNT DOUBLES..
AND HENCHMEN.
Shhh
our sponsors- and our spouses..
mom
NUTTY GO
thank you.
and all you who teach us to love more courageously...
THANK YOU ♡

Fig A.1

Afterword

The subtitle of this book, which I haven't really mentioned, yet refers to definitions, functions, and value of comics. At this point, it should be fairly obvious why that's appropriate.

We started out by getting our heads around what sorts of things are and aren't comics, then surveyed possible ways of defining the category essentially. While the latter might ultimately end up as a futile endeavor, in that an essentialist definition immune to counterexamples will never be forthcoming, it's worthwhile to have attempted. By engaging with comics philosophically in this way, we've achieved a greater understanding of the sorts of features they do and don't have, and have gained a greater appreciation for the sheer variety of comics that have been and continue to be made.

Even if an essentialist definition can't be found, something substantive can be said about the media characteristically used by comics and the norms that surround their use. These media, I've shown, exert interesting kinds of pressures on comics—captured by the position I call moderate medium specificity. Along with making comics particularly suitable for use in instructional and medical contexts, their media yield a tendency toward narrativity. Comics has evolved its own ways of regulating readers' attention. How individual comics function as delivery systems for temporal and spatial relationships is quite complex, and takes a good deal of work to unpack. And while what can be portrayed in comics isn't unique to them (contra strong medium specificity), there are some narrative techniques that emerge easily and smoothly from comics media that are much more challenging to achieve using media associated with other art forms. That's why comics can't be perfectly adapted into film, even though the two bear significant similarities such that adaptation from one to the other is about as straightforward as it's going to get.

Finally, I took up the little-discussed issue of evaluative standards for comics. I argued that some degree of relativism in evaluating particular comics is probably inevitable, but that we can make some moves to mitigate some of relativism's more counterintuitive consequences. Judging from what's cited in critical practice, four kinds of properties are relevant to the evaluation of comics: narrative properties, pictorial properties, historical properties, and referential properties. What they have in common is that they all contribute to valuable experiences that readers can have. Moreover, they're the properties selected as valuable from the comics world context, and given the media that comics use, it's no surprise that these types of properties were selected. Among the referential properties are those that contribute to the moral value of particular comics. While this value is sometimes negative, the comics category itself can't be condemned on moral grounds, and, ultimately, extant applications of the Platonic strategy toward comics are unsuccessful.

Although the book is called *The Philosophy of Comics*, a more appropriate, if less authoritative-sounding title might be *A Philosophy of Comics*. Use of the definite article implies a kind of finality or uniqueness that the indefinite article does not. And I'm under no illusion—nor do I want to give the impression—that what I've offered here in any way represents the definitive stance on the subject. The positions for which I've argued are contestable, controversial, and (in more than one place) probably wrong (for reasons I've not yet considered).

Furthermore, even a work of this length can't possibly cover all of the philosophically interesting features of comics. There are a host of topics that I've neglected. Let me suggest a few of these and then gesture at where the philosophy of comics might go from here. (Note that this is not an exhaustive list: others will have different interests and will be able to envision directions that I either haven't or can't.)

Though definitions of comics have been covered extensively at this point (relatively speaking), the ontology of comics deserves more attention. That is, while philosophers and others have offered plenty of ideas about how the category could be defined (if at all), less investigation has focused on whether comics are essentially multiples, the metaphysical status of the autograph copy as compared to reproductions of it, authenticity and forgery, and the like. Meskin (2012) has offered a characteristically thoughtful treatment of some but not all of these questions, but there's a lot more territory to explore.

While there's well-established theorizing about authorship and collective intentions for literature and film, there's considerably less for comics (see, for notable exceptions, Mag Uidhir 2012 and Mitchell 2017). But comics provide a marvelous variety of test cases for such theorizing. And there's the possibility that the authoring of comics is in some ways novel or incompatible with extant theories.

Like all art forms, comics is confronted with the digital revolution in intriguing ways. I think speculation about where comics are going is largely pointless and bound to be rapidly outdated. McCloud's *Reinventing Comics* (2000), significantly concerned with digital methods of making and disseminating comics, has not aged well. Rather, philosophers and other theorists could look at ways in which comics actually have evolved to use new, digital media, and what this evolution implies (if anything) about comics' metaphysical status, medium-specific tendencies, and value.

There's a lot of work that can be done on comics across cultures. That work is, admittedly, conspicuously absent from this book. Some of the more general claims I make could be problematized by attending to comics worlds that diverge in interesting ways from the Western tradition on which I concentrate, implying that what I've offered is more limited in scope than I make it out to be. My "standard history" ignores the alternate histories of comics across the globe, which are likely to provide correspondingly alternative exemplars and challenges than those I've considered.[1] To take a small case in point: Neil Cohn has established that the meaning-making linguistic functions of comics vary among American, Australian, and Japanese styles (2013, sec. 2). It would be interesting to investigate further to see what lessons can be drawn from these differences.

Just as the philosophy of art was enriched and revolutionized by the shift from attending predominantly to art in general to attending to individual art forms like comics, so the philosophy of comics can be enriched by attending to comics genres and subcategories. While I've framed this book around the properties that all types of comics have in common, there are also ways in which they differ. Some of this work has been done already (see the articles in Bramlett, Cook, and Meskin 2017, sec. 2), but mainly in an exploratory form.

Last, the social and political aspects of comics could use more attention than I've been able to give them. While I think that there's no good reason to condemn comics as an entire art form, digging into the ways in which particular comics or comics genres have functioned in the transmission and propagation of various worldviews, for good or ill, is a fascinating project. Books like Fredrik Stromberg and Peter Kuper's *Comic Art Propaganda* (2010) and Paul S. Hirsch's *Pulp Empire* (2021) are an excellent start.

In the preface to this book, I mentioned a previously obligatory disclaimer that had to be made when theorizing about comics. I indicated that this is no longer necessary, because the endeavor and the art form have become increasingly respectable. This raises an odd question: if it's now acceptable to take comics seriously, does that mean that comics have, in some significant way, died? Here's what I mean. Many popular art forms are at their most vital when they retain a whiff of disreputability. When they lose the latter, they tend to lose the former. Jazz, I think, might be a good example. To simplify rather drastically, jazz started out as dance music made by African Americans in rejection of European concert norms. It was seedy and dangerous. Now Wynton Marsalis and others play it at Lincoln Center. Philosophers and other theorists aren't looked down on for taking it seriously, but that's because what made it interesting in the first place has gone away.

I'm more optimistic about the present and future of comics than I am about the present and future of jazz. True, newspaper comics, in print form, began dying a slow death long before the decline of the daily newspaper, to the extent that many of the examples I use of them in this book might strike contemporary audiences as woefully bygone. Newspaper comics are rapidly passing into a phase in which the primary interest will be largely historical, and no philosophically or evaluatively noteworthy developments seem to be on the horizon.

Sales of comic books, too, are down in comparison to Wertham's time (television filled the void) and after the collecting and speculation craze died down. But here I think we should worry less. Economic trends might just be a matter of bubbles bursting and comic books settling into their natural audiences. And it's not like comic books are getting worse. While there will always be irredeemable stinkers, I firmly believe that the average comic book, across genres, is considerably better now than it was even twenty years ago. In this particular case, I think that comics is *benefiting* from increased respectability rather than being harmed by it. More respectability draws more talent. Comics isn't just a fallback for those who can't hack it in the fine arts, but a destination for serious writers and artists, many of whom deliberately move into comics after honing their skills working in traditionally respectable fare.

So, in closing, it's my hope that the publication of this book doesn't mark the death of comics at all. Rather, it's a reflection of their increased importance, influence, and fascinating qualities. Thank you for reading; perhaps something I've said will help you push the study of comics, or even comics itself, into the future.

Notes

Chapter 1

1. Throughout this book, I will use "author" as an umbrella term that encompasses all persons whose creative contributions produce the aesthetically relevant features of a comic (this roughly follows the account given in Mag Uidhir 2012). In most typical cases, these include whoever drew it and whoever wrote it: these can be the same or multiple persons. But authors can also, under some circumstances, include inkers, colorists, letterers, assistants, editors, and so forth.
2. This historical account is drawn from sources that include Carlin, Karasik, and Walker 2005; Crouch 2001; Duncan and Smith 2009; Harvey 1996, 1998, 2009; Kukkonen 2013; Kunzle 2009; Levitz 2015; Postema 2013; Robinson 1974; and Waugh 1947. Each of these historians of comics has a particular take on the category and its subcategories, and each is worth consulting for fuller, more accurate studies than I have given here. The major exception to the standard history is Scott McCloud, whose ahistorical formalist definition of comics implies that they go back thousands and thousands of years. We'll deal with this implication of McCloud's theory in Chapter 2.
3. It's worth emphasizing that the examples given in this thumbnail history are neither the first nor the only of their kind. I've included them mainly because of their influence and familiarity—some are even still in print, albeit by different authors.
4. Because of the "shop system," in which comics were produced in assembly-line fashion, authorship for comic books tends to be much more fraught than in the case of newspaper comics, resulting in numerous legal battles. Publishers had all the power (Siegel and Shuster notoriously sold all of the rights to Superman to National for $130), and in many cases continue to maintain that power. For this reason—not the minimization of the importance of authors and creators—I will in what follows sometimes associate particular comic books and superheroes with their publisher rather than their creators and subsequent authors.
5. Harvey's use of the Columbus Principle is instructive, but the reference to Waugh is shifty: Waugh (1947, 28) is actually writing about Bud Fisher's *Mutt and Jeff*, not Outcault, in the passage where he brings up Columbus.
6. Beaty offers an interesting discussion of American chauvinism in comics histories (2012, 28–30), in which he claims that a persistent effect thereof is ignoring the formal properties of comics in service of legitimating their place in society.
7. For a succinct history of manga, see Gravett 2004.
8. Though Grant Morrison makes some rather metaphysically extravagant claims to the contrary (see 2011, 274–78, 401).
9. For the inspiration for this sequence, one that includes two more pictures in the spectrum, see McCloud 1993, 29.
10. What I'm calling the cartoon style admits of plenty of variation in realism, as Joseph Witek has shown (2012, 29–34) in his discussion of what he calls the "cartoon mode" (more simplified) and the "naturalistic mode" (more realistic, but still cartoons).

11. For a good compendium of his images, see Ross 2005.
12. Indeed, Tom Scioli, artist and cowriter of *Transformers vs. G.I. Joe*, says, "That's something I realized about modern comics production is that the printing is so faithful, you can make very small bits of information that are perfectly legible, especially when you employ a cartoon visual vocabulary" (Scioli and Barber 2017, ch. 3 commentary). In comic books, at least, printing improvements are compensating for small size. Note, however, that Scioli is still working in a cartoon style—it's not like better printing has driven him to photorealism (perhaps due to the other reasons brought up in this section).
13. The authors I've listed were among those presented in the *Masters of American Comics* exhibition at the Hammer Museum and the Museum of Contemporary Art, Los Angeles in 2005–6 (see Carlin, Karasik, and Walker 2005). Beaty tells us (2012, 197) that the curators' explicit goal, posted at the exhibition, was to establish a canon of artists who work in comics. By the way, I don't think it's accidental that they're all men.
14. The evaluative sense is first described by Morris Weitz (1956, 33), and contrasted with what he called the *descriptive* sense. The chair analogy in the next paragraph is partially borrowed from Weitz. George Dickie (1974, 25–27) later used the term "classificatory" for the descriptive sense. I follow Dickie here as I think talk of classifying captures the practice I'm discussing better than talk of describing.
15. See Nzegwu 2019 for a provocative argument that Western art theory in general is systematically racist and a deracialized alternative.
16. In Pratt 2012d, I argue that when something is an artwork in the modern, classificatory sense of the term, it acquires *artistic recognition value*: it becomes the sort of thing that we can evaluate artistically. But that's rather different from acquiring *artistic appraisal value*, which an artwork only has to the degree that it has properties that merit a positive assessment. This distinction will become relevant again at the end of Chapter 6.
17. Qualitative identity is often contrasted with *quantitative* identity. To the extent that twins are identical, they're qualitatively identical: they look the same, but there's more than one of them. In contrast, Superman and Clark Kent are quantitatively identical: there's only one person there (in two different outfits).
18. This debate plays out in theories from Carroll (1994), Davies (1991, 1997), Dickie (1974, 1984), Levinson (1979, 1989), and Stecker (1997), among many others.
19. Beaty claims that comics have been studied and classified as literature within academia largely because they are all but ignored by art and art history departments (2012, 18).

Chapter 2

1. Some philosophical bookkeeping: while I am referring to properties in this explanation, I intend the term to be as metaphysically neutral as possible. That is, I intend no commitment to any particular account of properties: those with an aversion to "property talk" are welcome to substitute their favored alternative.
2. In fact, in metaphilosophy, there's a fairly popular position according to which philosophical problems are just *identified* by the uncertainty of their answers (see most famously Russell 1998, 87, 90).
3. See, for example, Levinson 2005.
4. See Dickie 1964.
5. For a full discussion of pantomime comics, replete with examples, see Postema 2016.

6. This notion of what it is to be a picture is highly controversial, and has been rejected by a number of prominent philosophers (see, famously, Goodman 1968). Settling the issue, or indeed taking much of a defensible stance on it is far beyond the scope of this book. However, as far as I can tell, nothing in Cook's theory discussed in this section hinges on any particular account of the pictorial. Hence, any criticisms I make of it shouldn't be operating under assumptions that he'd call into question—at least, not any assumptions about the nature of pictures.
7. It's not terribly unusual for trade paperbacks or other collections of comics to be filled out with illustrated prose stories that are, in form, exactly like *Batman* #663. For example, see "Jimmy Turtle and the Legendary Boxcar of Well-Made Ladies Shoes," which concludes *The Goon: Virtue and the Grim Consequences Thereof* (Powell 2006); or "Black Cybertron," bonus material at the end of *Transformers vs. G.I. Joe* (Scioli and Barber 2017). The only real difference between *Batman* #663 and these seems to be that the former, but not the latter, was published as a stand-alone issue within the series, and not mere bonus material. But why should that make it a comic while the others aren't?
8. That's not to say that any work that isn't pictorial isn't narrative. Obviously, nongraphic literature can be narrative even without any pictures. But when nonpictorial images are completely abstract, the idea goes, they don't represent anything, and if they don't represent anything, they can't represent events in a sequence in the way that narrativity requires.
9. To see that separation rendered literally, see Figure 4.7.

Chapter 3

1. Yes, Arnheim and Bazin have incompatible views. And yes, as Carroll has pointed out (2008, 202–4), this should make those who accept certain varieties of medium specificity uneasy.
2. Newsprint probably comes the closest, but it's been used for so many other things that it's even harder to connect uniquely to comics than it is to connect the material *film* to the category of film.
3. About this, at least, Carroll and I agree, based on his references to, e.g., "the media that are associated with artforms" (2008, 47). If media are *associated* with art forms, they can't merely *be* art forms.
4. It's worth noting that, for McLuhan, if a medium is used to deliver information, that information is also a medium (1964, 23)—that's the root of his famous claim that the medium is the message.
5. Just to eliminate one possible source of confusion here: Lopes is using "art medium" in the same way that I'm using "art form." Berys Gaut, whose views about medium specificity we'll encounter shortly, approvingly cites Lopes's views and offers a similar stance: "The medium is how one uses the material, so the medium is constituted by the set of practices that govern use of the material" (2010, 288). Those with a background in the philosophy of mind might appreciate the parallel Gaut establishes with functionalism: just as functionalists hold that the mind can be realized by multiple bases, so Gaut holds that a medium can be realized by multiple materials. While I agree with Gaut's notion that medium and materials differ, my own use of "media" will diverge from his substantially.
6. Indeed, Carroll's own definition of media is "(1) the materials (the stuff) out of which works are made and/or (2) the physical instruments employed to shape or otherwise

fashion those materials" (2008, 35). For the reasons given earlier in this section, I think it's more useful than not to expand the scope of media beyond stuff and tools.

7. While tu quoque considerations shouldn't count against Carroll's argument, I do want to point out that in a different work than those just cited, he writes, "Photography . . . is not the only constituent element that comprises film. In addition, there is, among other things, most notably, also editing" (2008, 30). If editing is a "constituent element" of film, then there is at least one non-material medium out of which films are crafted.
8. Theory-level endorsements of at least criterion (a) of moderate medium specificity, as I define it, can be found in Crawford 1970, Rimmon-Kenan 1989, and Herman 2004.
9. Gaut (2010, 301) uses a similar type of example.
10. Will Eisner and Frank Miller have an interesting discussion of this point in Chapter 2 of *Eisner/Miller* (2005, 11–19).
11. Note, by the way, that I'm not claiming that an actual comics artist in the 1970s could have made a work that looked like it used 2000s technology. *Pace* Danto (1964) and Gombrich (2000), I don't think the comics world was ready for that. It's not that artists of the time lacked the requisite skills in drawing, coloring, and lettering, but that they just couldn't have *thought* about making comics look like those that digital technologies are used to create.
12. The view I'm offering here is, for the record, closely related to the great art historian Ernst Gombrich's answer to the question, "Why does art have a history?" In *Art and Illusion* (2000), Gombrich produces a sustained argument that the evolution of art can be explained by two factors: temperament (the way artists have of seeing the world, typically culturally influenced) and technology (which I would include under the scope of my construal of media). Hence, e.g., Impressionism: the new technology of portable easels and premixed paints allowed artists like Monet, Renoir, and Pissaro to escape their studios and paint *en plein air*, which greatly affected the paintings they produced.
13. See Eureakalert! 2018. At the time of this writing, Hutton's work has been presented but not published. The main implication of Hutton's work has to do with the perils of screen time for children, but it should be evident that the results are interesting in our context as well.
14. Czerwiec's point resonates with an argument made by Kevin Melchionne in "Artistic Dropouts" (1998). Melchoinne argues that the system of art education in the United States is poorly conceived, in that it begins by exalting children with gifts for realistic drawing only to send them to art school where they find out that realistic drawing isn't important in contemporary art. (At that point, maybe they go draw superhero comics!)

Chapter 4

1. Though McCloud only says that comics consist in "images in deliberate sequence" (1993, 9), his subsequent discussion and choice of examples clearly show that he has narrative in mind as the chief sequential organizing principle.
2. For a good, brief overview of theories of narrative, see Abbott 2008, chap. 2.
3. The philosophical problem of what it is to be an event is, naturally, fraught with difficulty, and I don't plan on getting into it here. I refer the curious to Casati and Varzi 2015.
4. While this book is not in the business of offering practical wisdom: this is true, though most people are ignorant about it. Be careful what and how much you drink.
5. Just like comics, films are not literally read either, even if the art form might be language-like. On this point, see Bordwell 1985, 30.

6. For several other excellent illustrations of these possibilities, see Abbott 1986, 164–66.
7. It would take experiments using eye-tracking devices to confirm the extent to which Abbott's hypothesis generalizes.
8. This is also an implication of the Hayman/Pratt definition: "A comic's images must convey narrative information," we write: "The sequence of images does not merely contribute to the narrative—it contributes necessarily" (2005, 424).
9. My biases about the nature of narrative loom behind this whole paragraph. Single panels lend themselves (but are not necessarily restricted to) representation of only a single event. If narrative consists in the representation of the causal relations between multiple events, then the more panels that a comic has, the more events it can represent and the more narrative it can convey.
10. McCloud (1993, 109–14) offers an excellent catalog of different types of motion lines and effects.
11. For examples, see Hatfield (2009, 139–44) and Witek (2009, 153–55).
12. Reinforcing this, some years ago, I was fortunate to have dinner with Spiegelman, who told me in conversation that he thinks that the basic unit of comics is not the panel at all, but the page.
13. For a more complex and developed definitions of seriality, see Mag Uidhir 2013b.
14. The idea that suspense requires uncertainty about narrative outcomes (plus a desire for the outcomes to turn out a preferred way) is the more or less standard approach, which generates a paradox about our ability to feel suspense on repeat readings (see, e.g., Yanal 1996). Thinking about suspense as the frustration of desires is a plausible alternative proposed by Aaron Smuts (2008).
15. A favorite example of mine is the "Pizza Dog" issue (2013) of Matt Fraction and David Aja's run on *Hawkeye*, told from the perspective of a dog. Word balloons appear, but only the words the dog can understand are legible. Most other symbols are indications of what the dog can hear or smell—they're pictorial, but are pictorial indications of other kinds of spatiotemporal phenomena than are usually used to drive comics narratives.

Chapter 5

1. At the beginning of 2022, the website Flights, Tights, and Movie Nights lists over six hundred films globally that are based on comics (Bubbawheat 2022). Though its criteria are fairly liberal, that's a staggering number, and doesn't even include TV series.
2. If you read a lot of comics, you can probably think of some that blatantly ape filmic techniques, or are perhaps even created as movie pitches.
3. For more on enthymemes in art, see Danto's treatment in *Transfiguration of the Commonplace* (1981, 169–71).
4. I have heard, though cannot verify, that the Marvel Universe is the longest story ever told in human history.
5. It's possible for a film to depict everything shown on those pages, but the only reasonable way to do so, I expect, would be by means of creative zooming and cross-cutting, which produces rather different expressive and narrative effects.
6. This point is argued by Duncan and Smith (2009, 280–1).
7. This is Delmore Schwartz's view (see 2004, 57).

8. For the record, Cook doesn't put this point in terms of media. I'm translating his stance (charitably, I hope) into the vocabulary that's been developed in this book.
9. The comparatively individual nature of comics creation and comparative simplicity of production drive a potential ethical worry about the comics category in general, which we'll encounter in Chapter 7, Sections 7.2 and 7.3.
10. So-called motion comics, which you may have had the bad luck to encounter (never go looking for the *Watchmen* motion comic!), aren't comics at all. Rather, they're cheaply animated films based on comics.
11. See Caswell and Filipi 2008, 35–61, for further discussion of this part of *Bone*.

Chapter 6

1. Sophisticated relativists like David Wong (1991), who we'll encounter again shortly, have suggested ways to avoid this problem.
2. See, for example Shelley 1994.
3. Disagreement among true judges, if it exists, would be about the degree to which particular comics bear these properties and how significantly each property is to be weighed in overall critical verdicts. See Pratt 2012b for my account of how property weighting is possible.
4. It should be noted, however, that Meskin isn't asserting that the presence of these properties is either necessary or sufficient for value in comics.
5. For the record, this is just one way of thinking about the nature of the aesthetic, and it's controversial. Nothing special in this chapter hinges on classifying certain properties as aesthetic and others as nonaesthetic—it's primarily a matter of convenience and a result of the need to situate my views to some degree with respect to the history of philosophical aesthetics.
6. Beardsley's most influential views on this topic are expressed in a coauthored article (Wimsatt and Beardsley 1946) and in his book *Aesthetics* (1981, chap. 1).
7. I've argued elsewhere (see Pratt 2012a) for a more generalized version of the position I'll develop here.
8. See Kagan 2009 for a lucid summary of some alternatives to mental state views and their costs and benefits.
9. As of this writing, there's a company called Factum Arte that specializes in producing tremendously accurate reproductions of historically significant artworks and sites (e.g., the tomb of Tutankhamun, paintings by Caravaggio) via use of meticulous scanning and 3D printing. In articles archived on the website of the Factum Foundation, 2018, company representatives argue that while the reproductions don't make the originals obsolete, they actually provide a *better* and more epistemically valuable experience than the originals because of the degree of interactivity they afford. While the philosophical implications of Factum Arte's projects are unsettled, it's interesting to consider the possibility that a scan and exact reproduction of, for instance, *Action Comics* #1 could provide a more worthwhile experience than an original print. For one thing, the reader wouldn't have to get overly hung up about whether they were damaging it!
10. I'm just picking three prominent contemporary American comics awards with multiple categories to illustrate this point, but other American and international awards have similar categories and could be used for the same argumentative purpose.

11. It would be naive to claim that decisions about awards, in practice, are made exclusively on the basis of merit rather than also one the basis of reputation, personal affiliation, ethical and political orientation, and other biased factors.
12. For more on the distinction between and implications of recognition value and appraisal value, see Pratt 2012d.

Chapter 7

1. See Eaton 2003 for a fuller argument about how artworks in general can be assessed morally.
2. For an overview of this issue, see Kieran 2003.
3. For the record, this point holds even though relativism, also discussed in Chapter 6, is an issue in ethics, and even though there's disagreement about which moral values, if any, are the right ones.
4. The resulting Comics Code of 1954 and its descendants can be readily accessed via internet search.
5. I won't summarize Adorno's original argument here, but the curious can find it in Adorno and Simpson 1941 and Adorno 1975.
6. It might be pointed out that to the extent that film technology and dissemination approaches that of comics in these respects—as in many of the videos on YouTube, TikTok, or whatever the kids are into when you're reading this—it's subject to many of the same criticisms as comics.
7. See, e.g., Booth 1988 and Nussbaum 1990.
8. Given the increasing tendency to view films and TV shows on the smallest, most private screens possible (i.e., the smartphone), those would appear to be partners in guilt as well. That is, condemning comics along the lines of this arguments entails condemning literature *and* art forms that fall under the scope of moving images.

Afterword

1. See Bramlett, Cook, and Meskin 2017, sec. 1, for an overview of traditions that provide alternatives to the standard Western model.

References

Abbott, H. Porter. 2008. *The Cambridge Introduction to Narrative*, 2nd ed. New York: Cambridge University Press.

Abbott, Lawrence L. 1986. Comic Art: Characteristics and Potentialities of a Narrative Medium. *Journal of Popular Culture* 19: 155–76.

Adorno, Theodor. 1975. Culture Industry Reconsidered. *New German Critique* 6: 12–19.

Adorno, Theodor, and George Simpson. 1941. On Popular Music. *Studies in Philosophy and Social Sciences* 9: 17–48.

Arnheim, Rudolf. 1957. *Film as Art*. Berkeley: University of California Press.

Arnott, Christopher. 2007. Behind the Eight Ball. *New Haven Advocate*, September 27. http://www.newhavenadvocate.com/article.cfm?aid=3262 (accessed September 2008).

Bazin, André. 1967. *What Is Cinema?* Vol. 1. Translated by H. Gray. Berkeley: University of California Press.

Beardsley, Monroe. 1981. *Aesthetics: Problems in the Philosophy of Criticism*, 2nd ed. Indianapolis: Hackett.

Beaty, Bart. 1999. The Search for Comics Exceptionalism. *Comics Journal* 211: 67–72.

Beaty, Bart. 2012. *Comics versus Art*. Toronto: University of Toronto Press.

Blackbeard, Bill, and Dean Crain. 1995. *The Comic Strip Century: Celebrating 100 Years of an American Art Form*. Englewood Cliffs, NJ: Kitchen Sink Press.

Bolling, Reuben. 2001. *Tom the Dancing Bug*, July 7. http://www.gocomics.com/tomthedancingbug/2001/07/07 (accessed August 2017).

Booth, Wayne. 1988. *The Company We Keep: An Ethics of Fiction*. Berkeley: University of California Press.

Bordwell, David. 1985. *Narration in the Fiction Film*. Madison: University of Wisconsin Press.

Bramlett, Frank, Roy T. Cook, and Aaron Meskin, eds. 2017. *The Routledge Companion to Comics*. New York: Routledge.

Bubbawheat. 2022. All Superhero Movies by Date. *Flights, Tights, and Movie Nights*. https://flightstightsandmovienights.com/review-index/the-list/ (accessed February 2022).

Carlin, John, Paul Karasik, and Brian Walker. 2005. *Masters of American Comics*. New Haven, CT: Yale University Press.

Carrier, David. 2000. *The Aesthetics of Comics*. University Park: Pennsylvania State University Press.

Carroll, Noël. 1985a. The Power of Movies. *Daedalus* 114: 79–103.

Carroll, Noël. 1985b. The Specificity of Media in the Arts. *Journal of Aesthetic Education* 19: 5–20.

Carroll, Noël. 1994. Identifying Art. In *Institutions of Art: Reconsiderations of George Dickie's Philosophy*, edited by Robert Yanal, 3–38. University Park: Pennsylvania State University Press.

Carroll, Noël. 1998. *A Philosophy of Mass Art*. New York: Oxford University Press.

Carroll, Noël. 2003. *Engaging the Moving Image*. New Haven, CT: Yale University Press.

Carroll, Noël. 2008. *The Philosophy of Motion Pictures*. Oxford: Wiley-Blackwell.

Carroll, Noël. 2009. *On Criticism*. New York: Routledge.

Casati, Roberto, and Varzi, Achille. 2015. Events. In *The Stanford Encyclopedia of Philosophy*, edited by Edward N. Zalta. https://plato.stanford.edu/archives/win2015/entries/events/ (accessed May 2018).

Caswell, Lucy Shelton, and David Filipi. 2008. *Jeff Smith: Bone and Beyond*. Columbus, OH: Wexner Center for the Arts.

Chang, Ruth. 1997. Introduction. In *Incommensurability, Incomparability, and Practical Reason*, edited by Ruth Chang, 1–34. Cambridge, MA: Harvard University Press.

Chatman, Seymour. 1978. *Story and Discourse*. Ithaca, NY: Cornell University Press.

Church, Jok. 2016. Getting Things to Move. *UCan with Beekman and Jax*, April 10. http://www.gocomics.com/beakman/2016/04/10 (accessed May 2016).

Cohn, Neil. 2013. *The Visual Language of Comics*. New York: Bloomsbury Academic.

Coogan, Peter. 2006. *Superhero: The Secret Origins of a Genre*. Austin, TX: MonkeyBrain Books.

Cook, Roy T. 2011. Do Comics Require Pictures? *Journal of Aesthetics and Art Criticism* 69: 285–96.

Cook, Roy T. 2012. Why Comics Are Not Films: Metacomics and Medium-Specific Conventions. In *The Art of Comics*, edited by Aaron Meskin and Roy T. Cook, 165–87. Malden, MA: Blackwell.

Cook, Roy T. 2013. Canonicity and Normativity in Massive, Serialized Fiction. *Journal of Aesthetics and Art Criticism* 71: 271–76.

Couch, N. C. Christopher. 2001. *The Yellow Kid* and the Comic Page. In *The Language of Comics*, edited by Robin Varnum and Christina T. Gibbons, 60–74. Jackson: University Press of Mississippi.

Crawford, Donald. 1970. The Uniqueness of the Medium. *The Personalist* 51: 447–69.

Cwiklik, Greg. 1999. Understanding the Real Problem. *Comics Journal* 211: 62–66.

Czerwiec, M. K. 2015. The Crayon Revolution. In *The Graphic Medicine Manifesto*, ed. M. K. Czerwiec et al., 143–57. University Park: Pennsylvania State University Press.

Czerwiec, M. K., Ian Williams, Susan Merrill Squier, Michael J. Green, Kimberly R. Myers, and Scott Smith. 2015. *The Graphic Medicine Manifesto*. University Park: Pennsylvania State University Press.

Danto, Arthur. 1964. The Artworld. *Journal of Philosophy* 61: 571–84.

Danto, Arthur. 1981. *Transfiguration of the Commonplace*. Cambridge, MA: Harvard University Press.

Davies, Stephen. 1991. *Definitions of Art*. Ithaca, NY: Cornell University Press.

Davies, Stephen. 1997. First Art and Art's Definition. *Southern Journal of Philosophy* 35: 19–34.

Dickie, George. 1964. The Myth of the Aesthetic Attitude. *American Philosophical Quarterly* 1: 56–65.

Dickie, George. 1974. *Art and the Aesthetic: An Institutional Analysis*. Ithaca, NY: Cornell University Press.

Dickie, George. 1984. *The Art Circle: A Theory of Art*. New York: Haven.

Duncan, Randy, and Matthew J. Smith. 2009. *The Power of Comics*. New York: Bloomsbury.

Dutton, Denis. 2008. But They Don't Have Our Concept of Art. In *Arguing about Art*, 3rd ed., edited by Alex Neill and Aaron Ridley, 448–63. New York: Routledge.

Eaton, Anne. 2003. Where Ethics and Aesthetics Meet: Titian's Rape of Europa. *Hypatia* 18: 159–88.

Eisner, Will. 2008. *Comics and Sequential Art*, 2nd ed. New York: Norton.

Eisner, Will, and Frank Miller. 2005. *Eisner/Miller*. Milwaukie, OR: Dark Horse.

Eureakalert! 2018. New Studies Measure Screen-Based Media Use in Children. *Eureakalert.org*, May 5. https://www.eurekalert.org/pub_releases/2018-05/pas-nsm042618.php (accessed May 2018).

Factum Foundation for Digital Technology in Conservation. 2018. www.Factumfoundation.org (accessed June 2018).

Farinella, Matteo. 2018. The Potential of Comics in Science Communication. *Journal of Science Communication* 17: 1–17.

Fraction, Matt, and David Aja. 2013. *Hawkeye* #11, June 26. New York: Marvel Entertainment.

Gaut, Berys. 2010. *A Philosophy of Cinematic Art*. Cambridge: Cambridge University Press.

Gombrich, Ernst. 2000. *Art and Illusion*, 3rd ed. Princeton, NJ: Princeton University Press.

Goodman, Nelson. 1968. *Languages of Art: An Approach to a Theory of Symbols.*. Indianapolis: Hackett.

Gracia, Jorge E. 2007. From Horror to Hero: Film Interpretations of Stoker's *Dracula*. In *Philosophy and the Interpretation of Pop Culture*, edited by William Irwin and Jorge E. Gracia, 187–214. Lanham, MD: Rowman and Littlefield Publishers.

Gravett, Paul. 2004. *Manga: Sixty Years of Japanese Comics*. New York: HarperCollins.

Greenberg, Clement, 1982. Modernist Painting. In *Modern Art and Modernism: A Critical Anthology*, edited by Francis Frascine and Charles Harrison, 5–10. London: Harper and Row.

Groensteen, Thierry. 2007. *The System of Comics*. Translated by Bart Beaty and Nick Nguyen. Jackson: University Press of Mississippi.

Hajdu, David. 2008. *The Ten-Cent Plague*. New York: Farrar, Straus and Giroux.

Harvey, Robert. 1979. The Aesthetics of the Comic Strip. *Journal of Popular Culture* 12: 640–52.

Harvey, Robert. 1996. *The Art of the Comic Book: An Aesthetic History*. Jackson: University Press of Mississippi.

Harvey, Robert. 1998. *Children of the Yellow Kid*. Seattle: University of Washington Press.

Harvey, Robert. 2001. Comedy at the Juncture of Word and Image: The Emergence of the Modern Magazine Gag Cartoon Reveals the Vital Blend. In *The Language of Comics*, edited by Robin Varnum and Christina T. Gibbons, 75–96. Jackson: University Press of Mississippi.

Harvey, Robert. 2009. How Comics Came to Be. In *A Comics Studies Reader*, edited by Jeet Heer and Kent Worcester, 25–45. Jackson: University Press of Mississippi.

Hatfield, Charles. 2009. An Art of Tensions. In *A Comics Studies Reader*, edited by Jeet Heer and Kent Worcester, 132–48. Jackson: University Press of Mississippi.

Hayman, Greg, and Henry John Pratt. 2005. What Are Comics? In *Aesthetics: A Reader in the Philosophy of Art*, 2nd ed., edited by David Goldblatt and Lee B. Brown, 419–24. Upper Saddle River. NJ: Pearson Prentice Hall.

Hazlett, Allan, and Christy Mag Uidhir. 2011. Unrealistic Fictions. *American Philosophical Quarterly* 48: 33–46.

Herman, David. 2004. Toward a Transmedial Narratology. In *Narrative across Media: The Languages of Storytelling*, edited by Marie-Laure Ryan, 47–75. Lincoln: University of Nebraska Press.

Hirsch, Paul S. 2021. *Pulp Empire: The Secret History of Comic Book Imperialism*. Chicago: University of Chicago Press.

Holbo, John. 2012. Redefining Comics. In *The Art of Comics and Graphic Novels: A Philosophical Approach*, edited by Roy T. Cook and Aaron Meskin, 3–30. Malden, MA: Wiley-Blackwell.

Homer. 1951. *The Iliad of Homer*. Translated by Richard Lattimore. Chicago: University of Chicago Press.

Hume, David. 1996 [1757]. Of the Standard of Taste. In *Selected Essays*, 133–53. New York: Oxford University Press.

Inge, M. Thomas. 1990. *Comics as Culture*. Jackson: University Press of Mississippi.

Jog. 2007. Finally, I Didn't Have to Risk My Life for Comics. *Jog—the Blog*, February 15. https://joglikescomics.blogspot.com/2007/02/finally-i-didnt-have-to-risk-my-life.html (accessed September 2017).

Kagan, Shelly. 2009. Well-Being as Enjoying the Good. *Philosophical Perspectives* 23: 253–72.

Kieran, Matthew. 2003. Art and Morality. In *The Oxford Handbook of Aesthetics*, edited by Jerrold Levinson, 451–70. New York: Oxford University Press.

Kukkonen, Karin. 2013. *Studying Comics and Graphic Novels*. Malden, MA: Wiley-Blackwell.

Kunzle, David. 1973. *The Early Comic Strip: Narrative Strips and Picture Stories in the European Broadsheet from c. 1450 to 1825*. Oakland: University of California Press.

Kunzle, David. 2009. Rodolphe Töpffer's Aesthetic Revolution. In *A Comics Studies Reader*, edited by Jeet Heer and Kent Worcester, 17–24. Jackson: University Press of Mississippi.

Lambert, Josh. 2009. "Wait for the Next Pictures": Intertextuality and Cliffhanger Continuity in Early Cinema and Comic Strips. *Cinema Journal* 48: 3–25.

Lang, Berel. 1990. *The Anatomy of Philosophical Style*. Cambridge, MA: Blackwell.

Lessing, Gotthold Ephraim. 1962 [1766]. *Laocoön: An Essay on the Limits of Painting and Poetry*. Translated by Edward Allen McCormick. Baltimore: Johns Hopkins University Press.

Levinson, Jerrold. 1979. Defining Art Historically. *British Journal of Aesthetics* 19: 232–50.

Levinson, Jerrold. 1989. Refining Art Historically. *Journal of Aesthetics and Art Criticism* 47: 21–33.

Levinson, Jerrold. 2005. Erotic Art and Pornographic Pictures. *Philosophy and Literature* 29: 228–40.

Levitz, Paul. 2015. *Will Eisner: Champion of the Graphic Novel*. New York: Abrams ComicArts.

Lopes, Dominic. 2004. Digital Art. In *The Blackwell Guide to the Philosophy of Computing and Information*, edited by Luciano Floridi, 106–16. Malden, MA: Blackwell.

Louis, Joe. 2007. *Batman* #663 Sucks REALLY Badly. *FreakComics.com*, February 17. http://freakcomics.com/2007/02/17/batman-663-sucks-really-badly/ (accessed September 2017).

Mackie, J. L. 1977. *Ethics: Inventing Right and Wrong*. New York: Penguin.

MacPherson, Don. 2007. *Batman* #663. *Eye on Comics*, February 18. http://www.eyeoncomics.com/?p=106 (accessed September 2017).

Mag Uidhir, Christy. 2012. Comics and Collective Authorship. In *The Art of Comics and Graphic Novels: A Philosophical Approach*, edited by Roy T. Cook and Aaron Meskin, 47–67. Malden, MA: Wiley-Blackwell.

Mag Uidhir, Christy. 2013a. Epistemic Misuse and Abuse of Pictorial Caricature. *American Philosophical Quarterly* 50: 137–51.

Mag Uidhir, Christy. 2013b. How to Frame Serial Art. *Journal of Aesthetics and Art Criticism* 71: 261–65.

Matravers, Derek. 2000. The Institutional Theory: A Protean Creature. *British Journal of Aesthetics* 40: 242–50.

McCloud, Scott. 1993. *Understanding Comics: The Invisible Art*. New York: HarperCollins.

McCloud, Scott. 1995. An Interview (Conversation?) with Scott McCloud. Interview by Robert C. Harvey. *Comics Journal* 179: 53–81.

McCloud, Scott. 2000. *Reinventing Comics*. New York: HarperCollins.

McCloud, Scott. 2006. *Making Comics*. New York: HarperCollins.

McLuhan, Marshall. 1964. *Understanding Media*. New York: McGraw-Hill.

Melchionne, Kevin. 1998. Artistic Dropouts. In *Aesthetics: The Big Questions*, edited by Karolyn Korsmeyer, 98–103. Malden, MA: Wiley-Blackwell.

Meskin, Aaron. 2007. Defining Comics? *Journal of Aesthetics and Art Criticism* 65: 369–79.

Meskin, Aaron. 2008. From Defining Art to Defining the Individual Arts: The Role of Theory in the Philosophies of the Arts. In *New Waves in Aesthetics*, edited by Kathleen Stock and Katherine Thomson-Jones, 125–49. New York: Palgrave-Macmillan.

Meskin, Aaron. 2009. Comics as Literature? *British Journal of Aesthetics* 43: 219–39.

Meskin, Aaron. 2012. The Ontology of Comics. In *The Art of Comics: A Philosophical Approach*, edited by Aaron Meskin and Roy T. Cook, 31–46. Malden, MA: Wiley-Blackwell.

Miller, Frank. 2005. *Frank Miller's Sin City Volume 1: The Hard Goodbye*. Milwaukie, OR: Dark Horse Books.

Mitchell, Adrielle. 2017. Comics and Authorship. In *The Routledge Companion to Comics*, edited by Aaron Meskin, Roy T. Cook, and Franklin Bramlett, 239–47. New York: Routledge.

Molotiu, Andrei, ed. 2009. *Abstract Comics: The Anthology*. Seattle: Fantagraphics.

Molotiu, Andrei. 2017. Art Comics. In *The Routledge Companion to Comics*, edited by Aaron Meskin, Roy T. Cook, and Franklin Bramlett, 119–27. New York: Routledge.

Moore, Alan. 2008a. Alan Moore Still Knows the Score. Interview by Nisha Gopalan. *EW.com*, July 21. http://www.ew.com/ew/article/0,,20213004,00.html (accessed August 2017).

Moore, Alan. 2008b. *Alan Moore's Writing for Comics*. Rantoul, IL: Avatar Press.

Moore, Alan, and Dave Gibbons. 1987. *Watchmen*. New York: DC Comics.

Moore, Alan, and Dave Gibbons. 2000. The Alan Moore Interview: *Watchmen*, Microcosms and Details. Interview by Barry Kavanagh. *Blather.net*. October 17. http://www.blather.net/projects/alan-moore-interview/watchmen-microcosms-details/ (accessed August 2017).

Morrison, Grant. 2011. *Supergods*. New York: Spiegel and Grau.

Morrison, Grant, and Andy Kubert. 2014. *Batman and Son*. New York: DC Comics.

Nehamas, Alexander. 1988. Plato and the Mass Media. *The Monist* 71: 214–31.

Nozick, Robert. 1974. *Anarchy, State, and Utopia*. New York: Basic Books.

Nussbaum, Martha. 1990. *Love's Knowledge: Essays on Philosophy and Literature*. New York: Oxford University Press.

Nzegwu, Nkiru. 2019. African Art in Deep Time: De-race-ing Aesthetics and De-racializing Visual Art. *Journal of Aesthetics and Art Criticism* 77: 367–78.

Oudart, Jean-Pierre. 1977–78. Cinema and Suture. *Screen* 18: 35–47.

Plato. 1961. *Collected Dialogues*. Edited by Edith Hamilton and Huntington Cairns. Princeton, NJ: Princeton University Press.

Postema, Barbara. 2013. *Narrative Structure in Comics: Making Sense of Fragments*. Rochester, NY: RIT Press.

Postema, Barbara. 2016. Silent Comics. In *The Routledge Companion to Comics*, edited by Aaron Meskin, Roy T. Cook, and Franklin Bramlett, 201–8. New York: Routledge.

Powell, Eric. 2006. *The Goon: Virtue and the Grim Consequences Thereof*. Milwaukie, OR: Dark Horse Books.

Pratt, Henry. 2009a. Medium Specificity and the Ethics of Narrative in Comics. *Storyworlds* 1: 97–113.

Pratt, Henry. 2009b. Narrative in Comics. *Journal of Aesthetics and Art Criticism* 67: 107–17.

Pratt, Henry. 2011. Relating Comics, Cartoons, and Animation. In *Aesthetics: A Reader in Philosophy of the Arts*, 3rd ed., edited by David Goldblatt and Lee B. Brown, 369–73. Upper Saddle River, NJ: Pearson Prentice Hall.

Pratt, Henry. 2012a. Artistic Institutions, Valuable Experiences: Coming to Terms with Artistic Value. *Philosophia* 40: 591–606.

Pratt, Henry. 2012b. Categories and Comparisons of Artworks. *British Journal of Aesthetics* 52: 45–59.

Pratt, Henry. 2012c. Making Comics into Film. In *The Art of Comics and Graphic Novels: A Philosophical Approach*, ed. Roy T. Cook and Aaron Meskin, 147–64. Malden, MA: Wiley-Blackwell.

Pratt, Henry. 2012d. Respect, Recognition, and Appraisal: Are All Artworks Valuable? *Journal of Value Inquiry* 46: 147–58.

Pratt, Henry. 2013. Why Serials Are Killer. *Journal of Aesthetics and Art Criticism* 71: 266–70.

Pratt, Henry. 2016. Comics and Adaptation. In *The Routledge Companion to Comics*, edited by Aaron Meskin, Roy T. Cook, and Franklin Bramlett, 230–38. New York: Routledge.

Rabinowitz, Peter. 1977. Truth in Fiction: A Re-examination of Audiences. *Critical Inquiry* 4: 121–41.

Rimmon-Kenan, Shlomith. 1989. How the Model Neglects the Medium: Linguistics, Language, and the Crisis of Narratology. *Journal of Narrative Technique* 19: 157–66.

Robinson, Jerry. 1974. *The Comics: An Illustrated History of Comic Strip Art*. New York: Berkley Windhover.

Ross, Alex. 2005. *Mythology: The DC Comics Art of Alex Ross*. New York: Pantheon.

Russell, Bertrand. 1998. *The Problems of Philosophy*. New York: Oxford University Press.

Sava, Oliver. 2014. Doop Is the 21st Century's Most Important Superhero Comics Creation. *The A.V. Club*, April 9. http://www.avclub.com/article/doop-21st-centurys-most-important-superhero-comics-203174 (accessed September 2017).

Sava, Oliver. 2017. It's Movies vs. Comics in the Wild and Weird *Transformers vs. G.I. Joe*. *The A.V. Club*, March 24. https://aux.avclub.com/it-s-movies-vs-comics-in-the-wild-and-weird-transforme-1798259492 (accessed March 2018).

Schwartz, Delmore. 2004 [1952]. Masterpieces as Cartoons. In *Arguing Comics*, edited by Jeet Heer and Kent Worcester, 52–62. Jackson: University Press of Mississippi.

Scioli, Tom, and John Barber. 2017. *Transformers vs. G.I. Joe: The Quintessential Collection*. San Diego: IDW.

Shelley, James. 1994. Hume's Double Standard of Taste. *Journal of Aesthetics and Art Criticism* 52: 437–45.

Shiner, Larry. 2008. Western and Non-Western Concepts of Art. In *Arguing about* Art, 3rd ed., edited by Alex Neill and Aaron Ridley, 464–70. New York: Routledge.

Simone, Gail. 2000. *Women in Refrigerators*. http://lby3.com/wir/ (accessed October 2017).

Smith, Jeff. 2004. *Bone: The Complete Epic in One Volume*. Columbus, OH: Cartoon Books.

Smuts, Aaron. 2008. The Desire-Frustration Theory of Suspense. *Journal of Aesthetics and Art Criticism* 66: 281–90.

Sobel, Marc. 2007. *Batman* #663 Review. *Sequart*, November 28. http://sequart.org/magazine/16164/batman-663-review/ (accessed May 2018).

Soule, Charles, Javier Pulido, and Ron Wimberly. 2014. *She-Hulk*. New York: Marvel.

Spiegelman, Art. 2007. *Art Spiegelman: Conversations*. Edited by Joseph Witek. Jackson: University Press of Mississippi.

Spurrier, Simon, and Jeff Stokely. 2016. *The Spire*. Los Angeles: BOOM! Studios.

Stecker, Robert. 1997. *Artworks: Definition, Meaning, and Value*. University Park: Pennsylvania State University Press.

Stone, Tucker. 2007. *Batman* #663. *The Factual Opinion*, February 16. http://factualopinion.typepad.com/the_factual_opinion/2007/02/batman_663.html (accessed September 2017).

Stromberg, Fredrik, and Peter Kuper. 2010. *Comics Art Propaganda: A Graphic History*. New York: St. Martin's Press.

Tabachnick, Stephen E., ed. 2009. *Teaching the Graphic Novel*. New York: Modern Language Association of America.

Tan, Ed. 2001. The Telling Face in Comic Strip and Graphic Novel. In *The Graphic Novel*, edited by Jan Bataens, 31–46. Leuven, Belgium: Leuven University Press.

Tilley, Carol L., and Robert G. Weiner. 2017. Teaching and Learning with Comics. In *The Routledge Companion to Comics*, edited by Aaron Meskin, Roy T. Cook, and Franklin Bramlett, 358–66. New York: Routledge.

Tong, Ng Suat. 1999. An Open Debate about Closure. *Comics Journal* 211: 77–79.

Walton, Kendall. 1970. Categories of Art. *Philosophical Review* 79: 334–67.

Walton, Kendall. 1984. Transparent Pictures: On the Nature of Photographic Realism. *Critical Inquiry* 11: 246–77.

Waterson, Bill. 2013. Our Interview with *Calvin and Hobbes* Creator Bill Waterson. Interview by Jake Rossen. *Mental Floss*, October 17. http://mentalfloss.com/article/53216/mental-floss-exclusive-our-interview-bill-watterson#ixzz2iTAZaO00 (accessed July 2017).

Waugh, Coulton. 1947. *The Comics*. New York: Macmillan.

Weitz, Morris. 1956. The Role of Theory in Aesthetics. *Journal of Aesthetics and Art Criticism* 15: 27–35.

Wertham, Fredric. 1954. *Seduction of the Innocent*. New York: Rinehart.

Wimsatt, W. K., and Monroe Beardsley. 1946. The Intentional Fallacy. *Sewanee Review* 54: 468–88.

Witek, Joseph. 2009. The Arrow and the Grid. In *A Comics Studies Reader*, edited by Jeet Heer and Kent Worcester, 149–56. Jackson: University Press of Mississippi.
Witek, Joseph. 2012. Comics Modes: Caricature and Illustration in the Crumb Family's Dirty Laundry. In *Critical Approaches to Comics*, edited by Matthew J. Smith and Randy Duncan, 27–42. New York: Routledge.
Wolff, Robert Paul. 1970. *In Defense of Anarchism*. New York: Harper and Row.
Wolk, Douglas. 2007. *Reading Comics*. Cambridge, MA: Da Capo Press.
Wong, David. 1991. Relativism. In *A Companion to Ethics*, edited by Peter Singer, 442–50. Malden, MA: Blackwell.
Wright, Bradford. 2001. *Comic Book Nation*. Baltimore, MD: Johns Hopkins University Press.
Yanal, Robert J. 1996. The Paradox of Suspense. *British Journal of Aesthetics* 36: 146–58.

Index

For the benefit of digital users, indexed terms that span two pages (e.g., 52–53) may, on occasion, appear on only one of those pages.